Psychology of Religion

PSYCHOLOGY OF RELIGION

Paul E. Johnson

PROFESSOR OF PSYCHOLOGY OF RELIGION
BOSTON UNIVERSITY

Abingdon-Cokesbury Press
New York • *Nashville*

PSYCHOLOGY OF RELIGION

COPYRIGHT, MCMXLV
BY WHITMORE & STONE

K

PRINTED IN THE UNITED STATES OF AMERICA

Preface

There have been many psychological studies of religion in the past half century. Most of them are specialized, either in content or method. Whereas early studies concentrated on religious conversion and growth, later ones were restricted to educational or pastoral problems. Some have employed the questionnaire; others have used biographical, anthropological, and sociological data. A great deal of valuable information has been gathered for practical and theoretical use.

What is the next step for this growing psychology of religion? The time has evidently come for systematic integration of methods and data to see what has been discovered. What are the major problems, methods, and principles that have developed in the field? This book does not pretend to answer the question adequately. No single book can hope to perform so large a task, since no individual can see the whole perspective or tell the whole story. Yet one can aim to take a modest step toward meeting that need, by portraying the work of many minds and by inviting more minds to participate in the psychological study of religion.

To work or think clearly, we need a frame of reference. Every workman has some conceptual system or design to follow. We each have a point of view from which to see, an orientation making progress possible. So philosophy, science, education, politics, economics, and psychology all work from basic beliefs. In presenting this psychology of religion I shall declare my psychological creed:

1. This is a *dynamic psychology*. The progress of modern science has been increasingly toward dynamic concepts. Astronomy, physics, and chemistry find energy systems in constant tension and interaction. The biological and social sciences find life in con-

7

stant growth and interaction. The materialistic mechanism of the nineteenth century yields to the organic dynamism of the twentieth because it is now clear that we live in a dynamic universe. Psychology is wide awake to these dynamic facts. Dynamic psychology is no longer a rival school, but a basic point of view recognized by most psychologists today. H. A. Murray, in a Harvard University classroom, recently characterized the data of dynamic psychology as (*a*) a process in time, (*b*) spontaneous activity, (*c*) motivation driving goalward, and (*d*) emphasis on end rather than means. With this I agree, and my aim is to study religious experience as a spontaneous process in time motivated by value goals. Purpose rather than cause is the fundamental category.

2. This is *interpersonal psychology*. It is my conviction that interacting persons are the field of psychology. Nothing less than personality is an adequate functioning unit for psychology. Yet persons are what they are always in social context. To understand a person, see him in the social relations of family, school, vocation, church, and community activities. Isolation is impossible, for the solitary person is unreal, abstract, artificial, abnormal. No person is identical in two social settings, for one's style of life is responsive and adjustive to each relation he enters. Individualism leads to selfishness and anarchy; collectivism, to totalitarian oppression and exploitation. But interpersonalism does justice both to the individual and to society. The interacting units are persons; the interacting process is society.

The implications and applications of this interpersonal psychology will develop as the investigation proceeds. The stage will be a social psychology of interacting persons. The plot will be a dynamic interplay of energies and motives, personal goals socially influenced. This motivation arises not from unlearned instincts but from social interests and personal needs. Genetic growth of emotional responses, habits, language, beliefs, moral and religious attitudes is stimulated by social interaction. Subconscious (partly conscious) forces have larger influence than we often realize, as

8

dynamic products of biosocial factors in personality and culture.

Religion is essentially dynamic and interpersonal. Its dynamic character is evident in the power of interest and need to rouse tensions of desire and behavior. Dynamic religion is seeking, growing, believing, uniting for good. Living religion is ever responsive and devoted to value goals. The interpersonal character of religion is evident in its motif of enlarging co-operation. Religion is social reference to social realities by social responses for the sake of social values reinforced by social co-operation. Psychology of religion is inevitably a social psychology of interacting persons.

From this point of view we seek to understand what it means to be religious. The treatment cannot hope to be exhaustive. It will not even be comprehensive. Every problem selected for study excludes other possible problems. Yet no religion can be understood without psychological investigation, for the life of every religion is the experience that motivates its dynamic expression. Each reader will want to be his own psychologist to see for himself what the inner meaning of religion is. Each one will need to have his own religion in order to know from personal experience what it means. Each will find the full meaning of religion in dynamic interpersonal relations.

Acknowledgments

Many friends and colleagues have exchanged ideas on these questions. Fellow students and teachers have entered generously into critical discussions that penetrated easy assumptions and demanded further study. Edgar S. Brightman, Earl B. Marlatt, Francis L. Strickland, and Peter A. Bertocci have read the manuscript in whole or part and made valued suggestions. Edward S. Ames, George A. Coe, Frank S. Hickman, and Henry N. Wieman have explored productive agreements and differences. Roland P. Rice has assisted in the compilation of the index. Evelyn Grant Johnson, my wife, has given constant encouragement and collaboration in the preparation of the manuscript.

I gratefully acknowledge permission from the following copyright owners to quote material as cited in footnote references:

Floyd H. Allport and Daniel Katz, for *Students' Attitudes*.

American Council on Education, for H. M. Bell, *Youth Tell Their Story*.

D. Appleton-Century Company, Peter Blos, *The Adolescent Personality*.

Harlan C. Betts, for G. H. Betts, *The Beliefs of 700 Ministers*.

Bureau of Publications, Teachers' College, Columbia University, for A. H. MacLean, *The Idea of God in Protestant Religious Education*.

Christian Century, for P. E. Johnson, "Psychoanalyzing the Atheist."

Commonwealth Fund, for G. C. Robinson, *The Patient as a Person*.

Thomas Y. Crowell Company, for H. N. and R. W. Wieman, *Normative Psychology of Religion*.

Harcourt, Brace and Company, for C. G. Jung, *Modern Man in Search of a Soul*.

Harper and Brothers, for J. H. Leuba, "Religious Beliefs of American Scientists," *Harper's Magazine*.

Houghton Mifflin Company, for F. D. Brooks, *The Psychology of adolescence*; and L. F. Shaffer, *The Psychology of Adjustment*.

Longmans, Green and Company, for William James, *The Varieties of Religious Experience*.

The Macmillan Company, for E. T. Clark, *The Psychology of Religious Awakening*; Hartshorne and May, *Studies in Deceit*; Hartshorne and Maller, *Studies in Service and Self-Control*; J. B. Pratt, *The Religious Consciousness*.

John Wiley and Sons, for J. G. Miller, *Unconsciousness*.

Boston University, the Earhart Foundation, the Institute of Pastoral Care, and the Commission on Religion and Health of the Federal Council of Churches have provided me with significant opportunites for the psychological study of religion.

To these individuals, organizations, and foundations I express heartfelt gratitude.

PAUL E. JOHNSON

Boston University School of Theology

Contents

I

The Psychological Study of Religion

1. Approaching Religion

In approaching religion one may be naïve or critical. We are naturally naïve before we are critical. The word comes from the Latin *nativus,* meaning "native"; to be naïve is our native, unaffected attitude toward life situations. Naïve experience is the fountain of all human developments, the source of arts and sciences. Seeing and hearing provide the stuff of artistic appreciation. From these sensible delights come the raw materials to construct song and symphony, rhythmic dance and graphic portrayal, sculptured form and architectural symmetry. From naïve interest in nature and curiosity about how things work come the crude experiments and long progress of science and invention. In each field refinements outgrow naïve beginnings, yet without the latter the former could never be.

Naïve religious experience is the spontaneous interest that wakens life to awe and wonder.[1] The vastness of the heavens or the intimate delicacy of a petal may bate the breath in wonder. Thunder and tempest may overpower human frailty in awe of mysterious powers. The steady growth and decay of life through the seasons may suggest a controlling order of cause and effect. The quiet hush of forest or sunset may impress a man with a strange sense that he is not alone. What child of nature can escape these glimpses of another world around and yet within the familiar forms? Before investigation of these naïve experiences the sense of mystery grows within us. After examination there remains a feeling of invisible backgrounds that underlie and overarch the visible life of our world.

[1] W. E. Hocking says, "Religion is the mother of the arts."—*The Meaning of God in Human Experience* (New Haven: Yale University Press, 1912), p. 14.

In this state of innocence we are informed by social traditions. Words are spoken to indicate absent objects, and names refer to events beyond the range of pointing fingers. Invisible powers are designated by ideas and symbols that represent them. "Mana" among the Melanesians means a mysterious power that works good or evil. "Manitu" among American Indians is a great spirit whose power is sought and feared.[2] So everywhere people have their traditions by which the mysteries are named and clothed with character and function. Individuals growing up in such traditions accept and employ the concepts of their people to interpret the mysteries that confront them.

The naïve mind accepts traditions without question—that is, without questions implying doubt. For it, to question is not to doubt but to invite the answer from a respected authority. Children ask of parents, parents of grandparents, priests of sacred books. The answers are not individual opinions but the voice of tradition. There is no room for debate unless authorities disagree, in which misfortune the issue is to be decided, not on the merits of the case, but on the superiority of one authority over another.

The advantages of authoritarianism are well known. Authorities offer stability and security. But the cost of authority is high. Stability may block the way of progress, and security may rest on falsehood. When authorities err, no way is provided for correcting the established errors. A critical method is needed.

There are two critical approaches to religion: the philosophical and the scientific. Philosophical inquiry interprets the reality to which religion refers. All experience has objective reference—as in observation and knowledge we inevitably ask, Observation of what? Knowledge of what? Each religious experience refers to an object of religious concern. The philosophical task is to consider the claims of religious experience and investigate the whole system of reality to which it refers. Questions about God—his existence,

[2] See articles on these concepts in the *Encyclopaedia of Religion and Ethics*, ed. James Hastings.

nature, and purpose—are philosophical problems. The truth of particular religions and their teachings, the reality of the goods of life in this world and the next (if any), are questions for philosophy.

Theology is associated with philosophy in the study of truth and reality as a whole. Both search beneath appearances for the undergirding reality; both press beyond the local view to larger cosmic perspectives. Either may be taught by authority, yet both employ critical analysis freely. There is this distinction. A theology views the whole from the standpoint of one religion and draws more deeply from that historic tradition. A philosophy of religion aims to view all religions impartially and evaluate each from a universal point of view.

The scientific approach is, first of all, description. Its task is to gather, classify, and arrange facts in systematic order. From these facts general principles are inferred. The work of science is done with ever-increasing thoroughness, and new facts are continually added. Yet the inductive leap from data to conclusion comes to probability rather than final certainty. Science depends on philosophy for its presuppositions (for example, the presupposition of a lawful universe where cause and effect follow in regular sequence). And philosophy depends on science for its data and many of its inferences. An adequate philosophy of religion will employ all the facts available through scientific description and analysis.

Scientific studies of religion include the history of religion, the sociology of religion, and the psychology of religion. History of religion explores primitive cultures and buried antiquities to find the earliest forms, and traces the development of each religion through the centuries. Sociology of religion investigates the place of religion in group life and examines the interaction of social, economic, and political factors with religious values. The psychology of religion looks within human experience to understand what religion means to persons. It is intimately related to the other scientific studies. History and sociology both employ psychology to interpret the meaning of religious forms and activities, for they would otherwise be merely dusty records and lifeless patterns. Psychology of religion goes to primitive cults and historical faiths to secure data for its study. Social organizations, customs, and standards contribute to the psychological meaning of religion.[3]

2. HISTORICAL SURVEY

Psychology is one of the youngest of modern sciences. Yet the description of human experience and behavior is probably the oldest of all studies. The earliest records of every known culture relate the doings and sayings of men and women. Exploits of heroes, often magnified to superhuman stature, make up the songs and stories told and retold before writing was invented. The odes and legends of ancient China, Japan, India, Israel, and Greece recount events in which the ancestors dared to suffer and achieve. As these literatures unfold they reveal emotions and desires, ideas and ideals that constitute the inner side of behavior. Much of this lore is permeated with religious attitudes.

The psychological data of religion are therefore as old as human history. Facts are mingled with fancies, however, and interpretations are largely naïve. Heroes change at will from human to animal forms, become invisible, fly through air, journey into the earth and undersea. The sun stands still or rides too close to the earth and burns the crops, axheads float, waves become horses, dragons ride the clouds, armed soldiers spring up from dragons' teeth. Good and ill fortune result from charms, curses, fates, or unwitting mistakes. But gradually through these bewildering irregularities there develops a sense of order and justice. Glimpses of moral law appear in the Chinese Tao, the Greek Moira, the Hindu karma, and the Hebrew Decalogue. From these hints of law and

[3] Joachim Wach well demonstrates the labors of the social sciences of religion. See his *Sociology of Religion* (Chicago: University of Chicago Press, 1944).

order in man and nature come early premonitions of a scientific view.

So is the way prepared for psychology of religion. If psychology is the systematic description and critical analysis of human behavior, it appears astonishingly early on the human scene. We have found descriptions of human behavior at the dawn of recorded history. As these descriptions become more systematic and critical, the pioneer work is well begun. The naïve myths and crude legends are brought before the bar of reason and quite thoroughly overhauled. While yet in popular favor they are trimmed, refined, reinterpreted, or rejected entirely by more daring thinkers.

Ikhnaton (Egyptian Pharaoh *ca.* 1375–1358 B.C.) fearlessly rejected the religious traditions of two thousand years, departing from the priests and temples of the past to found a new religion of inner appreciations. Here is thoroughgoing criticism of a powerful intrenched religion and the systematic creation of a lofty monotheism. From the hymns and records that survive, it appears that religion was understood as an emotional experience.[4]

The ancient Hindu psychologists developed a remarkable science for analyzing religious experience. Vedanta thinkers explored the mystical rise of superconsciousness. Sankhya followers defined the powers of the individual soul as related to the organs of sense and motion. They formulated psychological problems clearly and analyzed processes with subtle understanding. They also invented yoga exercises for mental control and religious concentration.[5]

Gautama Buddha (563–483 B.C.) was systematic in his analysis of human behavior. He conducted experiments testing the typical methods of holy men, pursuing rigorous self-discipline and fasting even to the point of unconsciousness. When six years of such experiments brought no peace, he reached a solution similar to that of

[4] See Arthur Weigall, *The Life and Times of Akhnaton* (New York: G. P. Putnam's Sons, 1910; 1923).

[5] See S. Radakrishman, *Indian Philosophy* (2 vols.; New York: The Macmillan Co., 1923; 1929).

Freud in its premise that the cause of suffering is desire, but opposite in the conclusion that desire should be repressed.[6]

Jeremiah (650?-585?B.C.) is the psychologist of the Hebrew prophets. He identified himself with his people but was always their unyielding critic, reproving their follies (10:3) and pleading with them to return from their deceits to the true way of life (15:19). The profound stirring of his emotions and convictions reveals the distresses and progress of his faith.[7]

Socrates (470?-399 B.C.) represents the critical spirit in Greece. His conviction that "the unexamined life is not fit for human living" propelled him on a dangerous career of upsetting the established beliefs and popular illusions of his time. He rejected the traditional gods of his people and found his deity in conscience, a spirit that guides from within and sustains a man in life and death.[8]

Christian thinkers have notably advanced the psychological understanding of religion. To Jesus the heart of religion is the inner spirit, and he constantly turns from the external and formal to desires and motives, affections and thoughts that become the decisive issues of life. Murder begins in anger, adultery stems from lust, profanity from irreverence and insincerity, enmity from selfishness and hatred.[9]

Paul and Augustine expound conversion, the inner conflicts of flesh lusting against spirit, the frustrations of a divided will, "the expulsive power of a new affection," the integration of a greater purpose, the peace and power of devotion to a religious cause. They define issues that have engaged theologians down to modern times.[10]

The psychological approach to theology, so characteristic of recent discussions, received its modern impetus from Jonathan Edwards (1703-58) and Friedrich Schleiermacher (1768-1834).

---

[6] For source material see H. C. Warren, *Buddhism in Translations* (Cambridge: Harvard University Press, 1896; 1922).

[7] Note especially Jer. 12:1; 14:9; 15:17-18; 20:7, 9; 17:13-17.

[8] Plato's *Dialogues* are the best source of our knowledge of Socrates.

[9] Matt. 5-7 sums up the gist of this teaching.

Schleiermacher is generally considered the pioneer in revolting against the rationalism of philosophers and stressing religious experience as the feeling of absolute dependence. But in Boston, July 8, 1731, Edwards preached on "God Glorified in Man's Dependence," thirty-seven years before Schleiermacher was born. Elsewhere he argues the insufficiency of reason in religious revelation.[11]

Anthropologists and historians of religion have brought enlarging information toward the understanding of religion. Max Müller (1823-1900) conducted notable investigations in Oriental religions and edited the monumental series *The Sacred Books of the East* with the collaboration of many scholars. Pioneer studies of primitive culture by J. G. Frazer, R. R. Marett, E. B. Tylor, Emile Durkheim, Lucien Lévy-Bruhl, and others have encouraged a succession of valuable investigations of religious customs.

Religious experience became a leading interest of psychologists toward the close of the nineteenth century. The place of religious conversion in the awakenings of adolescence was studied by G. Stanley Hall in 1881. W. H. Burnham, A. H. Daniels, J. H. Leuba, E. H. Lancaster, and E. D. Starbuck investigated the traits of conversion experiences in a series of articles appearing in the nineties. Pioneer books on this subject were: E. D. Starbuck, *The Psychology of Religion* (1899); G. A. Coe, *The Spiritual Life* (1900); William James, *The Varieties of Religious Experience* (1902).[12]

Psychological studies were made of primitive religion by Wilhelm Wundt, *Elements of Folk Psychology* (1900); Irving King, *The Development of Religion* (1910); Emile Durkheim, *The Elementary Forms of Religious Life* (1912). Then almost simultaneously

---

[10] Biographical accounts of Paul's religious experience appear in his epistles and in Acts 7:58–28:31. Augustine's *Confessions* contains his psychology of religion.

[11] See Jonathan Edwards, *A Treatise Concerning the Religious Affections* (Philadelphia: Cressy, 1921).

[12] The history of psychology of religion is treated by G. A. Coe, *The Psychology of Religion* (Chicago: University of Chicago Press, 1916), pp. 1-2; Sante de Sanctis, *Religious Conversion*, tr. H. Augur (New York: Harcourt, Brace & Co., 1927), pp. 1-26, 263-318; and D. M. Trout, *Religious Behavior* (New York: The Macmillan Co., 1911), pp. 397-434.

came systematic and critical surveys of the whole field of religious psychology by E. S. Ames, *The Psychology of Religious Experience* (1910); G. M. Stratton, *The Psychology of the Religious Life* (1911); J. H. Leuba, *A Psychological Study of Religion* (1912); G. A. Coe, *The Psychology of Religion* (1916); J. B. Pratt, *The Religious Consciousness* (1920).

In the twenties the field was enriched by the studies of Rudolf Otto, W. B. Selbie, F. L. Strickland, W. S. Bruce, R. H. Thouless, F. S. Hickman, A. C. Underwood, Sante de Sanctis, J. C. Flower, H. W. Dresser, E. T. Clark, C. C. Josey, and E. S. Conklin. In the thirties D. M. Trout, A. D. Nock, A. T. Boisen, T. H. Hughes, A. C. Knudson, E. M. Ligon, the Wiemans, and K. R. Stolz added other interpretations. Recent works fall into diverse areas of special interest, applying psychology to religious and character education, to the work of the pastor as counselor, and to problems of health, social leadership, and like matters. There is need for more systematic studies in psychology of religion.

3. Points of View

Psychological investigations inevitably possess points of view. In the effort to be scientific one may seek to rule them out as being "unwarranted assumptions." But some point of view is implicit in every view, whether scientific or otherwise, and it is the part of rigorous, honest understanding to be explicit. It is well to bring these assumptions and presuppositions to the light of open consideration rather than to conceal them in busy efforts to look the other way in order to avoid seeing where we stand in the looking.

Psychology is the science of mind. There are three ways of looking at mind: subjective, objective, and synoptic points of view.[13]

[13] Historical information about psychologies is given by E. G. Boring, *A History of Experimental Psychology* (New York: D. Appleton-Century Co., 1929); Edna Heidbreder, *Seven Psychologies* (New York: D. Appleton-Century Co., 1933); Richard Müller-Freienfels, *The Evolution of Modern Psychology*, tr. W. B. Wolfe (New Haven: Yale University Press, 1935); and Gardner Murphy, *An Historical Introduction to Modern Psychology* (New York: Harcourt, Brace & Co., 1928; 1932).

Let us examine each standpoint in the order in which it is named.

a) The subjective view studies *mind from within*. Introspection or looking within is the method of examining one's own conscious experience. The structural psychologies of Locke and Hume analyzed the mental contents into sensations and ideas. Titchener sought a scientific dissection of mind by taking consciousness apart and dealing with its elements as sensations and images. Dynamic psychologies have described the stream of consciousness (James), stimulus-response (Thorndike and Woodworth) representing the mind in action. Depth psychology also views mind from within. The psychoanalytic work of Freud employed dream analysis, free association, and symbolism to explore the urges and complexes beneath the surface of consciousness. Jung, Adler, Rank, and others have broadened the investigations of subconscious processes for diagnosis and treatment of personality disorders.

There are difficulties in introspective methods: *(a)* Consciousness is private; it is not readily open to the scientific comparison and verification of common objects in public view. *(b)* Language is inadequate to communicate inner experiences to others. *(c)* Self-observation is difficult because the observing interferes with the naturalness of the experience. Few people are expert or accurate in describing their own feelings. And yet in spite of the difficulties introspection does provide the only immediate, firsthand evidence of the inner experiences so necessary to an understanding of human behavior. To comprehend the motives and feelings of others, one must infer from his own. Rather than giving up the introspective task, it is wise to become more expert in such observation.

b) The objective view studies *mind from without*. Experimental work in psychology began a century ago to study reaction time with a chronoscope invented by Wheatstone in 1840. By 1880 psychological laboratories were opened in Europe and America. In 1903 the Russian scientist Pavlov conducted his famous experiments on conditioning the salivary reflex of dogs. These and other experiments encouraged the hope of an objective psychology based entirely upon external observation and measurement. Behaviorism describes behavior as a physiological process, while functional psychology treats mind as an instrument for biological use in evolutionary survival.

The objective approach aims to be strictly scientific in its study of facts open to public observation and verification. But it is limited to the extent that it is external and consequently remote from the sources, motives, and inner meanings of behavior. As a method, behaviorism is useful; as a philosophy denying consciousness, it is unscientific and nonpsychological. Objective studies of behavior have succeeded in gathering significant data (of animals and children notably) and treating them in scientific manner. But taken alone, without the data of consciousness, the objective method is quite inadequate to understand the insights, values, and motives of human experience.

c) The synoptic view studies *mind in perspective.* Finding neither subjective introspection nor objective measurement adequate alone, psychology undertakes to employ both together. In the perspective of man as a whole operating in environmental situations there is better opportunity to understand behavior. Gestalt psychology seeks the meaning of behavior in the total pattern of experience. In perception objects are seen not one by one but as a larger whole; for example, the whole face is recognized rather than one feature at a time. In a maze or problem solving, the individual reacts not to one stimulus at a time but with insight to the total situation. Hormic psychology describes behavior as a purposive seeking of goals. Instincts, impulses, and dispositions are urging life toward the realization of some end anticipated by the individual. Personalistic psychology sees every aspect of experience and behavior as belonging to a unitary person that gives meaning and integration to conscious activity. Interpersonal psychology views personality as interacting with other persons in social relations.

Classifications are of course artificial, and many psychologists today feel the time has come to outgrow rival schools by finding common ground on which to agree. Two trends may be noted in recent psychology: *(a)* to reject atomistic elements in favor of organic wholes, and *(b)* to subordinate static structures to dynamic processes. These holistic and motor trends are so widely accepted as to govern the work of most psychologists today. The schools are outgrowing former limitations, emphasizing other facts, and putting new meaning into old concepts. The leading structural psychology today is Gestalt (also topological), and it has entirely rejected atomistic and static concepts for dynamic wholes. Dynamic psychology is moving beyond instinct and stimulus-response to purpose and goal-tensions.

The dynamic, interpersonal psychology of religion here presented follows these holistic and motor trends. It is synoptic in viewing whole persons as interacting with other persons in a social environment. It is dynamic in seeking the personal and social goal-tensions that motivate behavior. Every person is in dynamic interaction within and without. Religious behavior is social co-operation, human and divine, to attain value goals.

4. DATA AND METHODS

The psychology of religion is not remote from the points of view described above. The pioneer work of general and experimental psychology, genetic and educational psychology, anthropology and social psychology, mental hygiene and therapy, have exerted no little influence upon the study of religion. The data of psychology of religion are drawn from these investigations as well as from distinctly religious sources. In tracing the methods of securing and treating religious facts we shall classify them as subjective, objective, and synoptic.

a) Subjective studies of religion:

(1) The *biographical* method opens a rich source of information about religious experience. Autobiographies of men and women to whom religion was life have revealed its vivid meaning to them. The confessions and journals of Augustine, St. Teresa,

Wesley, Fox, Woolman, and other religious leaders, and the devotional writings of Thomas à Kempis, Richard Baxter, Jeremy Taylor, and others provide primary sources of great value in knowing the inner life. Individuals whose religious perceptions are keen and whose literary expression is facile continue to enlarge the source material of religious experience.

William James made effective use of these resources in his *The Varieties of Religious Experience* (1902), which has become as classic as the biographies he draws from, and for the same reason. A vivid sense of reality pervades authentic religious testimonies; they hold perennial interest, bearing witness to the life that is in them. Biographical data are used by other psychologists of religion, for how can they be ignored? Like the case studies so valuable in medical, legal, and social records, they are histories of what happens to and by the principal actors on the scene. They may not always be typical, for those who write of vivid experiences are apt to be exceptional persons. To separate fact from fiction is difficult in all experiences; but experience is the place to begin investigation. Illusions are as much the data of psychology as sober judgments. Empirical sciences begin with experience and work therefrom.

(2) The *questionnaire* method is a systematic way of guiding confessions and accumulating a quantity of comparative data upon topics of interest. Lists of questions are carefully constructed and submitted to a number of people selected as typical of populations whom they represent. The responses are then classified, analyzed, and treated statistically to indicate characteristic trends in religious life. E. D. Starbuck pioneered in questionnaire studies, basing his *The Psychology of Religion* (1899) largely thereon. Coe, Pratt, Leuba, Clark, and others have used questionnaire procedures in their psychologies of religion. They have been widely employed in educational research, as in religious and social surveys. More recently they have been used by psychologists to secure cross sections of political opinion (Gallup polls) or discover the interests of customers, readers, and radio listeners.

Defects in the questionnaire method have been noted and freely admitted by those who employ it. G. A. Coe points out six limitations: (a) the unintentional selection of data by fragmentary questions and answers; (b) answers suggested by the questions; (c) inaccurate observation, especially when introspection is required; (d) inaccuracy of memory; (e) inaccurate or inadequate description; (f) the necessity of interpreting returns.[14] And yet increasing use proves usefulness. A large part of data gathered in various sciences results from defining problems, asking questions, and reporting information as accurately as may be possible. Some of the defects may be corrected by clarifying issues, giving better directions, eliminating ambiguities, and comparing answers. Numerous refinements, such as true-false, multiple-choice, completion, matching, crossing out terms, verbal association, together with statistical procedures for checking and weighing the data, increase their value. Personal interviews used with questionnaires also make them more trustworthy.

(3) *Psychometric* techniques, outgrowths of the questionnaire, are more accurate scientific instruments. Mental testing, pioneered in 1908 by Binet and Simon in France, has been refined and elaborated into batteries of tests for measuring nearly every aspect of personality. Rating scales for traits of character and conduct, adjustment inventories, attitude and temperament tests, introversion-extroversion tests, emotion and interest tests, information, judgment, opinion, and ethical discrimination tests, free association lists, environment scales, and performance tests have come into wide use. They are not foolproof or free from error. They are experimental and somewhat artificial. But when carefully constructed and validated statistically by correlation with other factors, they serve in gathering data for understanding personality in ways that are significant for religion.

b) Objective studies of religion:

(1) *Archaeological* research has uncovered a vast amount of

[14] Coe, *The Psychology of Religion,* pp. 43-49.

information about the ancient manifestations of religion. Tools, artifacts, and burial customs of prehistoric men yield religious evidence. Egyptian tombs and buried cities of the Near East have opened amazing treasures of inscriptions, statues, pictorial and architectural designs, hymns, prayers, and chronicles that show what religion meant to those peoples. These remains are fragmentary, yet they offer objective data for scientific study and psychological inference.

(2) *Anthropological* studies have investigated the religious customs of primitive culture. Myths and legends; tribal ceremonies and traditions in reference to birth, initiation, and death; prayers, charms, and curses; totem emblems and sacrifices; the placating of spirits and magical practices, contribute to the data of religion. It is in evaluating this material that difficulties arise. To the external observer it may appear a mumbo-jumbo hocus-pocus of groveling superstition, or it may be seen as the prototype of almost every modern religious belief and practice. Every fact has to be interpreted, and hasty generalization often lifts marvelous rabbits out of innocent old hats. The evolutionary hypothesis assumes that all forms of religion are somehow one, thus blurring contrasts and melting differences into the common lump. Is religion the child of magic? Are the gods heroic myths or emblems of tribal unity? Are beliefs in the soul and immortality by-products of ghosts and dreams? Is sex the root of all religion? Is interest in God a manifestation of the father complex? It is well to avoid the fallacy of primitivism, claiming that origin determines value, and falling into the pit where high religion is nothing more than low.[15]

(3) *Experimental* methods have proved useful in many fields of science. In psychology they are less impressive than in physics because the subject matter is more complex and unpredictable. Psychologists have devised ways of measuring physiological reactions and sense discrimination, but they turn to testing and

---

[15] See E. S. Brightman, *A Philosophy of Religion* (New York: Prentice-Hall, Inc., 1940), pp. 37-39; and Coe, *op. cit.*, pp. 51-53.

statistical methods to discover the mental traits of personality. Religious behavior does not readily yield to laboratory techniques, and yet experimental methods may be employed. Coe experimented with hypnosis in connection with questionnaires,[16] and psychoanalysts have examined mythologies and dreams. William James and Benjamin Blood were interested in "anaesthetic revelations," tracing similarities between the sensations and hallucinations produced by drugs and those observed in religious ecstasy.[17] Psychic research has experimented with alleged communications of departed spirits. More practical than these borderland experiments is the controlled observation of worship and religious education, measuring the effects of setting and symbols, items of prayer, scripture, music, suggestion, instruction, projects, and other activities.

c) Synoptic studies of religion:

(1) *Historical* study of religion is synoptic in the effort to see religion in perspective. It employs the data of archaeology and anthropology with literary documents and records to trace the course of civilizations. While using all available sources it is not confined to any one type of data or method of research. Sacred literature is usually written in historical form interpreting the religious meaning of events. Biographical studies show the history of individuals in reaction to contemporary events. Interpretation is a large part of the historical task, and from a synoptic view the intrepretations are more likely to be fair and comprehensive. On the broad stage of history causes and effects stand out more clearly, and a steadier light is cast upon the essential nature of religion in all times.

(2) Social and religious *surveys* are employed to gather information on a large scale. The religious needs and facilities of a whole community, state, or country may reveal significant condi-

[16] See Coe, *The Spiritual Life* (New York: Methodist Book Concern, 1900), pp. 104-50.

[17] See James, *The Varieties of Religious Experience* (New York: Longmans, Green & Co., 1902), pp. 387-91.

tions and trends. Questionnaires, interviews, report sheets, and statistical procedures join to make the survey a serviceable method. What is unique about this method is not the techniques employed but joining them together in a comprehensive investigation. By this means the interrelations of many social factors and forces— economic conditions, heredity, environment, population trends, cultural levels, customs, ideals, vocational interests, amusements— may be seen together in larger relationships.

(3) *Systematic observation and interpretation* is needed to complete these studies of religion. It should be present in each of the foregoing methods and finally should draw together all data into systematic perspective. Biographical data may be gathered by personal interviews recording the life history, family and social influences, health, interests, problems, and purposes. Questionnaires and tests, experiments and surveys, to reveal social and cultural factors, bring other data into the picture. When all possible information is secured, it may be cast into a profile or psychograph, that we may view the situation as a whole. In this way guidance centers, behavior clinics, medical services, and educational, psychological, and religious counselors are able to diagnose and plan more wisely. This exemplifies the systematic observation and interpretation needed to understand any human situation. Our psychology of religion cannot rest content in any knowledge short of the most thoroughgoing investigation. To understand religion psychologically, arm-chair theories must give place to accurate information and working principles that grow out of such information. Interpretation must walk step by step with observation from facts to principles.

5. RELIGION AND PERSONALITY

Defining religion is a difficult task because religion is so complex. It is one of the broadest terms that language provides, for religion works with the largest ideas man has ever conceived. As a collective noun it covers a vast array of human interests and activities. In the name of religion what deed has not been done? For the sake of religion men have earnestly affirmed and contradicted almost every idea and form of conduct. In the long history of religion appear chastity and sacred prostitution, feasting and fasting, intoxication and prohibition, dancing and sobriety, human sacrifice and the saving of life in orphanages and hospitals, superstition and education, poverty and wealthy endowments, prayer wheels and silent worship, gods and demons, one God and many gods, attempts to escape and to reform the world. How can such diametrical oppositions all be religious? Yet which of them can be excluded without an arbitrary denial of historical facts?

An adequate definition of religion must be general enough to include all types. Many definitions are constructed by the doubtful device of taking (or mistaking) some part for the whole. It is possible to classify definitions of religion by the chief aspect indicated. Leuba classified them in three groups as emphasizing the intellectual, emotional, or volitional aspect.[18] To these should be added three more groups: social and institutional definitions, value definitions, and synthetic definitions that seek to unite these aspects in a larger view. We may well begin with a general definition.

Religion is response to a Sustainer of Values. This statement aims to include as many aspects and varieties of religion as possible. Any response, whether fear or trust, any action or attitude that recognizes a power able to control values, is religion in the broad sense. Any Sustainer—or many—who can save or destroy, give or withhold what one may need or desire, is indicated. A Sustainer may be personal (as a Father) or impersonal (as a process), human (as a parent) or divine (as a Wholly Other), natural (as scientific forces) or supernatural (as magical powers), individual (as in monotheism) or societal (as in humanism) and institutional (as in Nazi devotion to the nation). This definition excludes neither magic nor demons, neither codes of laws nor ethics; it includes devotion of animals to

[18] See J. H. Leuba, *A Psychological Study of Religion* (New York: The Macmillan Co., 1912), pp. 339-60.

masters, children to parents, lovers to beloveds, and patriots dying for a fatherland. The essentials of religion are *(a)* desire for values, *(b)* conscious dependence upon a power who is able to sustain such values, and *(c)* responses considered appropriate to secure the values by aid from such a power.[19]

With this inclusive view as a background, a more distinctive definition is needed to differentiate religion. It must distinguish what is meant from what is not meant, drawing clearly the line between the designated and the undesignated. For a term that connotes everything denotes nothing. Religion will need to be distinguished from magic and myth, social custom and organization, science and philosophy, ethics and aesthetics, though it may have points in common with them. A differential definition will point to what is essentially unique.

Religion is personal co-operation with a trusted Creator of Values. The most unique trait of religion is belief in a Creator of Values. Psychology can neither prove nor assume the existence of such a Creator. But psychology cannot ignore human belief in a Creator. Religious devotion usually refers to a superhuman being great enough to create good things. Not every deity is credited with creation of the world or life. But every deity is worshiped because he is trusted to create some value. Lesser spirits, men, and animals may sustain values, but to create new values is distinctly a godlike achievement. Mere power is not the object of religious devotion, but power for good. Demons and evil spirits may be feared and exorcized either by magic employing mechanical coercion or by religion seeking to persuade a good power to help. Religion worships only good powers, though it may fight against evil ones. The whole

[19] Cf. the statement of J. B. Pratt that "religion is the serious and social attitude of individuals or communities toward the power or powers which they conceive as having ultimate control over their interests and destinies."—*The Religious Consciousness* (New York: The Macmillan Co., 1920), p. 2. Our view of a Sustainer of Values is quite in accord with his Determiner of Destiny, though it is less deterministic, and accents present values more than the ultimate outcome of final destiny. "Response" is a larger and more dynamic term than "attitude," used by Pratt.

range of its activities is to save the good and to overcome the evil.

A second characteristic of religion is social co-operation. Many are the responses of religion, but the most essential of all is co-operation. Desiring values and believing in a higher power able to help, the religious person seeks to co-operate in realizing them. Creation of values is co-operation. God is understood to need man, even as man needs God. Also men need each other, and religion seeks the common good by mutual action. Religious co-operation is not mechanical, as magic and science may be, but social. Prayer is a person-to-person request. Religions may be pantheistic and super-personal or naturalistic and impersonal, but these are more like magic or science and less distinctively religious. Historically and essentially the distinctive faith and work of religion is co-operation with a Creator of Values.[20]

Values are personal. They belong in every case to someone for whom they have meaning and worth. A religious value may refer to an object, but it also refers to a subject who cherishes it. Religion therefore moves and has its being in the realm of personality. The experience of religion is a personal experience; its value is intelligible only to persons. Psychology of religion seeks to explore the meaning of religion in human personality.

There are two ways in which religious studies may evade personality. One may take a microscopic view of religion by studying the minutiae of its minor details, the jots and tittles (dots of *i*'s, crossings of *t*'s) in literal devotion to words, or the postures and genuflexions of formal ceremonies, thus missing the vital meaning of religious experience for personality as a whole. Another may take a telescopic view of religion as a cosmic process in a comprehensive

[20] Cf. Brightman's definition: "Religion is co-operation with God and man for the realization of individual and shared values."—*Op. cit.*, p. 435. This is submitted as a normative definition of what religion ought to be. A good example of a less personalistic definition is Wieman's: "Religion is devotion to what one holds to be supremely worthful not only for himself but for all human living."—*Normative Psychology of Religion* (New York: Thomas Y. Crowell Co., 1935), p. 29. Both agree in co-operation and sharing values; the former refers to God as personality.

unity of impersonal pantheism, submerging personality in the larger whole as a wave subsiding into an ocean of engulfing being. Either view, whether miscroscopic or telescopic, lacks the perspective of personality and distorts the understanding of religion. These distortions psychology of religion seeks to correct by focusing upon religion as personal experience.

Personality is the organizing unity of experience directed by insight and purpose.[21] As experience is organized around religious insights and purposes, we become religious persons. Scientific psychologies have sometimes been microscopic, explaining behavior in atomistic terms without recognizing the organizing work of personality as a whole. The reflex arc, stimulus-response, association of ideas, instinctive urges, unconscious mechanisms, may be useful concepts but are fractional segments of the whole person in action. While the specializing tendency of a science may be to know more and more about less and less, the generalizing tendency of a philosophy may be to know less and less about more and more. Some psychologies of religion are overphilosophical, taking a telescopic view of distant processes beyond the legitimate range of psychology. Psychology will recognize the objective reference of all experience, but it does not investigate the nature of God or the engulfing causation of a cosmic continuum.

The psychology of religion here set forth aims to follow a moderate course between the rocks and shoals of microscopic and telescopic fallacies. In so doing we must consider personality the unit of our investigation. Responses are to be seen as intra-activities of personality, even as society is the interactivity of personalities. This may be called interpersonal psychology, for the person is the essential unit of interaction in a social order.

[21] See P. E. Johnson, *Who Are You?* (New York and Nashville: Abingdon-Cokesbury Press, 1937), pp. 16-23.

II

Religious Experience

1. THRESHOLDS OF RELIGIOUS AWARENESS

To be conscious is to have experience. The limits of experience are called "thresholds" or "limens." Experimental work has been conducted to discover the points at which persons become aware of auditory, visual, and gustatory stimuli.[1] But these sensations, once thought to be the final elements of psychological analysis, are neither specific nor reliable data but abstractions from larger empirical unities. Gestalt psychology has demonstrated that perceptions are total patterns of meaning, not summations of atomistic sensations. Perceptions are organized by persons into meaningful wholes. "No Gestalt without a Gestalter."[2] Thresholds are, therefore, boundaries of personal significance that are raised or lowered by the person's selective responsiveness.

What does it mean to be conscious and have experiences? In waking from deep slumber you have a typical experience to analyze. One may be roused by some disturbing stimuli such as light or sound waves. The effort to wake up meets resistance and perhaps resentment at being disturbed from drowsy comfort, but one responds by groping for a meaning. "What's that?" The light may then be recognized as coming from a window—which means morning. The noise may be identified as the ringing of an alarm clock meaning, "Time to get up." With that recognition a dilemma arises, "Do I have to get up, or can I stay in bed a while longer?"

[1] Consult W. F. Vaughan, *General Psychology* (New York: The Odyssey Press, 1936; 1939), pp. 106-8; E. G. Boring *et al.*, *Introduction to Psychology* (New York: John Wiley & Sons, 1939).

[2] William Stern, *General Psychology*, tr. H. D. Spoerl (New York: The Macmillan Co., 1938), pp. 114, 179.

33

Then one gropes for perspective by recalling yesterday with its unfinished business and forecasting today with its plans and responsibilities until a decision is made and action taken—or action deferred.

There are evidently four steps in this procedure of becoming conscious: (*a*) There is *awareness*, or selective attention. From waves of stimuli beating upon his receptors, a person selects relevant ones by attending responses. Intensity, suddeness, or repetition of light or sound stimuli have arousing effect. Yet the motor set, interest, or response of the person also directs attention (literally, a "tension" toward something). (*b*) With this comes a process of *search*.[3] What is going on? One is alert enough to be aware of a disturbance without yet fully knowing what it means. Awaking is an exploratory process, focusing perception upon the total situation, seeking more information about it. (*c*) The next step is a *judgment* of recognition. This is the daylight that means morning, the sound of an alarm clock meaning "Wake up!" Perception grows clearer as the mind gropes for understanding. Every judgment is a relating act, bringing this event into relation with others and seeing them together. The range of interpretation is enlarged by other items from the memory of the past and the prospect of the future. (*d*) From these insights conscious experience now becomes more *purposeful*. There have been purposive, or goal-seeking, tendencies throughout in selectivity, search, and judgment. But the purpose now becomes the problem, or focal issue, in a conscious effort to make a decision. Something needs to be done, in this case the getting up and on to the tasks of the day. As one recognizes the morning time that means another day, he foresees goals and engages in the telic consideration of means to serve the ends in view.

Religious experience is not so simple as this, yet the religious

[3] For a psychological exposition of search see D. M. Johnson, "A Modern Account of Problem Solving," *Psychological Bulletin*, XLI (1944), 201-29.

consciousness, upon analysis, yields the four operations noted above. There is *awareness* of religious stimuli[4] and *search* for religious meanings. There is interpretation issuing in *judgments* of recognition and value. There will be *purposes* to do something to attain religious goals. Religious consciousness is not a world separate from the secular consciousness. The structure of all experience appears to have these four characteristics though the content may vary. The nature of religious experience does not contradict or escape the natural order of consciousness.

Does the person, in religious awareness, use the natural perceptions, or does he have a special sense beyond them? To begin with, we should admit the place of sensory perceptions in much of our religious experience. To perceive the beauty of a sunset, or the splendor of a starlight night, may call forth joyous reverence. To sense the boisterous terror of a storm at sea may impel men to call upon their God for mercy and help. To hear persuasive preaching, scripture reading, and singing of hymns may lead to a religious conversion. To see the holy symbols of a High Mass may hold one in rapt attention upon the divine meanings. Religious awareness stoops to use the lowliest of perceptions and elevates them to sublime heights of admiration and devotion.

The language of religion is rich in sensory imagery:

O taste and see that the Lord is good.

I will lift up mine eyes unto the hills. Whence cometh my help?

I saw the Lord . . . high and lifted up, and his train filled the temple.

Speak Lord; for thy servant heareth.

When I consider thy heavens, the work of thy fingers, the moon and the stars, which thou hast ordained; what is man, that thou art mindful of him?[5]

[4] A religious stimulus may be defined as any event which initiates a religious response, as toward a Creator of Values.

[5] Pss. 34:8; 121:1; Isa. 6:1; I Sam. 3:9; Ps. 8:3-4.

By enlarging perspectives of interpretation, perceptions are woven into the meaning of an eternal presence.

This brings us to the other part of the question: Does religious awareness employ a special spiritual sense? William James finds evidence for an affirmative answer. In his chapter on "The Reality of the Unseen" he cites numerous illustrations of supersensible recognitions, leading him to conclude:

It is as if there were in the human consciousness *a sense of reality, a feeling of objective presence, a perception* of what we may call "something there," more deep and more general than any of the special and particular "senses" by which the current psychology supposes existent realities be originally revealed.[6]

One is not reassured by his comparison of this type of experience with hallucinations, but he considers vivid experiences of divine presence convincing to the one who has them and decisive in the permanent fruits of character. The outcome of his investigation seems to be that intuitions may be either illusory or real but are more apt to bring certainty than shallow rationalism.[7] Gestalt psychology also finds perception a direct insight into the meaning of a situation as a whole.[8]

Rudolf Otto criticizes the above passage from William James as naïve, contending that James resorts to mysterious hypotheses to explain religious perception.[9] To Otto this feeling of reality is objectively given as "a primary, immediate datum of consciousness" not deducible from other data. This unique datum of a

---

[6] *The Varieties of Religious Experience*, p. 58. Italics are in the original.

[7] "If you have intuitions at all, they come from a deeper level of your nature than the loquacious level which rationalism inhabits. . . . The unreasoned and immediate assurance is the deep thing in us, the reasoned argument is but a surface exhibition."— *Ibid.*, pp. 73-74.

[8] See Kurt Koffka, *The Growth of Mind*, tr. R. M. Ogden (New York: Harcourt, Brace & Co., 1924; 1928), and Wolfang Köhler, *The Mentality of Apes*, tr. E. Winter (New York: Harcourt, Brace & Co., 1926).

[9] *The Idea of the Holy*, tr. J. W. Harvey (London: Oxford University Press, 1923), p. 10, note.

"Wholly Other" he calls the "numinous," from the Latin word *numen*, meaning the divine force or potency ascribed to objects or beings regarded with awe. "This mental state is perfectly *sui generis* and irreducible to any other." [10] It is a direct perception of reality independent of other forms of knowledge.

A. C. Knudson joins with Otto and Troeltsch in finding the source of religious experience in a unique religious a priori. He distinguishes four different kinds of experience: sense experience, aesthetic experience, moral experience, and religious experience. "Man has a native capacity for each of these." They are "structural in human nature, . . . unique and underived." No one of them can be deduced from, or reduced to, another. The religious a priori is a unique endowment, or potentiality, consisting not in specific content but in the capacity to have religious experiences. [11]

That men have religious capacities can be heartily endorsed. But that religious capacity is independent of sense, aesthetic, and moral capacities would seem questionable. Human capacities inter-mingle freely, and surely religion is not to be divorced from aesthetic and moral experiences, when beauty enters so largely into worship and the moral imperative into religious conduct. Religious capacities may be unique, but can they be independent and separate? If so, human nature falls apart into segregated faculties like the splitting off of dissociated personalities. Is religious devotion so fractional that it employs only a fragment of the self? We agree that religious capacity is too dynamic to be the mere sum of other parts, but it is also too unified to be only one part. Do not all capacities (religious, social, moral, aesthetic) work together in the whole man who achieves religious integration?

What makes awareness religious? Is the uniqueness in data or interpretation? Religious data may be unique, but no datum is

[10] *Ibid.*, p. 7.

[11] See Knudson, *The Validity of Religious Experience* (New York and Nashville: Abingdon-Cokesbury Press, 1937), p. 146; also "Religious Apriorism," *Studies in Philosophy and Theology*, ed. E. C. Wilm (New York: The Abingdon Press, 1922), pp. 93-127.

religious without interpretation. Analysis shows that the same data may be interpreted toward either religious or secular meanings. This would indicate that the distinctly religious process is in the interpretation. After all, religion is a question of what life means to you. There are experiences that seem to be uniquely religious, like the feeling of God's presence, the strength and comfort of his sustaining power. But these mean only what they are judged to mean. Pure data without interpretation (if such there be) do not even constitute a sensory perception, much less religious understanding and devotion.

What empirical tendencies may be taken as clues to distinguish religious from nonreligious experiences? Religious awareness will be seen to arise in devotion to values. Briefly we may note three characteristics of religious experience. (*a*) Religious experience is a value experience: a preference for interests and needs worth realizing. (*b*) Religious experience is a divine reference: an objective outreach to a supreme value and source of values. (*c*) Religious experience is a social response: an effort to co-operate with a divine power in the creation of values. These movements in religious experience will be explored as we proceed.

2. INTEREST, NEED, AND WORTH

At thresholds of religious awareness we have discovered psychological tendencies that are present in all experience. This raises the question of the uniqueness of religious experience. What makes some experiences religious and others nonreligious? The previous section reached the conclusion that religious traits arise in value experience. The next step will therefore be to analyze the psychological development of values, particularly religious values.

Worth stems from interest and need. Whatever satisfies interest or need has value. R. B. Perry defines a value as "any object of any interest." [12] Interest is a personal response of attention. It literally means tension between events. From our viewpoint, inter-

[12] *A General Theory of Value* (New York: Longmans, Green & Co., 1926), p. 115.

est may be defined as an attentive attitude toward situations that seem to affect one's values. Perry describes interest as a motor-affective act, attitude, or disposition of favor or disfavor. It is characteristic of human attitudes to be for or against things. This spontaneous response of preference is what recognizes objects of interest as values. Yet Perry unduly enshrouds his concept with mystery: "An act is interested in so far as its occurrence is due to the agreement between its accompanying expectation and the un-fulfilled phases of a governing propensity." [13]

Expectation is clearly an aspect of interest, but his reference to a "governing propensity" is a more difficult puzzle. By this term he makes reference to a general determining tendency in control of the organism. The implication is that interests are controlled by instincts or mechanisms that push them into action. In relating these determining tendencies to instincts he does not mean heredi-tary reflexes. Behavior is too variable and modifiable for that. To him, instinct is an inherited propensity, a specific disposition to learn. This is called a "driving adjustment" that responds to ex-ternal and internal stimulating conditions by tending to release particular sets of random acts to particular goals. The propensity is thus merely a tendency to respond to stimuli by repeated efforts until "success" is attained. If instinct is reduced to nothing more than a persistent tendency to react to stimuli, we may wonder what after all is left of the instinct.

William McDougall [14] contends that the inherited and relatively unchanging tendencies of human character are of two main classes: general and specific. In addition to the general tendencies arising from the constitution of mind, he describes a number of specific tendencies, or instincts. Each of the instincts is related to a primary emotion arising therefrom. Some of these are:

[13] *Ibid.*, p. 183.

[14] *An Introduction to Social Psychology* (Boston: J. W. Luce & Co. [1908], 1918), pp. 47-84.

Instinct	Emotion
Flight	Fear
Repulsion	Disgust
Curiosity	Wonder
Pugnacity	Anger
Self-abasement	Subjection
Self-assertion	Elation
Parental instinct	Tenderness

To multiply instincts in this way raises the dilemma of where to stop. In later writings [15] McDougall adds food-seeking, gregariousness, mating, acquisitiveness, constructiveness, appeal, laughter, comfort, rest, the migratory instinct, and other propensities. E. L. Thorndike finds almost as many instincts as situations to which organisms respond. His catalogue of unlearned tendencies or "gene-caused propensities" seems to approach infinity. In defense of their large number, he argues that the genes provide tens of thousands of specific details in making the sizes and shapes and colors of the parts of man's body—why then, should instinctive tendencies be less elaborate? [16] He does omit the religious instinct as well as McDougall's instincts of self-abasement and self-assertion, Freud's death instinct and perverse sexuality, and many others, such as the herd instinct, the maternal instinct, rivalry, acquisitiveness, pugnacity, and self-preservation. Why omit some of these and not others? His reply is that genes are not deities and do not deal in magical powers. But why is one instinct less magical than another?

McDougall agrees in rejecting the religious instinct; for religious emotion is no single and specific expression of one instinct. It is too complex and diversified to be the product of a single motive, but develops in various ways from multiple causes.[17] Formerly,

[15] *Outline of Psychology* (New York: Charles Scribner's Sons, 1923), pp. 130-76; *The Energies of Men* (New York: Charles Scribner's Sons, 1933), pp. 97-98.

[16] *Human Nature and the Social Order* (New York: The Macmillan Co., 1940), pp. 300-301.

[17] *An Introduction to Social Psychology*, pp. 91-92.

religious instinct was generally accepted, but today one can scarcely find a psychologist to defend it. Religious experience grows out of many needs and interests basic in human nature, but to single out one of these is oversimplification; and to reduce empirical facts to instinct is unempirical.

The difficulty in every instinct theory is a fallacy of abstraction. Instincts are not facts, as popular thinking may assume, but theoretical inferences from facts. The inability to agree upon the nature and number of instincts is a typical difference in dealing with concepts that reside not in concrete facts but in the mind of the theorizer. Instincts are defined as unlearned tendencies "prior to experience and independent of training." But who can know what is prior to experience and independent of modifying conditions? It is maintained that sucking is an instinct because it appears so early in life. And yet the baby makes random motions, exploratory and experimental, in the first feedings that indicate learning is taking place. There is further possibility of prenatal practice in thumbsucking and experimenting to learn. Other so-called instincts are delayed, and defended on the principle of maturation. Yet who can deny that learning is possible during the maturation period? If there is any situation where every possibility of learning is excluded, a test case might be made. The best experiments appear in animal behavior, but it would be careless analogy to infer that human learning is identical with animal behavior.

G. W. Allport and P. A. Bertocci have conducted a stimulating debate on these theories of motivation. Allport views the purposes of different people as too diverse to be traced to a few primal motives shared by all. When they seek the same goals it is obvious that they are influenced by a similar environment and culture; they learn from each other the methods of attaining them. Interests and traits develop in response to situations that invite them.[18] Bertocci replies that one cannot explain the similarity of

[18] Allport, *Personality: A Psychological Interpretation* (New York: Henry Holt & Co., 1937), p. 112.

goals by appealing to similarity in culture, for the culture itself needs to be explained by reference to the cause of cultural similarity.[19] If individuals did not have common motives to begin with, would they ever create a common culture? Is not human life equipped with common goal-seeking propensities or purposes? Allport also recognizes purposive motivations, but arising from contemporary goal-seeking (functional autonomy), modified by learning, and individualized by divergent temperaments and abilities.[20] Bertocci proposes a synthesis of propensities, sentiments, and traits. He suggests that traits can be one of the levels at which hormic energy organizes itself into the life of an individual. Sentiments to him are "not adequate to explain the persistent and continuously functioning characteristics of given individuals which are uniquely expressive of their form of adjustment rather than their environment."[21] Allport cannot accept the proposal to regard attitudes, sentiments, and traits as merely proximate factors in motivation. "To my way of thinking they offer so ultimate a representation of human motivation as psychological knowledge today warrants."[22]

In view of the abstract and fallacious implication of "instinct," it would be wise to give up the term for a better one. The better concept from our point of view is "need." Needs may be organic (as hunger is), arising from lacks in the vital processes. They may be psychological and sociological in the growing range of interests and activities. This avoids the ambiguity of unlearned inheritance by recognizing that needs are constantly changing through learning and modifying conditions. Needs are "dynamic, unique, personal, and ultimate." They meet the purposive goal-seeking of Bertocci and the demand of Allport that "what matters most to

[19] Bertocci, "A Critique of G. W. Allport's Theory of Motivation," *Psychological Review*, XLVII (1940), 509.

[20] Allport, "Motivation in Personality: Reply to Mr. Bertocci," *Psychological Review*, XLVII (1940), 535-45.

[21] Bertocci, *op. cit.*, p. 531.   [22] Allport, *op. cit.*, p. 553.

me is that all of these units of motivational structure be regarded as dynamic, unique, personal, and ultimate." [23]

The dynamic psychology of H. A. Murray arises from the discovery of specific needs that motivate personality.[24] He classifies needs as viscerogenic and psychogenic. The organic needs which he calls viscerogenic include air, water, food, sex, lactation, urination, defecation, harmavoidance, and sentience. The psychogenic list of twenty-nine items includes such needs as acquisition, conservance, order, recognition, defendance, dominance, deference, blamavoidance, affiliation, succorance, and exposition. The effort to specify concrete needs is useful, but his recourse to universalized needs common to all falls again into the abstraction of instincts. In fact, the resemblance of his list of needs to familiar instincts is striking, as is also his concept of a hidden force which drives the organism.

A need is a construct (a convenient fiction or hypothetical concept) which stands for a force (the physico-chemical nature of which is unknown) in the brain region, a force which recognizes perception, apperception, intellection, connotation, and action in such a way as to transform in a certain direction an existing, unsatisfying situation.[25]

An abstraction is "a convenient fiction or hypothetical concept," and if there is any single organic force that does all that the above statement claims, it is as mysterious as the magical genes of Thorndike. We can agree with Murray (*a*) that need is the immediate outcome of certain internal and external occurrences, (*b*) that it is not a static entity but comes and goes and changes, (*c*) that each need is unique, and (*d*) that there are similarities among human needs. A need arises from an inner feeling of tension that seems to impel striving toward a specific goal. Yet needs tend to attach themselves to objects by a cathexis of desire or purpose. The focusing of needs upon specific objects and the images, interests, and emotions thereby excited become a need-integrate or complex.

[23] *Ibid.*
[24] *Explorations in Personality* (New York: Oxford University Press, 1938), pp. 52-96. [25] *Ibid.*, p. 123.

43

From interests and needs develop values. To be aware of a need is to value the object which will fulfill it. To be interested in an object is to desire and prefer it enough to give attention and goal-seeking effort in that direction. A value is a goal of conscious appreciation and preference, which one strives to realize. In seeking such a valued goal, the means that promise to serve that end are also valued. Instrumental values are means that serve intrinsic values as ends.

Andras Angyal undertakes a holistic approach to the rise of values in a chapter entitled "Biospheric Dynamics." [26] "Biosphere" is his term for the realm in which life carries on its bipolar organization. In this living system *tensions* are specific instances of dynamic subject-object relationships. The conscious experiences of these psychophysical tensions are *interests*. Viewed from the subject pole, tensions are *drives*, the conscious experience of which is *craving*. Readiness to behave in certain ways is termed *attitude*. When attitudes are traced back to more general ones they become unquestionable *axioms of behavior*. When intellectually elaborated, a system of personal axioms becomes a *philosophy of life*.

Biospheric tensions viewed from the object pole appear as environmental attractions or repulsions, termed positive and negative *valences*. The valences prompt specific behavior and, when conscious, may be called *demand quality*. When an object has the potentiality of exerting a prompting influence on the organism, it has *biological relevance*. Objects are relevant for the person by virtue of their *meaning* or content. The content is highly individualized by cultural variations and personal experiences. The personally relevant object represents a *value* for the individual. Specific values can be traced back successively to more general ones, until one eventually reaches a set of fundamental personal values. These *axiomatic values* are intrinsic, usually unquestionable,

[26] Angyal, *Foundations for a Science of Personality* (New York: The Commonwealth Fund, 1941).

for a given person. They form the *system of axiomatic personal values.*

This may help us to understand religious values. From the needs of personality, tensions occur in dynamic subject-object relations of interest. In the craving for objects or goals of value, attitudes of preference and desire become potent, overlaid with other attitudes of fear of thwarting and failure. In this mingling of desire and fear the person longs for help to succeed in reaching his goals. He is therefore apt to seek divine aid, the larger resources of supernatural power, to secure his values. In these efforts to co-operate with what he believes to be a divine Creator of Values, he is religious. To the extent that divine resources are sought to attain other goals, religious values are instrumental. To the extent that a divine Creator is viewed as the supreme value and all resources devoted to him, religious values are intrinsic. Admiration, awe, and wonder are typical responses to the Creator as intrinsic value. Anguish of need and joy of gratitude are typical responses to the Creator as instrumental to other values. So religion becomes a system of axiomatic personal values.

Wherever need and interest become focal in conscious experience, values are recognized. Not all values are religious, yet if needs are urgent enough and human abilities to meet them inadequate, religious search for divine aid is likely to occur. In turning to a Sustainer of Values for help, in feeling confidence and gratitude, and in earnest devotion to the value cause, the characteristic religious attitudes and emotions develop. These are reverence for a supreme value, the sense of need for greater resources than one's own, and the desire to give one's self in mutual purpose and comradeship to the One trusted to create and sustain values.

3. HUMAN RESPONSE TO DIVINE VALUE

No religious experience is merely subjective without objective reference. An argument for solipsism, contending that mind has knowledge of nothing beyond itself, is a *reductio ad absurdum.*

Like the dunce cap, solipsism is a device to put on others and is not intended for one's own head. Those who wield solipsistic threats intimidate by waving absurdities over the heads of opponents in argument. If one actually believed that doctrine, and wanted to be consistent, he would not attempt to convince others, who are as nonexistent as empty space and as unapproachable as the other side of the moon. Psychologists and philosophers, with rare exceptions, are all engaged in studying mind in relation to the objective world.

William Stern shows that general psychology is one of the "disciplines that treat mental phenomena not for themselves but in their *relation to the world*," including both the world of nature and the world of culture.[27] J. S. Moore declares that psychology, like every science, is based on postulates. The four indispensable presuppositions of psychology he finds to be: (a) the existence of the objective world, (b) the existence of consciousness, (c) the interrelation of consciousness and the world, (d) the uniformity of mental life.[28]

When J. H. Leuba suggests that the religious person invents his own god,[29] he surely does not mean to say such a person is entirely cut off from reality. For he recognizes the co-operation of men not only with other men but with "hyperhuman" forces of the real world. What he seems to mean is that the gods of religion are inductions from experience, and that human experience manifests "a Force tending to the creation of an ideal society." The reality is actually there; the invention is man's interpretation of it.

What we insist is that religious experience is response to objective reality. The presence of objective reality seems undeniable, at least it is assumed by everyone in practical activity and scientific labors. What reality is like is a question of interpretation. To

[27] Stern, *General Psychology*, p. 21.

[28] *The Foundations of Psychology* (Princeton: Princeton University Press, 1921), pp. 159-63.

[29] Leuba, *A Psychological Study of Religion*, p. 10.

physics it is a system of electronic forces, largely invisible yet moving at high speed and power in orderly ways. To religion, reality is also powerful and largely invisible, but vastly different from physical nature in value and responsiveness.

Psychology of religion does not undertake to prove the existence or describe the nature of a Divine Being. That is the task of philosophy and theology, beyond the limitations of psychological studies. But psychology, in company with every science, must assume an objective reality related to subjective experience. Without this postulate human experience and activity are unintelligible. In this larger setting of reality each experience appears as response to stimuli. Religious experience is response to stimuli that represent an active reality viewed as divine, or as creative of values.

The object of religious interest is a power or powers with which man may co-operate for good. Religion is human search for divine values. With divine powers we seek to co-operate in a way different from that employed with physical powers. Physical powers are treated mechanically by push and pull, prediction and control. Divine values can neither be pushed nor pulled, predicted nor controlled arbitrarily. The Divine Value is treated as a Person to be respected and invited. He responds not to command or coercion but to petition and persuasion. Even though the Divine Value may not be recognized clearly as personal, yet he is treated as a person should be treated.

The distinction between physical and spiritual is not one of amount of power. It is one of quality and kind of power. Things may be as powerful as high explosives, but they are not talked to as capable of understanding ideas. Spirits may be vaguely and weakly conceived, but they are viewed as responsive in personal ways to offering and invitation. Man responds socially to spirits because he expects spirits to respond in kind to him. There is a kinship of interest and comprehension, of asking and answering, that makes personal relations so widely different from impersonal relations.

In the face of this kinship there is also sharp contrast between human and divine. Like God, like people, is a well-established rule. Essential likenesses are not to be denied. But there are differences just as essential. The Creator stands over against the creature as "Wholly Other." The Divine Value is what man would like to be and is not. Divine attributes are the ideal and the despair of earnest seekers for a better life. "Be ye therefore perfect, even as your Father which is in heaven is perfect." [30] Whatever man most aspires to be is found in his ultimate ideal and represented in his heroic conception of the Divine Life.

It has often been noted, since the time of Edwards and Schleiermacher, that religion expresses man's sense of dependence. The recognition of this dependence upon resources other than one's own turns desires outward in objective reference to a more-than-human Resource. God is believed to be the Creator and Sustainer of the values man most needs. Before this Creator man stands in deep humility as one who does not make, but receives, his cherished life. In conscious dependence he realizes the chasm that separates his creaturehood from the Creator. In need he petitions, in gratitude he praises, the Creator of Values as the source of life and its goods.

The divine reality is therefore more than human in value as well as in power. As the Creator of Values, he is more than any other value. He not only makes values but is also the supreme value. He helps us in our needs and we come to need him for more than help. Humility in need and gratitude for help rise to reverence for, and joy in, the greatest of values. There comes a growing realization that the Sustainer is the chief good to be desired, more precious than any gift he might give. From this supreme valuation rises the decision to consecrate other goods to the highest good. Offerings increase in value until the worshiper offers himself as the most complete offering which it is in his power to dedicate. Reli-

[30] Matt. 5:48.

gious devotion is the continuous expression of this purpose to give one's self and all to God. In so doing the devotee may ask nothing for himself but the peace of harmony with the Source of Values. He is blessed with a sense of destiny fulfilled, of finding in losing, of a communion that is life's largest completion.

4. Religious Emotion

Motions and emotions go together. They are related in language and life. In language both come from the same root, "to move." In life they represent dynamic or motivating tendencies. Psychologists and psychiatrists give enlarging place to emotional factors controlling behavior. Devious experiments have been conducted to discover and measure emotions. But emotional life is not well understood and remains one of the baffling obscurities of present-day psychology.

This difficulty results from the prevailing style of conceiving emotions impersonally. The usual approach has been to analyze them into elements and to classify them by abstract and atomistic schemes. They have been reduced to sensations of pleasantness and unpleasantness. The somatic basis of feeling has been studied, and graphs have been made of pulse rate, breathing rate, and electrical changes of the body under emotional excitement. Emotional effects of glandular secretions and biological needs and strivings have been noted. But the outcome has been contradictory and inconclusive.

William Stern believes that feeling will be properly understood only as this atomism yields to a view of personality as a whole.[31] Emotions encompass all experience and subordinate all other mental activity to them. Feelings and moods are nuances, casts, and tones that pervade and suffuse the entire consciousness. He calls feeling embedded experience characterized by subjective nearness to the person. It has a formlessness that is difficult to describe directly without crystallizing it into ideational patterns. Cognition

[31] *Op. cit.,* pp. 513-74.

and acts of will are *Gestalten* and tend to form salient patterns; feeling is *Ungestalt,* fluid and diffuse, yet very influential in both ideas and action.

Emotions are dynamic and telic tensions of personal experience. They are usually aroused by interacting external and internal conditions of personality. Stimuli from the external world and stimuli from within organic processes and consciousness mingle with attention, perception, memory, anticipation, purpose, and judgment to produce emotional tensions. Needs, interests, and values arise in these emotional processes and play the role of both cause and effect. They too are telic and are never experienced without emotional qualities. Organic and psychic needs awaken interest in values that will satisfy them. To need something is to endure the risk of gaining or losing it. To value something is to have satisfaction in its realization and dissatisfaction in its loss. Emotion is thus the qualitative experience of tension toward goals.

Emotions have polarity because "the activity of the person maintains multiple polarized tensions" [32] that are reflected in consciousness. The telic polarity consists of the fluctuating success and failure which every person experiences in reaching his goals. The dynamic polarity appears in the expending and accumulating of energy, as felt in experiences of excitement and tranquillity. Transitive feelings are exciting when striving toward goals, pleasant while approaching goals, and unpleasant when receding from them. Resultant feelings are tranquil when telic activity is concluded, pleasant when fulfilled, and unpleasant when not fulfilled. These unstable fluctuations of mood result in an inner strain known as ambivalence. One may have ambivalent religious feelings in the alternating love and fear of God. Gradations of feeling occur, with variations in intensity, breadth, duration, depth, and genuineness of personal experience.

What stimulates emotion? In animals whose brains have been

[32] *Ibid.,* p. 533.

removed, scratching the back or pinching the tail may produce snarls from a dog or hissing and clawing from a cat; but these are evidently reflex actions. Conscious beings respond emotionally to situations that mean danger, success, or frustration. The same object or event, such as lightning, frightens one and not another according to its meaning for him. A child knows not whether to laugh or cry at a parental slap until it is clear whether it is a "spank" or a "love pat." The James-Lange theory that emotions result from bodily actions rather than causing them is a partial view of the total situation. Bodily action may accentuate emotion (as in the famous case of fear caused by running from a bear), but running away from a rabbit does not cause fear. Is it not the recognition of danger from the bear and no danger from the rabbit that makes the essential difference? And the recognition of this meaning is the idea that stimulates the emotion.[33]

We may talk of a pure emotion, but who has ever met one? If we should have a pure emotion, we could not recognize it, for recognition adds an idea to the emotion. Emotions are not things to be separated or divided, but activities of persons responding. A dynamic and synoptic view sees the various aspects of life united in total responses of the personality as a whole. The half truth in the James-Lange theory is the fact that body and mind interact. Bodily activity accentuates fear, even as fear whips up the circulation and neural tonicity for vigorous activity. Yet both the emotional and bodily activity are responses to occasions that mean danger by persons who recognize the need for flight or resistance. The whole truth points to emotions as interrelated with every interest and activity of the psychophysical life. To be emotionally aroused is to feel with the whole body from the tip of the toes to the roots of the hair, impulses that interact with conscious

[33] "The intensity of the anxiety is proportionate to the meaning the situation has for the person concerned. . . . The therapeutic task, therefore, can only be that of finding out the meaning certain situations have for him."—Karen Horney, *The Neurotic Personality of Our Time* (New York: W. W. Norton & Co., 1937), p. 44.

ideas and judgments of need and value. If in any situation one decides it does not matter, the emotion subsides. If he sees purposes threatened and thwarted, he is stirred up to excited responses of the total personality to defend his values.

Religion is deeply rooted in human emotions. There are those who find the origin and development of religion specifically in the emotional life. In my view, religious interests permeate every aspect of experience. No experience is vital or dynamic without emotional support, and since religion is concerned with the deepest needs and highest worths of life it will naturally be charged with emotional urgency. The most intense feelings appear in the most vital experiences, as E. S. Ames points out. "And it is just because religion involves these immense concerns of individual and social welfare that it is characterized by intense feeling." [34] Indifference results from lack of interest; and when religious interest fades, emotional content drains off and religion dries up in formalism or neglect. Liberal religious sects that neglect emotion for rationalism fade and decline. Without dynamic emotional motivation religion is of doubtful value except as a relic in a museum. Even museum relics have value only as they awaken interest and stir responses. Yet what a far cry from the warmly intense emotion of personal religious experience to the detached curiosity touching museum interests!

What stimulates religious emotion? Religion is affected by any and all interests vital enough to satisfy needs and increase values. Persons need to survive and grow in constant development of values; they need to share values in social participation; they need to create and construct new values for the enrichment of all; they need to mingle admiration and humility in reverence of supreme value. Religion is deeply involved in efforts to meet all these needs and to sustain all these values. And the more clearly their worth is recognized, the more emotional we become about them.

[34] *The Psychology of Religious Experience* (Boston: Houghton Mifflin Co., 1910), pp. 329-30.

We have so much at stake in the risks of life and society, in creating and appreciating these values, that we are rightly aroused emotionally to protect them from loss and enjoy them more abundantly. The complex organization of interests and emotions around a value object is known as a "sentiment." The organization of sentiments around permanent goals is known as a "disposition."

It is in the reverent sentiments and dispositions that we become most directly and vividly aware of religious values. When man confronts the Creator of Values, he may well be stirred to the depths of his being by the supreme significance of that event. The most thorough analysis of such emotions is made by Rudolf Otto in *The Idea of the Holy*. He finds the essence of religious experience in a constellation of emotions of creature-feeling. The fundamental element in strong and sincere religious emotion is the *mysterium tremendum,* which combines (*a*) a sense of awe more solemn than fear, a dread of the divine wrath; (*b*) a realization of the unapproachableness and power of the divine majesty; (*c*) energy and excitement in the urgency of the living God; (*d*) a stupor of wonder and astonishment before the "Wholly Other"; and (*e*) fascination, alluring rapture, and complete surrender to the supernatural object of devotion.

How are religious emotions different from other emotions? The distinctive feature is the meaning, the recognition of values related to personal emotional needs. Otto considers awe, wonder, and fascination nonrational, but these emotions are aroused by cognitive reference to a superhuman power. The more tremendous this supernatural object is judged to be, the more emotion rises to significant intensity. Fear of a bear is as different from "fear of the Lord" as one perceives the objects to be different. One may judge the bear to be vicious and run frantically for safety, or one may interpret the bear to be tame and offer to feed him in calm assurance rather than fear. One may fear a God of wrath; but if God is interpreted as a Father who pitieth his children, fear gives place to trust and love. "Fear of the Lord" is a misnomer, for this complex of emotions is actually the sentiment of reverence. Otto vividly describes emotions arising from recognizing a God of power, wrath, and unapproachable mystery. But to those who interpret God as forgiving, tender, redeeming love, the religious emotions will be quite different from Otto's analysis. They are more apt to be the gentler feelings of gratitude, comfort, trust, assurance, peace, and eagerness to commune and co-operate in loyal service.

J. H. Leuba ably disposes of the theory that fear is the primary emotion in religion. If fear is conspicuous in primitive religion, it is not because of the intrinsic qualities of primitive religion but rather because of the insecurity and danger that dominate primitive life. Even there, fear is mingled with other emotions and steadily yields to modification. In the emotional progression of religion, fear changes to awe, reverence, admiration, gratitude, a sense of the sublime, and to the tender emotions. And in the higher civilizations today fear and awe have been largely displaced by other religious emotions. In contrast to the wave of fear that provoked religious revivals in the time of Jonathan Edwards, quite different emotions prevail in our generation. The theology that stressed God's wrath, the wretchedness of this life, and the torments hereafter aroused fear. Changing ideas of God, man, and eternity have changed these emotions. Leuba finds three causes for the decline of fear: (a) in civilized society occasion for fear have become fewer (except in war and calamity); (b) modern education make us more reflective and less emotional, thereby converting emotions into controlled reactions; and (c) recognition of the inadequacy of fear as a method of meeting danger turns us to more intelligent responses. The characteristic religious sentiments of our time are sympathy, love, trust, hope, courage, fortitude, and forgiveness; these prove more effective for the needs of modern living.[35]

[35] *Op. cit.*, pp. 126-50.

Religious emotions, sentiments, and dispositions are complex. No single feeling or meaning characterizes all varieties of religious experience. Objective situations condition emotional responses. Whatever God means to you will define your religious emotions. Your ideas of the divine good and the goal of human destiny will be significant. Your view of the supremely worthful, the ideal most real and the real most ideal, will stimulate emotional overtones and undertones that are typical of your religion. Your specific interests and needs will indicate what emotions evoke your religious reactions. And, subjectively, how you feel about religious values will decide what you do about them. Religion may be as flat as your indifference, or as vital and urgent as your sense of great issues at stake. If you believe in a Creator of Values and feel deeply your need of divine assistance and co-operation, you will feel keenly about religion. Emotions arising from such beliefs reverberate through all of life and affect every deed and decision.[36]

Emotions may be constructive or destructive. Fear spreads panic, and anxieties result in hesitation and inefficiency. Anger and despair, likewise, produce inaccurate fumbling and random responses. These distress emotions are destructive of poise, stability, and efficiency. They defeat the values sought by disorganizing the personality. And their effects are undesirable—indigestion, circulatory and nervous disorders, illness, weakness, and unhappiness. Other emotions are constructive in creating stability, joy, and success. Faith, hope, and love are the justly famous trilogy that serve as constructive forces in personality and society. D. M. Trout takes these three emotions as "the only general experiential differentia which characterize every religious act," distinguishing it from nonreligious behavior.[37]

How does religion influence the emotions? Can we expect

[36] "There is no such thing as feeling apart from idea; 'the idea' is an integral part of all feeling; and it is the whole meaning and destiny of feeling to terminate in knowledge of an object. . . . A religion of feeling always and rightly tends to transform itself into a religion of idea."—Hocking, *The Meaning of God in Human Experience*, p. 64.

[37] *Religious Behavior*, p. 27.

religion to control the emotional life so that the destructive tendencies will be curbed and the constructive tendencies strengthened? There is convincing evidence to this effect. Faith, hope, and love are more characteristic of the great religions than fear, despair, and rage. The typical religious object is a Sustainer of Values who works for good and is willing to co-operate with man. This essential hope that characterizes religious experience is a constructive emotional force, giving the worshiper more stability and integration for effective living. Trust and love cast out fear and despair, transforming destructive emotions into constructive energies of harmony, confidence, and peace.

William James shows the value of religious emotions. He distinguishes the constructive and destructive impulses as healthy-mindedness and morbid-mindedness. His lecture on "The Religion of Healthy-Mindedness" gives numerous case studies to demonstrate how religious optimism helps one to live serenely and successfully. By positive suggestions of personal faith, enthusiasm, recollection, and the eloquent example of others, many are cured of diseases and kept from evil and despair. This is not achieved by the moral methods of effort and strain, but by religious methods of surrender and trust in a supernatural power. His lecture on "The Sick Soul" explores the destructive tendencies of morbid fear, pain, despair, and their urgent need of a redemptive religion of deliverance. No refined optimisms or moral consolations can meet these deeper needs, but only a religion that is complete enough to offer a way of salvation. The divided self has to be united, and the natural man born again to a spiritually adequate personality.

What brings about such changes, says James, is "the way in which emotional excitement alters." [38] New interests become "hot parts" of the field of consciousness, former interests become cold. From these centers of dynamic energy come the constructive emotional forces for the remaking of personality. How this hap-

[38] *The Varieties of Religious Experience*, p. 195.

pens we do not know. He uses mechanical figures of speech, points to the unconscious, and suggests a wider self through which saving influences come. Psychology will trace results more clearly than causes, and beyond the immediate environment does not presume to explain the reality that causes these decisive re-creations.

This we know: religious motivation rouses life from indifference to interest, from inhibiting to facilitating energies. Hope casts out despair, faith dispels fear, love dissolves anger and scorn. Conflicts and repressions are released and directed by devotion to a larger good than selfish advantage. Joy in value achieved brings more effective action. Calm assurance gives poise and stability. Forgiveness and reconciliation bring peace in ultimate harmony. As religious emotions progress, they sublimate the desires and fulfillments of life to higher purposes in loyal devotion.

5. TYPES OF RELIGIOUS EXPERIENCE

The varieties of religious experience are many and profuse. To classify them accurately is next to impossible, and yet they cluster and come together in polarities of similarity and contrast. The resemblances that draw religious persons together are most clearly seen in contrast to the differences that set them off from each other. Those whose religious experiences are alike tend to affiliate sympathetically into sects aware of this mutual interest. At the same time they are often joined by opposition to another point of view, which they unite against. In tracing types of religious experience we shall present them in pairs of contrast.

a) The *individual* versus the *social*. One type of religion emphasizes individual experience. Ezekiel was an individualist who declared, "The soul that sinneth, . . . it shall die." [39] Each person is individually responsible to his Creator. Hermits have forsaken society for the privileges of solitude. Others find religion a social experience and do not understand why people ever want to be alone. To them, religion has a social origin and a social purpose

[39] Ezek. 18:4.

in the development of social values. Religious life is a fellowship, and salvation is through brotherhood in a beloved community. Introvert and extravert tendencies have been noted by Jung[40] and others to affect all experiences of life; these basic individual differences turn religious interests inward or outward. Between these extremes are many, perhaps the majority of us, who need and find room for both individual and social experience. Complete experience will enjoy both, though emphasizing now the individual and now the social.

b) The *active* versus the *passive*. The active type of religion is well known. The first religious facts are religious acts, F. L. Strickland points out.[41] Primitive religion is active in ceremonies, dances, sacrifices, and ritual. Religious leaders demand action. "This do, and thou shalt live."[42] Good deeds are required of the Buddhist, deeds of penance are expected of the Catholic, deeds of service are stressed among Protestants. Moral achievement and reforming zeal appeal to many. The passive type finds meaning in silence and quietism. Hours spent in meditation and prayer seem more important than busy rounds of frantic activity. Salvation is not by deeds of merit, but by faith and divine grace. Self-surrender is a way to let go of the world and make room for spiritual power. A Buddhist controversy over this point was represented by the "monkey-hold" sect teaching that man must exert himself to be saved, reaching up and holding on as the baby monkey to its mother; and the "cat-hold" sect teaching man not to struggle but to relax in faith and be saved by the upholding divine power, as the kitten is held by its mother.

c) The *formal* versus the *informal*. These contrasting types are evident in services of public worship. Formal services are rich in symbolism, ritual, and ceremonies. Idols and images, incense and

---

[40] *Psychological Types* (New York: Harcourt, Brace & Co., 1926).

[41] *Psychology of Religious Experience* (New York and Nashville: Abingdon-Cokesbury Press, 1924, pp. 46-53.

[42] Luke 10:28.

rhythmic beats, impressive architecture and elaborate decoration, processions and recessions in dramatic pageantry, traditional prayers, genuflections, and intonations make up the content of formal worship. It has dignity, antiquity, and a funded meaning to excite emotions and aspirations. But others may react against this weight of formality and seek religion in simplicity. A Friends' meeting, with its bare walls and silence, is an austere protest against formality, offering instead the spontaneous utterance of prayer and testimony as the spirit moves. Aesthetic symbols give way to free and democratic comradeship, where everyone is his own priest and God dwells in the heart as an inspiring, guiding inner light.

d) The *conservative* versus the *progressive*. Religion is seen by Höffding[43] and others as an effort to conserve values. The conserving tendency to save what is worthy is evident in every religion. To this extent everyone is conservative who cares for any value enough to maintain it. But when effort to preserve outreaches the effort to grow, we have the conservative type. The traditional ways of the past are then considered unquestionably superior to the new ideas of the present. The new departures are resisted as betrayals of the glorious treasure of the past. In opposition to the conservative is the progressive, who is more eager to grow than to preserve the past. He welcomes change confidently, believing that progress is possible, ready to forego the security of the attained for the adventurous gains of the not yet attained. The progressive is liberal in his generous welcome to the "wave of the future," and he may be radical in uprooting the past to reform the present.

e) The *tolerant* versus the *intolerant*. The tolerant person seeks to be open-minded and broad-minded. He delights in differences, seeing in diversities the enlargement of the interests and values of life. He expects to find good in all religions; he may consider one religion as good as another. To the intolerant this is "fatal apostasy" from the one and only true revelation. Tolerance is

[43] *The Philosophy of Religion*, tr. B. E. Meyer (New York: The Macmillan Co., 1906; 1914), pp. 209-72.

feared as a betrayal of unique and unapproachable superiorities, and despised as a weak and foolish compromise that degrades the best to the level of the worst. To one of strong and dogmatic convictions there is only one true religion or right way of life. Other creeds are false, other gods are no gods, other churches a scandal of false pretension. It may be observed that formal and conservative types tend to be intolerant. But this is not the whole story, for informal and progressive types may be just as dogmatic and scornful of any who disagree with their enlightenment.

f) The *affirmative* versus the *negative*. Affirmative religion is optimistic and healthy-minded. It stresses the abundant life and seeks to enlarge all values. It looks up, not down, forward, not backward; "facing the sun, the shadows fall behind." Evil is forgotten or excluded as unreal and unhealthy; sin and error are to be avoided by filling the mind with truth and goodness. Trust, rather than fear, is the dominant emotion. It emphasizes the desirable by positive suggestion and constructive development. Negative religion is pessimistic and suspicious of human nature. It sees every desire as a temptation luring life to destruction, and it hopes to save life from evil by cutting off desire. It prohibits with "thou shalt nots" and hedges the good with stern commands to keep it pure from corruption. It glories in sacrifice, denial, and a martyr's crown. The ascetic discipline strengthens character by the enduring of hardship and by training for great labors.

Here are twelve types of religious experience set in six pairs of contrast. They are not exhaustive, but they are typical of prevalent tendencies in religion. Any type pushed to its ultimate extreme means distortion. Each needs the corrective of its opposite to save the religious life from partiality and imbalance. The dialectic of Hegel indicates that progress is possible by uniting antitheses in a higher synthesis, moving on to other oppositions and yet higher unities, canceling out the unworthy and reclaiming the worthy.

Hocking shows in his law of alternation [44] our need of passing from one emphasis to another to fulfill the rhythm of life. We advance best by stepping forth on alternate feet. Religious experience will be enriched by alternating interests and reconciling contrasts.

[44] *The Meaning of God in Human Experience,* pp. 405-27.

III

Religious Growth

1. Developing Religion

The best place to begin is at the beginning. But, like the end of the rainbow, beginnings are difficult to find. Artificial events can be staged and scheduled so that the public may be seated in neat rows to see the curtain rise or hear the whistle blow. Natural events are different. They come silently and unexpectedly, without publicity or fanfare. And before we arrive on the scene the beginning is lost in later developments. Historical beginnings are notably obscure. Something is beginning every minute, but those present lack the perspective to know what is going to be significant enough to preserve for posterity. When posterity gathers sufficient perspective on a development to ask how it began, the origin is erased by the passage of the time that made the history.

The origins of religion are hidden. Somewhere in the prehistoric ages men somehow developed religious traditions that were well established when the first written records were made. The discoveries of archaeology and anthropology have pushed history back thousands of years into the formerly unknown past and have added priceless records to the early chapters of man; but religious beginnings are still beyond view. More light will yet be shed on these distant antiquities as the results of further research accumulate. What do we know about the early development of religion?

a) The beginning of religion was *humble*. As Jesus was born in a stable, so religion first appeared in lowly surroundings—unworthy, one may think, of its later glory. Primitive superstitious beliefs and rites may seem repulsive to refined tastes, but origin does not determine value.

b) Religion from the first was *complex*. Most explanations oversimplify the origin of religion. It has been suggested that religion begins in fear or wonder, totem or magic, instincts or spirits. But these are partial explanations, half truths or less, for the whole truth is far more complex. Whatever concerns life in the complexity of its interests and values concerns religion.

c) Religion aims at social *welfare*. As far back as we can see, religion is devoted to human welfare. It performs strange and sometimes destructive acts, but always for what is thought to be a larger good. Its basic motive is to create, conserve, and increase values. The highest values and purposes are the concern of religion.

d) Religion is therefore *urgent*. To the primitive mind, the mysterious powers are not to be taken lightly. They control destiny and must be approached cautiously and reverently. Religion was serious business then, perhaps more so than today, if needs were greater and resources fewer. When the values of life are at stake, there is reason to be earnest. In times of crisis religion usually comes into the foreground. The more urgent the need, the more men seek for aid.

e) Religion develops in *persons*. This includes the intrapersonal adjustive activities of the individual as well as the interpersonal activities of individuals in social relations. Persons are creators and sustainers of societies. Primitive tribes may appear to submerge persons, but the person is the subject of every religious experience, the one who serves and is served by religious values.

Growth is the basic need of life. Every living thing seeks to complete itself. "Fullness of life is the goal of life, the urge to completeness is the most compelling motive in life." [1] Hadfield shows how this law of completeness works physiologically toward health by restoring wounds and deficiencies to wholeness, and psychologically toward self-realization by seeking to harmonize

[1] J. A. Hadfield, *Psychology and Morals* (New York: Robert M. McBride & Co., 1925), p. 61. See also Arnold Gesell, *Infancy and Human Growth* (New York: The Macmillan Co., 1929), p. 409.

all complexes and sentiments into unified expression. Morally we strive toward perfection and religiously toward holiness or spiritual wholeness. Other needs may be tangential, but the urge to grow is the never-ending demand for completion. We are born to grow and our natures are eager to be moving along lines of progress. Without growth, life slips instantly into decay and decline. There is no standing still. We must either grow or die.

Religion is life seeking completion. Without growth, religion declines. To grow is, therefore, a religious imperative. Otherwise, religious experience is but a memory, and religious activity an empty shell of hollow formality. Religion is a resource for human growth, serving the growing needs of persons and societies. To serve life well, religion must keep apace with human growth at every stage of development.

What produces religious growth?

a) Situations of *need* are conducive to religious growth. Crises often turn men to religion because they are dramatic exposures of urgent need. But for those who have eyes to see, life is constantly in need. Only the blindness of conceit misleads us to suppose we are self-sufficient. To realize that we are forever inadequate is to sense our deep need of a more adequate Creator of Values. To know insecurity from hour to hour, to meet disappointment and loss is to feel the need of eternal treasures and larger resources.

b) Experiences of *fulfillment* encourage religious development. If there were no answers to prayer, who would continue to pray? Unless something is found, would it not be futile to search? No illusion can long survive its exposure. Religion does not live except where something happens. Those who earnestly and intelligently seek religious values find their needs satisfied, and trust because they trust not in vain. Magical superstitions pass away as cumulative experience shows them to be unfounded and useless. False religious ideas and foolish petitions also fall before the tests of experience. But true religion survives and grows through its successful results. Fulfillment is essential to religious growth, to encourage and nourish its developing life.

c) Between every vital need and its true fulfillment stands a skillful *effort*. Religious success must be earned by religious labor. "Faith without works is dead." Without exercise religion decays. More people lose their religion through neglect than from any other cause. Mere activity is not enough, for it may be nothing more than random motions and meaningless repetitions. Saying prayers is a meaningless exercise if the mind wanders while the tongue mumbles careless syllables. Religious efforts need to be as skillful as intelligent understanding and purposive activity can make them. Religious growth requires growth in skill to practice its finer arts. To live with God and fellow men in harmony and service, for the sake of meaningful values, is the artistry of religion.

2. RELIGION OF CHILDHOOD

Children are born very young, yet birth is not the beginning of growth. Heredity is delivered complete at conception, and with the potentialities of that heritage the embryo begins to grow. During the prenatal period of forty weeks important developments occur: cells subdivide and multiply; organs develop specialized functions, such as those of heart and brain in relation to circulation and the nervous system; digestive and glandular processes begin. Embryologists report a remarkable schedule of prenatal developments: (*a*) heartbeat at 3 weeks (*b*) limb buds at 4 weeks, (*c*) arm and leg movements at 6 weeks, (*d*) flexing of fingers at 12 weeks, (*e*) prerespiratory movements at 5 months, (*f*) complete set of 12 billion nerve cells at 5 months.[2] The Chinese count the age of children from conception, not birth—and with good reason, for it is then that life history begins.

[2] Arnold Gesell, *The First Five Years of Life* (New York: Harper & Bros,, 1940), pp. 10-12; C. A. and M. M. Aldrich, *Babies Are Human Beings* (New York: The Macmillan Co., 1940), pp. 4-5.

Are there any prenatal influences that have a religious bearing? The relation of dependence, so characteristic of religion, is clearly established in this period. The fetus is so dependently co-ordinated with its intimate environment that every need is instantly satisfied. Temperature and sustenance are so constantly maintained that the contrast with later life is evident. There are psychologists who find in this contrast the source of the later discontents, sharp distresses over the painful gaps and lacks of postnatal life, and homesickness for the perfect environment that is no more. Religious aspiration seeks in God the perfect environment not provided in the world of physical things.[3]

At any rate, birth is a crisis. The trauma, or shock, of birth is significant in personality development.[4] At birth, life gains its first independence, launching its own circulation, respiration, vocalization, and other functions. The infant comes to consciousness in a very different environment. This new world is larger, more remote, more changeable, and therefore less constant and adequate. It is far more complicated and puzzling, offering both good and bad, painful and pleasant, experiences. In this strange and confusing world new wants appear as the life needs air, nourishment, warmth, and attention. The senses are at first uncoordinated; motor responses are gross, random, and unorganized; meanings and comprehensions are virtually nil.

But there are hopeful capacities to grow. These capacities may be classified as maturation and learning. The organism is loaded with potentialities, ready to develop on growing schedule. Maturation is growth which originates from within the organism in regular sequence. It is both physiological (such as the cutting of teeth) and psychological (such as progress in locomotion and

---

[3] "Mother sea," as James calls it. "A wider self through which saving experiences come."—*The Varieties of Religious Experience*, p. 15. Freud discusses and rejects this oceanic sense in *Civilization and Its Discontents*, tr. J. Riviere (New York: Cape & Smith, 1930), pp. 7-22.

[4] See Otto Rank, *The Trauma of Birth* (London: K. Paul, Trench, Trübner & Co., 1929).

co-ordination). Psychological maturing is aided by social inter-action.

Learning is motivated by stimuli from the dynamic environment, especially by interpersonal relations. It begins at birth (maturation before birth) and continues to death. Learning is most important for growth, and contributes to the majority of human developments. It is also more manageable and responsive to social influences. Learning conditions all forms of behavior and experience: motor skills, language, personality traits, social adjustments. Religious development results almost entirely from learning. The rate of learning is probably highest in early childhood. It has been contended that persons learn more in the first year than in any other. Aptitudes for learning are present from birth, and the list of first-year achievements is very notable.

When is the best time to begin religious training? The earlier the better. Before birth is not too soon, or even before the birth of the parents. For the family is the first school for childhood learning. If the parents are sincerely religious, there is the first requirement for the religious development of children. Long before formal instruction is set up, the child is learning by suggestion, imitation, and adjustment to the attitudes of others. The religious opportunities of infancy are greater than we realize. First impressions are indelibly lasting. To neglect the first years and begin later, is to omit the foundations without which the whole structure is insecure.

What are the religious needs of childhood? It will be well to consider three periods: infancy, ages 1-2; early childhood, ages 3-6; and later childhood, ages 7-12.

a) *Regularity* is the first need of infancy (ages 1-2). This is physiological, as somatic rhythms call for regular supply of nourishment, sleep, and exercise. But it is even more a psychological need. Infants learn only by repetition. Their pattern of life must have stability and order to establish associations and meanings. No single item has meaning until it is associated with another item in a series of relationships. Chickens learn to associate the appearance of the farmer with food and flock eagerly around him because he regularly supplies the food. The rapidity of learning is shown by an experiment with newborn infants who were given the bottle just after a buzzer had been sounded for five seconds. By the time they were four or five days old they had established the association, so that when the buzzer sounded they opened their mouths, performed sucking motions, and decreased other activities.[5] Desirable habits and trustworthy character require regular associations, in which causes and effects of conduct are consistent enough to teach lessons of good and bad.[6] A secure basis for religious experience is a dependable, trustworthy environment. The infant's first revelation of God may come through this experience of order and regularity.

b) *Affection* is another religious need of infancy. Infants who are not shown affection develop withdrawing attitudes that lead to antisocial traits and to unhealthy emotions of fear and antagonism. Lack of affection is a major cause of neurotic and delinquent tendencies.

In examining the childhood histories of a great number of neurotic persons I have found . . . the basic evil is invariably a lack of genuine warmth and affection. A child can stand a great deal of what is often regarded as traumatic—such as sudden weaning, occasional beating, sex experiences—as long as inwardly he feels wanted and loved.[7]

Gentleness, kindness, and tender care develop social responses and healthy emotions. Yet child care may be overprotective. Too constant solicitude encourages a helpless dependency that retards growth. Infants need to be left alone enough to develop their own

---

[5] D. P. Marquis, "Can Conditioned Responses Be Established in the New-born Infant?" *Journal of Genetic Psychology*, XXXIX (1931), 472-92.

[6] "A moral being can be produced only by a moral environment." See Hugh Hartshorne, *Childhood and Character* (Boston: The Pilgrim Press, 1919), p. 9.

[7] Horney, *The Neurotic Personality of Our Time*, pp. 79-80.

resources and grow self-reliant. God is first known to children in the love of parents and friends. If our love were wiser, it would be more divine.

c) *Worthy example* is also needed in infancy. Example is one of the first and best ways of learning. Long before a vocabulary is acquired for verbal instruction, children learn by observation. How is a child to develop a sense of values? By sensing what parents hold worthy. To the infant, parents stand for God. They perform the functions of God, creating and sustaining the living values of their children. They provide whatever is needed and receive from the infant the responses of dependency, trust, petition, and gratitude that are nearest to the religious emotions. Now when these godlike parents show attitudes of reverence and devotion to a yet higher source of values, the child is deeply impressed. Whatever moral and religious traits parents desire children to have may best be shown in themselves. Emotions are very contagious. Parents who maintain harmony instead of conflict, faith not fear, hope not despair, will inevitably communicate these emotions to their children. Trust in God and fellow men need not be argued for. If trust is practiced, it will be eloquent.

d) In early childhood (ages 3-6) the *discovery of persons* is a constant adventure. The infant at first may not distinguish between persons and things. Pets and parents are pushed and patted around as mechanically as inanimate objects. Then comes a dawning recognition that persons respond in ways that things do not, and do things that squeaking, rolling toys cannot do. Crying brings attention, cooing invites affection from parents. Persons are thus appealed to as understanding and as responsive to persuasion. In the discovery of other persons the infant comes to know himself as a person. Social consciousness is prerequisite to self-consciousness and religious awareness. When God is accepted by parents as present in the home, he seems to the child a member of the family. Prayer is as natural as family conversation. The invisibility of God may be a problem, and yet parents are also invisible when they leave the room. Pictures and stories of God that portray him falsely are to be avoided, yet the fatherhood of God is meaningful to any age. Ideas of God can and should grow steadily with enlarging understanding, until his traits are viewed in a cosmic sense.

e) *Co-operation* is another need of early childhood. As soon as persons are discovered, they are sought to play the game of co-operation. Nothing interests children more than the give-and-take of interaction. Games as simple as tossing a ball back and forth or picking up and throwing down seem never to become stale. For co-operation is a social adventure and those who take time to play with children win their loyal devotion. If parents are too busy to respond to these invitations, they miss the finest opportunities to demonstrate co-operation. Seeing the aloof individualism of adults, children also take on that stubborn social resistance that blocks effective co-operation. Religion is co-operation with God, and co-operation with others for the sake of God. To co-operate for the good of all is to be religious in the most practical way. Lessons in co-operation are therefore basic to religious growth. Every co-operative root does not bear religious fruit, but without the roots no fruit may be expected. In early childhood co-operation is so eager and spontaneous that its cultivation is a natural development. For the happiness of the child and the welfare of his future society, co-operation belongs in the first lessons of life. In this way families will learn the meaning and value of religion.

f) *Sharing* is a desirable art to learn in early childhood. It is a mutual response of giving and receiving values. Children usually receive more than they give, with consequent danger of selfishness. By and large, selfishness does more damage and breeds more misery than any other practice. And selfish habits are firmly rooted in childhood from infancy. Personality disorders and social failures of later life have their beginnings in selfish attitudes of childhood.[8]

[8] Fritz Künkel, *What It Means to Grow Up* (New York: Charles Scribner's Sons, 1936), shows the consequences of egocentricity in growing children and youth.

Learning to give up desires and possessions to others, learning the joy and justice of exchanging gifts and services, are lessons essential to religious as well as social success. For religion is a social experience of sharing the best values of life. When prayer is selfish petition for private advantage, it dips beneath the religious level to unsocial magic. Prayer becomes religious in asking good for others and seeking mutual welfare. As soon as children begin to pray, they may learn to pray unselfishly and find religion a way of joyous sharing with others.

g) In later childhood (ages 7-12) *curiosity and exploration* are leading interests. Having acquired a vocabulary, the child uses it violently to ask questions. His stay-at-home days are over. At school and roaming about the neighborhood he is eager to find out everything there is to know about his world. These jumping, shouting question marks often drive adults frantic with their insatiable curiosity. Busy and impatient parents may resist the noise and resent the questions as a nuisance to be outlawed for disturbing the peace. But a question is the best tool of understanding. Every question should be respected, for it is a sign of readiness to learn. Questions about sex and the story of life are not to be evaded but calmly and clearly explained, for no other time will be so appropriate to understand these vital mysteries. Questions about God and religion are not easy to answer well: first, because they are difficult to explain, and second, because, like sex, they have emotional halos. Wise parents will think ahead and clarify their own religious concepts against that day when they must justify the faith that is in them. No man knoweth the hour when a leading question opens the mind of childhood, but blessed is he who is prepared to answer well. Even better is the mutual search with the child that shares with him the exploring adventure.[9]

h) Organization and self-control are important agenda of later

[9] Marguerite H. Bro, *When Children Ask* (Chicago: Willett, Clark & Co., 1940), is a useful guide for parents from one who understands the value of sharing.

childhood. In these years physical growth is slower but firmer, knitting bones, muscles, and nerves together in closer co-ordination. Explorations collect oddly assorted curiosities, as incoherent as the contents of a boy's pocket or a girl's dresser. These fragments, dumped into a heap, need to be organized into an orderly system. And the older child cannot be organized permanently by anyone but himself. The mother may clean his room periodically and put things in order, but they do not stay that way. The important thing is to learn for one's self the satisfaction of being neat. Fortunately, the child has at this age strong tendencies toward independence—toward making his own decisions and thinking for himself. Co-ercion is resented by children, who respond better to invitations that captivate interest than to orders that forbid. Tempers and moods need to be controlled from within by developing the poise and dignity of self-respect and social adjustment.

Life should grow increasingly purposive and responsible. A religious purpose can give meaning and unity to life. Children at this age may become earnest, loyal followers of a religious purpose. They may take definite responsibilities in the junior church program, and do home tasks cheerfully as a welcome religious expression. They find new interests to live for in devoting themselves to a program of concrete activities in co-operation with and for the sake of others. Church and character-forming organizations demonstrate the remarkable progress children can make at this period, when their energies are organized along constructive purposes. Successful organization and control may be stimulated from without, but actually it develops from within.

3. Religion of Adolescence

Youth is what everyone wants but those who have it. Why does everyone want youth? First, because it seems so gay and bright with promise. Second, because we miss it later on and find no way to return to it. Why is it not desired by all who have it? First, because it is not so easy as it looks; no age has more perplexing problems and inner tensions to work out. Second, because youth is impatient for the not yet attained—impatient to explore the future, cross frontiers, and win a responsible place in the world.

Adolescence means "growing up to," or growing toward, maturity not yet attained.[10] Youth has the advantages and disadvantages of a halfway house; it is on the way yet not at the goal. It is somewhere between childhood (vehemently disowned as helplessly innocent) and adulthood (often resented as somber and subdued by the cares of the world). A young person is very sure that he has outgrown and rejected his childish past, while at the same time he secretly suspects that he has not come into his future estate of manhood or womanhood. Reluctant as he may be to admit it, he is not yet all here, and he knows it to his sorrow.

There is no more decisive time in life than adolescence (ages 12-21). For the young life is then at the threshold of many opportunities. Children are so busy growing they have little time for anything else. The developments of childhood should build sturdy foundations of health, neuromuscular skills, social adjustments, mental abilities, moral and religious ideals. Taking a step at a time as they do, children are not in a position to gain perspective and understand themselves. Physical growth is very rapid in the early months of adolescence. And then youth has time to pause long enough to size up his situation, take his bearings, and gather resources to go ahead.

Physiological changes of puberty are significant in growing up. Maturation of organs, glands, hair, voice, and figure indicates a new cycle of life. A person is the same yet not the same. Certain habits, attitudes, and characteristic features maintain identity. The continuity of growth preserves the developments of the past, and nothing ever learned is entirely lost. But the changes of

[10] Our word "adult" comes from the Latin *adultus* ("grown up"), past participle of *adolescere*.

adolescence renew almost every aspect of personality.[11] Psychologically, adolescent personality expands in many directions. Four dimensions at least should be noted.

a). Personal experiences deepen. Emotions have a depth heretofore unknown to the adolescent personality. Periods of storm, well known at this age, are reverberations from glandular developments violently stimulating the emotions. Mood swings from elation to depression, outbursts of temper, and variations of temperament are unpredictable and often unmanageable while he is trying to learn how to live with his new feelings. To ask him why he feels as he does is futile, for he probably does not understand his own unexpected emotions. These upsurgings of vitality are indications of larger capacities for sensing the values of life. Appreciations are awakened and refined. There is keener sensitivity to ranges of values undiscovered before.

Religious experience is enriched by deeper reverence and satisfaction in communion with God. Church symbols, traditions, and fellowship become meaningful and mysteriously inviting. Worship, once mere formal repetition, glows with vivid reality. Prayer may inspire ecstasy, and meditation aspire toward heroic sacrifices and achievements. Life changes to technicolor of rainbow brightness. It is not surprising that religious awakenings come so naturally in adolescence, for new capacities and sensitivities make possible richer experiences and deeper appreciations of all values.

Under favorable conditions, religion occupies a very important place in the life of the maturing boy or girl. It satifies his groping for a fundamental synthesized understanding of the whole realm of experience. It gives him a sense of values, a sense of personal relationships and obligations. It facilitates the formation of high ideals of unselfish service. It gives him help in attaining self-control and self-discipline which characterizes strong personality. It reinforces his moral character. It aids him in resolving

[11] L. S. Hollingsworth, *The Psychology of Adolescence* (New York: D. Appleton-Century Co., 1929), p. 17, warns against the myth of a magical change at puberty, showing the gradualness and continuity of development.

many conflicts of impulses and desires, and thus assists him in attaining sound mental health. Praise, prayer, and other elements of worship may enrich and deepen his life, and add much to its wholesomeness and happiness. Religion in reality involves personal devotion to a Supreme Being, and can provide a unifying force for all that is highest and best in the youth's nature.[12]

b) Social interests broaden. The discovery of persons has been noted as one of the great events of early childhood. Now the adolescent discovers persons in a new sense. Persons were then convenient or inconvenient objects to do things for you and with you. Now they become creatures to admire, to exclaim and wonder about. When boy meets girl the heart beats faster, and, though they have been in the same neighborhood for years, they now see each other as for the first time. Social attentions are more intensive in emotional response and eager desire to be together. Social interests are more extensive as one friend after another comes into favorite focus and circles of friends grow larger. Children often prefer older friends, but adolescents are devoted to associates of their own age and count every minute lost that is not spent in the company of one or more of them. To be with the crowd is the life, until couples begin to pair off and the later adolescent comes to prefer the only one. In either case social consciousness is keen and social approval means everything.

A boy of seventeen writes: "And in the last year I made a wonderful discovery. That is that the people one sees all about and who seem a formless mass with no individuality at all are composed of vitally different personalities all of whom are more or less disposed to talk about themselves. Experience is practically tapping on your back if you will only turn around. There was the taxi driver whose father had been a blacksmith in Haiti and who after having married a Negro woman refused to send his half-breed children to a Negro school. Incidentally, this fellow

[12] F. D. Brooks, *The Psychology of Adolescence* (Boston: Houghton Mifflin Co., 1929), pp. 341-42.

had about the most sensible political views I have ever heard. All this I gathered in while riding a few miles."

Another boy the same age writes: "I now also realized that it was not enough to classify a teacher as nice or not nice (a nice teacher could have bad qualities and vice versa), in fact it grew on me that a teacher had to be classified in two separate ways: as a teacher, and again as a person. With the ability to see a teacher in more than one light came a real interest in the characters of the people around me; each of my friends took on a new color." [13]

Religion at this time expands socially.[14] The conscience becomes sensitive to new social values and responsibilities. The anguish of guilt and remorse broods over social blunders and personal inadequacies. Ideals of perfection and hero worship tantalize the ineptitudes of adolescence. The pain of self-consciousness causes one to pass through awkward stages to increasing grace and skill, learning thereby to aspire and work for desired progress. In this time of high idealism youth dreams of turning the world upside down and building a better world. Such dreams are not to be discouraged; they are the best hope of human progress and deserve a larger place in the councils of adult leadership. The religion of youth develops social enthusiasms that are worthy of being encouraged. The sharp sense of social need, the courageous challenge of old and intrenched wrongs, the eager desire to serve, and the readiness to make sacrifices for a cause are characteristic of youth. They are likewise essential to religious and social progress. Unless we keep our religion young in this sense, and our social order

[13] Quoted by Peter Blos, *The Adolescent Personality* (New York: D. Appleton-Century Co., 1941), p. 298.

[14] K. C. Garrison contends that "religion, to most adolescents, is but an extension of their social life."—*The Psychology of Adolescence* (New York: Prentice-Hall, Inc., 1934, 1940), p. 189. See also G. Stanley Hall, *Adolescence* (New York: D. Appleton-Century Co., 1904), II, 304, who says every individual is born twice, once as an individual, and again as a member of a species. The function of religion is to facilitate the change to a social consciousness.

flexible to constant change in every generation, the good we cherish will fall into decay.

c) Intellectual powers heighten. This social sensitivity does not, however, mean slavish servility. The normal adolescent has a mind of his own and intends to use it. The center of authority moves inward from external commands to self-demands. It is not unusual for young people to flaunt their independence.[15] In struggling for a sense of worth and a place of respect in society they insist, rightly or wrongly, upon making their own decisions. Freedom to think and decide is their right and should be exercised throughout childhood. College freshmen show wide contrasts at this point. Those who have had practice in deciding for themselves at home sail out, into the larger freedoms of college on a steady keel, but those who have had everything decided for them are helplessly at sea. They either flounder in depths of dependent homesickness or careen wildly about tossed by every wind of opinion and wave of impulse. Parents who tire of sharp criticisms and long arguments should recognize that adolescents need to try their logical wings and heighten intellectual powers if they are to grow in wisdom.

Religious experience needs to grow intellectually. Childish concepts of God and miracles, heaven and hell, biblical inspiration and revelation, religious duties and devotion, need to grow up. Doubts are not to be feared, but welcomed, as symptoms of independent judgment. Adolescent doubt may be exaggerated by some writers, and doubts are often induced by social expectation and imitation. But the basic cause of doubting is the emerging reason, seeking to understand and to find coherent meanings for the contradictions of experience. Children may be taught narrow, inflexible religion incapable of expansion or of harmony with mature experience. To teach this kind of religion is to court needless conflicts that finally turn many away from religion, which they come to identify

---

[15] D. A. Thom considers the struggle for intellectual independence the most difficult and painful part of growing up. See his *Normal Youth and Its Everyday Problems* (New York: D. Appleton-Century Co., 1932), p. 142.

with superstition.[16] Foolish teaching of religion, like the popular stories of Santa Claus, makes bitter skeptics who distrust the whole business and resent those who have deceived them. Everyone needs a sound philosophy that will meet the tests and stand the shocks of modern life. As intellect develops in childhood and adolescence, continuous growth should enlarge religious concepts. Young people need freedom to think, stimulating problems to solve, and democratic guidance through comradeship with mature minds who are honestly facing and creatively thinking through their own problems.

d) Life purposes lengthen. The aims of childhood are transient and temporary. A baby cries for the next meal and reaches for what dangles before his eyes. Children live from day to day, an hour at a time, a hand-to-mouth and step-by-step existence. Young people begin to sum up days into weeks, months, and years. They save pennies and dimes until they have enough to purchase some long-desired treasure. Through a round of social dates, whirling off with one friend after another for the thrill of the moment, they come to think of "going steady" and planning for marriage and a home. After many years of doing one task at a time, and hoping the next one will not turn up too soon, they come eventually to think about a vocation to follow through life. As purposes lengthen into destinies, the most important decisions of life are made. We may ponder why these far-reaching decisions are made before young people have the wisdom of age. Older and less democratic societies have permitted the elders to decide these questions for youth. But our observation is that youth do about as well as their seniors and that with added responsibility judgment matures and ability increases.

The long purposes and destinies of life involve religion. "Why live?" and "What shall I do with my life?" are essentially religious

---

[16] L. A. Averill, *Adolescence* (Boston: Houghton Mifflin Co., 1936), p. 395, shows that the degree of an adolescent's skepticism is commensurate with the superficiality and narrowness of the concepts instilled into him in childhood.

questions. They raise perspectives of the total meaning of life that draw together beginnings and ends. If we are here for a purpose, we ought to discover what that purpose is. If there is a purpose, it concerns not only us but the world at large. A vocation is more than a job to finish or an occupation to consume time and space. A vocation is essentially a purpose as long as life. Literally "a calling," it meant called of God to do his will. It was a commission, or sending forth, under divine orders. "Who will go?" "Here am I; send me." To have a vocation one must find an imperative purpose to work for. No religious experience is adequate without this sense of divine vocation to give direction and continuity to living. To find such a life purpose is to settle the deepest issue of life, not once for all, but every day. For purposes may fail unless they are reaffirmed and renewed from day to day. Living on purpose means enacting that purpose into every thought and mood, every deed and development.

4. Religious Maturity

Every age is a crisis, the crisis of how to grow. For life is a constant battle with decay. Health is a winning battle of victorious living; disease, senility, and death are losing battles. In biological terms this is known as metabolism, the ratio of building up (anabolism) to the destruction (katabolism) of living cells, by which energy is provided for vital processes and activities. Retarded growth is one of the most pitiful tragedies of life. Nature sometimes falters and leaves human wrecks—in stunted forms, withered limbs, or defective organs. Mental retardation is even more serious, as seen in those whose clouded intelligence is unable to rise above the mental ages of infancy or early childhood. Social retardation is evident in the maladjustment of those whose immaturities appear in timid withdrawing or aggressive delinquency.

Religious immaturity is not so startling, yet it is quite as tragic as other retardations. When religion fails to grow, the results are religious cripples who are stunted, deformed, blind, or deaf in spiritual life. Jesus evidently considered this more serious than bodily injury.[17] But not many take the spiritual life as seriously as that. Religious cripples and morons are so common that we scarcely notice them. Many adults cherish a retarded religious experience that misfits present needs and disqualifies them for larger adventures.

To arrive at maturity is something, but not enough. To continue growing through the long years of adulthood is the problem. For maturity is one of the most dangerous threats to growth. It is the age of settling down into hardening forms that resist change. The average man develops very little after the age of twenty-five. Whether a college graduate or an unskilled laborer, he is not likely to change radically the established pattern of his life. He learns no more than is necessary, develops almost no new interests, makes no major reforms, and acquires surprisingly few ideas beyond those needed in the daily routine of his business. This stagnation does not mean that he is incapable of further growth, for educational experiments have shown as great, or greater, capacities for learning in the later years. We stop growing psychologically, not because we must, but because it is easier to keep familiar habits and follow the settled ways of the good old days.

Childhood delights to grow; adolescence demands it. We expect children to grow, sending them to school and to play that they may have every growing advantage. We are sure that adolescents have much to learn, and we urge them to cast aside childish pranks and take on the full stature of manhood and womanhood. But when young people get their growth, as we say, when they have a steady job and a home of their own, they are to settle down and tread the old beaten paths of those who have gone before. Having taken their last fling and bidden farewell to youth, these young adults are put in lock step with their grandparents and expected to keep in line. Why should there be no more adventures after

[17] Matt. 5:29-30.

the age of twenty-five? Why complete one's education so prematurely when learning ought to be as long as life? Our society is sadly at fault to establish these humdrum customs of treadmill routine as the style for maturity. Is it the machine-age civilization or short-sighted, dumb assent that truncates growth so sharply at the threshold of maturity, making drones and robots of adults?

There are at least five major tasks for maturity to accomplish. They involve the whole personality and yet are distinctly religious problems for mature religious growth.

a) *Self-knowledge.* It takes years of living to know oneself. To understand one's abilities is the product of many experiments to see what one can do best. A child is ready and eager to try anything, not knowing where his aptitudes lie. By maturity one should have a fairly clear idea where he can best succeed. Quite as important is it to know his limitations and realize what he cannot do. Knowing his limitations, the next problem is to accept them and live cheerfully within his own range of growth. Religion seeks perspective in humility before the Creator, yet hoping that all limitations are relative and trusting in the power of continued growth. Religious self-knowledge corrects both conceit and inferiority in the devotion to a larger cause. It seeks the optimal pattern of life—to learn what is best and then proceed without hesitation to do it.

b) *Controlled desire.* Children are attracted like flitting butterflies to every bright spot of interest. They want what they want when they want it, but not for long. Youth is overpowered with desires. New powers and waking capacities supercharge them to excesses. Like inexperienced drivers, excited to have so much power, they open the throttle recklessly, forgetting the need of control. A mature person, like an experienced driver, knows the dangers that go with power and is more alert to the value of control. Control of lower desires for the sake of higher ones is a religious art. If one is sincerely religious, he lives for a purpose, and by that purpose he controls his unruly impulses. To accept a divine calling is to have a larger responsibility, to trust a higher guidance, and to find the peace of resignation to a higher will.

c) Maximum efficiency. Motor skills are learned in early childhood. Social skills are won at the expense of awkward attempts and constant adjustment. By later adolescence a fairly complete set of habits has been acquired for the ordinary routine of later years. It is the misfortune of most adults to be content with habits already acquired and to coast along on past achievements. It is estimated that human beings are twenty per cent efficient most of the time. In a crisis we may rise to the occasion and make some heroic rescue by a superhuman feat of strength and endurance. Then, without further incentive, we drop back into the familiar mediocrity. More constant stimuli are needed to rouse us to the higher ranges of possible achievement. Religious motivation is a constant source of greater achievement. A divine purpose is a tremendous incentive to heroic living, and those who are committed to working with the Creator of Values are more apt to rise to their best efforts. By religious aspiration and inspiration, by faithful practice and progress, maturity may approach maximum efficiency.

d) Wisdom of experience. Intelligence has been defined as ability to learn by experience. Experience increases self-knowledge, control of desire, and efficient skills—that is, if one is able to learn from his experiences. Otherwise he makes the same mistakes over and over again. But if one can learn, every experience becomes his teacher. Wisdom is more than facts or skills; it is a true sense of values. Wisdom is a sound judgment—not a hasty opinion, but a sense of the whole meaning of life. Religious maturity has this wisdom of experience. A religious person is intent upon the business of living. He cultivates the inner life and evaluates every experience as a possible divine revelation. He refers his perplexities to larger perspectives and seeks divine leading. It is therefore in religious maturity that experiences may ripen into the fruit of wisdom.

e) Seasoned faith. The faith of childhood is a flower of innocence. The faith of adolescence drops childish petals to put forth intelligent fruit. But the faith of maturity is like a tree whose roots are deep in the stream of experience, whose trunk is sturdy enough to bear the brunt of the elements, that brings forth fruit in season. Having weathered many storms, such faith is proved worthy and able to stand. Faith so tested is more than dumb assent; it grows into faithfulness. Belief grows into trust; it rises above the merely intellectual and becomes an act of will. "Though he slay me, yet will I trust in him." [18] The faithful are full of faith. They are also filled with courage, patience, and unshakable determination to march in the line of duty. Seasoned faith is the salt of the world that loses not its savor but flavors, purifies, and preserves. [19]

5. EXPERIMENT AND INTEGRATION

Growth is an interacting process of experiment and integration. To grow, we must try the untried. The infant begins his experiments in random motions to explore and develop potentialities. Walking and talking are difficult skills to be learned by repeated efforts. Social adjustments to enlarging circles of persons are exciting experiments in the fine art of living with others. Mental growth is measured by the mastery of problems of increasing difficulty.

But experiments alone never produce growth. Whatever is gained by experiment needs to be appropriated by integration; otherwise experiments would remain forever in the futile disorder of random activity. A chicken runs frantically about a coop, dashing against one side and then another in foolish experiments. A

---

[18] Job 13:15.

[19] See E. M. Ligon, *The Psychology of Christian Personality* (New York: The Macmillan Co., 1936), and *Their Future Is Now* (New York: The Macmillan Co., 1939), for a good discussion of growing Christian personality.

child of two years will look around, take in the situation as an integrated whole, and walk straight to the door. Many people had seen lamps swinging, apples falling, and teakettles steaming before Galileo, Newton, and Watt drew their conclusions therefrom. Learning by experience is bringing the lessons of experimentation to a synthesis of understanding and progress.

Experiments without integration are centrifugal. They strike out and fly off in various tangents like the knight of Stephen Leacock who mounted his steed and rode furiously in all directions. They decenter life in distraction and confusion. The multiple appeals and distracting stimuli of the contemporary scene shred interests and scatter purposes. The speed at which we dash along is not conducive to poise or concentration. There is no lack of exciting adventures, but how to unify the many fragments of living into a whole life is the unsolved problem.

Integration of personality means the effective co-ordination of interests, emotions, and purposes. This unified, harmonious functioning of all one's powers brings success and happiness. The balanced wholeness of a character formed by good habits is referred to as integrity. The unintegrated person is disorganized, loose, contradictory, and unpredictable. Careful studies show that the average child in grades 5 to 8 is ethically unorganized. Integration of character traits is a specific achievement, not well provided for in current education.[20]

Dissociation is a disintegrative tendency. Many problems are so perplexing and distressing that, instead of making a direct attack upon them, one may dispose of them by ignoring or evading them. Running away from, postponing, or repressing unwelcome issues are well-known devices of escape. Ligon defines lust as "an intense emotional attachment of any sort which is not integrated with the total personality."[21] A lustful eye roves and a lustful

---

[20] See Hugh Hartshorne and F. K. Shuttleworth, *Studies in the Organization of Character* (New York: The Macmillan Co., 1930).

[21] *The Psychology of Christian Personality*, pp. 142-43.

heart is never satisfied but is always craving new excitements and experiments. Pure desires are integrated to a faithful purpose, but lusts refuse to remain true or constant. These evasive tendencies lead to serious nervous disorders.

Integrations are often incomplete and immature. A childish devotion to a father or mother may become a fixation that prevents mating and marriage. Childish impressions of God as a kind of Santa Claus may preclude larger theistic perspectives. Dogmatic devotions to the old-time religion may block normal growth to religious maturity. Integrations are needed at every stage of growth to consolidate gains and prepare for continued advance. But no integration should be final. Finality paralyzes growth.

What prevents normal integration of personality? L. F. Shaffer [22] finds ten conditions harmful to the integration of growing persons:

1. Lack of orderly living.
2. Lack of proper guidance and constructive discipline.
3. Too repressive discipline.
4. Vacillating and conflicting control.
5. Pulling and hauling children to keep up with parents' impatient haste.
6. Neurotic parents.
7. Quarreling and inharmonious home, and conflict of loyalties.
8. The broken home, from which one parent has deserted.
9. Conditions that repress and inhibit against giving confidence and receiving advice.
10. Emotional maldevelopments.

It is evident that most of these conditions are preventable. Religious conversion can unify a divided self in devotion to a great cause. One function of religion is seen in the Latin root *ligare*, "to bind." [23] Religious devotion binds together the diverse forces of personality into a unified whole of inner peace and steady action.

[22] *The Psychology of Adjustment* (Boston: Houghton Mifflin Co., 1936), pp. 385-87.
[23] There are other possible meanings. See the *Oxford New English Dictionary* (1933).

Maturity grows toward symmetry, and religious maturity aims at nothing short of perfect. Yet perfection is not to be attained once for all as something final but, rather, as a fleeting goal is continuous creative progress. Religion, as Professor G. W. Allport suggests, is "the most comprehensive of all the possible philosophies of life," because it is "the search for a value underlying all things." [24]

In the early stages of religious growth, experiment outruns integration. Curiosity invites the child to search for the new and unknown. Questions fly off alert minds at amazing speed. Answers and traditions that satisfy the elders only stir up the younger generation to more questions. Every suggestion is worth trying; every idea might be a revelation. The not discovered is more challenging than the already found, for it offers new adventures. This is one reason for the bewildering variety of religious beliefs and activities. In the history of religion every possible interpretation and experiment seems to have been tried (as also in science, morals, and politics). Whatever experiments have not been tried will no doubt have their turn. The experimental times are the progressive stages in growth.

Then come the conservative tendencies of maturity. As experiments are sifted out, men tend to agree more upon common conclusions. The random adventures of immaturity become the purpositive directions of maturity. A new science (like psychology) is still in a state of volatile disagreement, but an old science (like chemistry) has a larger body of integrated and accepted knowledge. Experiments continue, but they tend to fill in the gaps of theory rather than overthrow the established order. When a revolutionary hypothesis, like relativity, comes along, it offers a new integration and experiments are devised to verify it. Religious progress has the advantage of a long history, and there are now

[24] "A deeply moving religious experience is not readily forgotten, but it is likely to remain as a focus of thought and desire."—Allport, *Personality: A Psychological Interpretation*, p. 226.

signs of converging among creeds and practices. Maturity settles many of the conflicts and distractions of youth, but its danger is in surrendering experiment for the comforts of integration. In order to keep growing, religion needs to be equally vigorous in experiment and integration.[25]

---

[25] Gerald Heard shows that growth is a balance of expansion and cohesion.—*Man the Master* (New York: Harper & Bros., 1941), p. xi.

IV

Regenerative Powers

1. RELIGION DEAD OR ALIVE?

Religion is life. When religion dies, as religions have, it is no longer religion, but a relic. As a fossil leaves a fragmentary trace of extinct life embedded in the rock, so a dead religion may leave records of its history long after the life has departed. The death of a religion is not easy to explain, but it has significance for us. Religions of Babylonia, Assyria, and Crete were buried in the ruins of dead civilizations. Internal strife undermined the religion of Egypt. Confusion of many gods and cults sapped the religious faith of the Roman world, where tolerance became a disease causing decay. The religious superstitions and divine immoralities of Greece fell deservedly before philosophical criticism and scientific progress. More recently, Russian churches were closed by a revolution against an unjust society.

The shell of religion is often mistaken for the life. Imposing architecture, impressive ritual, and sonorous repetitions may represent hollow formality. Whited sepulchres of dead bones, is the verdict of history upon religious decadence. For a while they seem to stand securely intrenched, yet as life departs they become antiques containing memories but not hopes. From generation to generation religion may be lost, or even from day to day the life of religion may decline unless regeneration occurs.

Religion has died in persons who are otherwise living. Individuals may lose interest and turn elsewhere. Some are offended by unworthy examples of religious profession, or disappointed by unanswered prayers seeking rewards in vain. Others busy themselves with secular activities, too absorbed in material gains to be concerned about spiritual values. Some take doubts and intellectual conflicts as final, rather than working through to clearer understanding. Others are unwilling to accept the discipline or make the sacrifices in unselfish service that religion requires. Religious growth is not the line of least resistance, but calls for constant experiment and integration, as noted in the preceding chapter. Growth in higher values is more hazardous, even as the attainments are more difficult. Religious growth aims toward perfection, and, as Spinoza knew from his own disciplined life, "All things excellent are as difficult as they are rare." [1]

When Nietzsche said that God is dead, he was confessing the death of his own religious experience. [2] Religion without experience is dead because experience is the life of religion. Religion has survived without temples, priesthood, or ritual. It has outlived the society that sheltered it and has survived every other aspect of civilization—as Judaism did after the destruction of Jerusalem and Christianity after the fall of Rome. But it has never survived without experience; when religious experience goes, religion is no longer alive.

In the psychological study of religion we are concerned about religious life. The inner aspect of life is experience and the outer expression is behavior. Religious living is therefore a matter of experience and behavior. The specific question of this chapter is: How does religion live? Four hundred years ago the battle of science and religion was in astronomy, in the contests of Copernicus and Galileo with the Roman theologians. Fifty years ago it was in biology, in the Darwinian controversy over the question of evolution and creation. Today the battle is in psychology. Does psychological analysis reveal that religious experience is unique, vital, and valid? Or does it vanish into neurological reflexes and neurotic complexes? Dynamic life is the issue at stake in the scientific efforts of psychology to assay the meaning of religion in personality and society.

Life is a mystery greater than our knowledge. We usually know

[1] The closing sentence of his masterpiece, *The Ethics*.
[2] *Thus Spake Zarathustra*, Prologue 2.

life when we see it. We distinguish living from dead things, and point to life here and there. Forms of life vary over a wide range —from the amoeba under a microscope to primates and man. What has life in common among the wide range of its variations?

Life has the same raw materials as appear in many inanimate objects. It has electrical energy and contains many chemicals. But we kill live tissue by chemical analysis, and miss its unique characteristics. It is not the elements, but the organization of them that constitutes life. Organisms are vastly more complex, plastic, and interdependent than inorganic structures. They function so that parts serve the whole and the whole serves the parts. Biologists find the following traits in all organic life: nutrition, growth, repair, reproduction, sensitivity, and adaptability. The most conspicuous traits of living organisms, according to Seba Eldridge, are: (a) their community with the environment; (b) continuous interaction among cells and tissues of the organism; and (c) a structure that is stable, yet variable.[3]

Most of these traits, such as growth and reproduction, sensitivity and adaptability, interaction and community, appear also in the religious life. We do not need to wait until explanations are complete to understand what it means to be alive. We know life because we feel it coursing in our veins and tingling in our nerves. Some are more alive than others, overbrimming with vitality and energy. There are times when we are less alive than at other times. Fatigue, sorrow, depression, and despair devitalize the energies for living. Again, we may be high-spirited, sparkling in wit, thrilling with exhilaration, living to our fullest and best.

It is evident that psychological interests make us more or less alive. The moments of more adequate living are times when emotions are stirred by appealing ideas that call forth vigorous and effective responses. Religious resources can enlarge and renew life in this way by interests and aspirations, insights and meanings, motives and emotional responses, goals and purposes. Artists who

[3] *The Organization of Life* (New York: Thomas Y. Crowell Co., 1925), pp. 1-13.

seek to catch on canvas or film the vitality of a subject declare that the spirit or psychological interest of a person is the most significant factor in beauty. It is the spirit of a man or woman that counts most in the way he lives.

Herbert Spencer, in his search for a formula that would be inclusive of life in its biological, psychological, and sociological aspects, defined life as "the continuous adjustment of internal relations to external relations."[4] Life is adjustment. To adjust is to be flexible and adaptive enough to meet changing conditions by appropriate responses. To live is to respond well to the multiple, and often confusing, demands of the outer world. Life forever seeks harmony of inner and outer relations. Every life chooses its world, selects its stimuli, and controls its responses for some value sought. The range of adjustment measures the life. Life grows toward whatever it reaches for. Religious experience is the largest adjustment of life; religious aspiration seeks cosmic harmony on the grandest scale. Not content with local adaptations of the moment, religion seeks adjustment to the whole meaning of everything, everywhere, forever. To follow the outreach of religious response is to see man seeking the largest values in the most complete life. "Whatsoever is good for thee, O Universe, is good for me."[5]

2. BIRTH AND REBIRTH

Human personality is at once the best known, and the least understood, of all facts. Great as scientific knowledge is today, we are baffled by the simplest questions of a little child. What am I? Where did I come from? What kind of person will I become? Somewhat is known about the generation of life: When the ovum is fertilized by the spermatozoon, a new individual develops according to the pattern of the species—yet unique in its own identity. Hereditary traits are packed in genes, whose pairs of chromosomes match and select characters to be transmitted to the

[4] *Principles of Biology* (New York: D. Appleton-Century Co. [1867], 1897), I, 80.
[5] Marcus Aurelius Antoninus (A.D. 121-80).

new generation. Such knowledge as this is but a flicker in the dark of vaster unknowns. How did life begin in the first place? What makes fertilized germ plasm reproduce? Where do the genes gain that marvelous power to select and transmit characters? Why does life grow into the intricately functioning powers of personality?

To complicate the mystery and enlarge the range of life, generation is accompanied by regeneration. Birth opens the way for rebirth. Nicodemus was astounded when Jesus declared, "Except a man be born again, he cannot see the kingdom of God." [6] Nicodemus was laboring with a narrow view of biological birth and did not comprehend the meaning of psychological rebirth. It is customary to label physical birth "natural" and spiritual birth "supernatural." Jesus seems to mean that rebirth is as normal as birth. The mystery and creativity of life are equally wonderful in birth and rebirth.

Psychological rebirth is a major reorganization of interest and purpose. At birth, the infant has been called a candidate for personality. Let theologians debate where and when the soul begins. Psychologically, the soul is equivalent to personality, which is potential at birth. Neurophysiological powers develop before birth. Birth, however, marks the dawn of consciousness. The first breath may be a reaction to a helpful slap on the back, to startle life into waking consciousness. Yet consciousness is not self-consciousness. Numerous explorations and discoveries are needed during the period of infancy before the baby is conscious of himself as a person. He is born not a personality but a bundle of dynamic potentialities normally capable of achieving personality.

Many are the attainments of psychological growth through childhood and adolescence. Noteworthy religious developments have been traced in the chapter above. Each of them may be seen as a spiritual rebirth. Sensory perception and ability to recognize meanings, communication by language, discovery of persons, social

[6] John 3:1-12.

92

co-operation and sharing, organization and self-control, are psychological rebirths taking place in childhood. When personal experiences deepen in adolescence, social interests broaden, intellectual powers heighten, and life purposes lengthen, young people are actually born again. Religious awakenings and conversion experiences come to a peak in the adolescent years. As maturity brings self-knowledge, controlled desire, maximum efficiency, wisdom of experience, and seasoned faith, there is reason to expect a reconstruction of personality. For personality can and must be born again to grow into the full measure of developing powers. Such rebirth is natural in the normal growth of human life, to be expected and encouraged, for otherwise growth is retarded. It is supernatural in the higher creativity that transcends one level after another.

Why be born again? One answer is found in the basic need of *growth*.[7] Birth is only a beginning in the adventures of a human being. If one neglects to take the next steps in the course of normal development, he fails to grow. Not to grow is to defeat the progress of life, to be abnormal in retardation that lags behind expectation. The tragic symptoms of failure to grow spiritually appear in juvenile delinquency and crime, in quarrels and bad dispositions, in desertion and broken homes, in evasions and irresponsibilities, in selfishness, greed, and the personal instabilities that defeat the larger fulfillment of moral and social achievements. In the total progress of life, continued growth may well be seen as essential for human success.

Fatigue is a recurring need for rebirth. Every act and process of living drains off energy. To maintain bodily temperature, to restore tissue, to co-ordinate the synapses of the nervous system, to think, feel, and decide, to organize and carry forward the

---

[7] "At bottom all growth or change, like the birth process which is its prototype, is seen to contain the elements of death as well as life. As a rule the death aspect is only partial and is more than compensated for by the new life created thereby."— Jessie Taft, *The Dynamics of Therapy in a Controlled Relationship* (New York: The Macmillan Co., 1933), p. 284.

activities of daily life, require constant replenishment of energy. In the wear and tear of going we tend to run down. Children, starting fresh in the morning, are too tired by night to keep up the pace. As we approach middle age the burden of fatigue weighs the more heavily. And this is not mere muscular fatigue, for without active exercise one may also be exhausted. It is nervous fatigue that becomes the greater health problem in modern living. Exhausted resources must be restored, or we perish by degrees in slow stages of decline. Medical prescriptions tide patients over for a while, in the hope that they may build up their vitality. But every wise physician knows it takes more than vitamins to maintain the vitality needed. Spiritual resources of poise, confidence, and hopeful purpose are essential to successful living. Rebirth in spiritual vitality is what religion has to offer.

Error and *sin* are problems for everyone. To err is human, and we all come in for our share of it. But no one has the right to keep on making the same mistakes. For intelligent progress means that we learn by experience to overcome the errors of the past. Yet mistakes become habits, and the line of least resistance is to repeat the familiar old faults. Sins are the serious errors that turn life in false directions. To correct sin is to redirect life more truly toward the goal of its largest fulfillment. Otherwise an increasingly bitter harvest of consequences destroys values that we can ill afford to lose. The curse of sin is this tendency to pursue its persistently destructive course in fatal disregard of the consequences. The cure of habitual sin is not less than a spiritual rebirth.

Fragmentary living is another frustration. We are finite and inevitably limited in vision, understanding, purpose, and energy. But we add to our necessary limitations unnecessary ones. By prejudice, isolation, and selfishness we confine ourselves to petty interests. Narrow interests and loyalties may be good as far as they go, but they fall short of going far enough. It is easy to mistake the part for the whole and devote the whole life to partial concerns. Religion seeks the complete life in the larger wholeness of true integration; if we desire vaster values, wider perspective, unselfish interest and service, religion offers a way out. It is the way of new birth, awakening life to see and to dare new adventures in spiritual progress.

What is this new life of religion? Rebirth at every stage in the growth of life is a creative synthesis. The potential powers of the past reorganize, and come to actual achievements heretofore unknown. C. Lloyd Morgan [8] has called this progress of life to new levels "emergent evolution," showing that new powers come into being when matter moves up to the level of life, and life emerges to the higher level of mind. Each significant development in the historic advance of life on this planet is a creative synthesis of new birth. In the progress of individual growth plateaus appear while life gathers its resources for the next step in its development. To speak of a religious awakening as the second birth is too meager, for there are many rebirths along the way of growth from infancy to maturity. In more ways and times than we count we are reborn into new life. Religion refers to this new spiritual attainment as eternal life, indicating its larger dimension and deepening quality.

a) Eternal life is *unitive*. It is by inner conflicts that we most often defeat ourselves. Impulses clash, desires doublecross and cancel each other. Poise is disturbed and satisfaction deflated by divisions within. We want too much, or too many contradictory things, and pay the price in distractions and distresses. A house divided against itself does not stand well. So the individual who is serving too many masters rebels against himself and becomes his own enemy. Most of us are restrained by inhibitions. Worries, anxieties, and fears hold us in leash, bound by nervous tensions. Health is affected, and power for adequate living is drained off or damned up by these inner conflicts. Rebirth means coming into eternal life that is unified around a great cause in loyal devotion.

[8] *Emergent Evolution* (New York: Henry Holt & Co., 1924). The "creative synthesis" of Wundt and "creative evolution" of Bergson are similar concepts. See Henri Bergson, *Creative Evolution*, tr. Arthur Mitchell (London: Macmillan and Co., 1911).

Committing life to a cause releases inhibited energy and directs scattered interests along the channel of continuous purpose. It gives man something to live for, to lose himself in and find himself through. A "magnificent obsession" is a passion that consumes trifling anxieties in the flame of a great cause.[9] To offer all to God is a transforming experience that draws the eddies and backwashes of selfish and fearful timidity into the strong current of new life.

b) Eternal life is *resourceful*. When a man is self-conscious and watching for every sign of fatigue, he soon comes to the point of exhaustion. But if he forgets himself and concentrates upon his goal, he comes into a "second wind" that permits him to keep on going vigorously. In time of crisis, trying to meet the urgent needs of others, one's strength is surprisingly increased. Mothers nursing sick children, men engaged in hazardous rescues from fire or flood may keep on far beyond the limits of ordinary endurance. We smile at the absurdity of Ponce de Leon's searching through Florida for a fountain of eternal youth. There is no liquid that has magical power to restore youth, or quench forever the thirst to drink again. But there are spiritual resources whereby one may find more adequate energy for the tasks at hand. Psychologists speak of motivation as the key to effective learning and achievement. Fountains of eternal life are inexhaustible resources of motivation. To have purposes and powers to carry on is a question of spiritual energies. Eternal life is everlasting motivation. It does not run dry but, like a fountain, rises day and night. To find such resources for living is one of the secrets, perhaps the greatest secret, of success as a human being.

c) Eternal life is *expansive*. Religious interests and purposes are outward bound. In religious progress one outgrows puny self-interest, turning outward to others. "Nothing human is alien to me," said a Roman Stoic who discovered his kinship with everyone

----

[9] The psychological value of loyalty to a cause is well shown by Josiah Royce, *The Philosophy of Loyalty* (New York: The Macmillan Co., 1908).

everywhere.[10] "The world is my parish," said an English clergy-
man whose responsibility to serve outgrew his church and became
a world mission.[11] One of the urgent problems in expanding growth
is how to extend the range of values. The introvert turns inward
to center attention on himself, and suffers shyness, escapism, and
the inferiority feelings of ingrowing selfishness. The extravert turns
outward to find enlarging joys in the social identification of self
with others. Tagore quotes a Hindu line, "Man seeks the man in
me and I lose myself and run out," to show how religion opens
doors and invites lonely individuals out into a larger world of
comradeship.[12] The Chinese philosopher Mo Ti taught universal
love as the will of Heaven.[13] Eternal life is universal in its extension toward the whole. Like a brimming cup, such life is overflow-
ing to larger values.

3. CONVERSION EXPERIENCES

The climax of rebirth is best known as conversion. Epoch-mak-
ing conversions appear in the history of many religions. Moses was
converted from a fugitive murderer to a deliverer of his people
by an experience of meeting God on a mountainside. The long
struggle of Gautama for peace and enlightenment finally reached
a climax under the Bo tree, changing his life and influencing the
many followers of Buddhism. The mystery cults of Greece, Rome,
and Persia brought new life to those who were converted in emotional upheavals.[14] The conversion of Paul from a persecutor to a
missionary of the Christian faith came to a crisis on the Damascus

---

[10] Terence (*ca.* 185-159 B.C.).

[11] John Wesley (1703-91).

[12] *The Religion of Man* (New York: The Macmillan Co., 1931), p. 110.

[13] Y. P. Mei, *The Ethical and Political Works of Motse* (London: Arthur Probsthain, 1929).

[14] H. R. Willoughby, *Pagan Regeneration* (Chicago: University of Chicago Press, 1929); A. D. Nock, *Conversion* (London: Oxford University Press, 1933). See James, *The Varieties of Religious Experience*, 127-58, and J. B. Pratt, *The Religious Conscious-ness*, pp. 122-64, for interesting case studies in conversion; also A. C. Underwood, *Con-version: Christian and Non-Christian: A Comparative and Psychological Study* (New York: The Macmillan Co., 1925.)

Road and extended its influence along other roads of the Roman world. Augustine, in his *Confessions,* traces step by step his long progress from pagan profligacy to Christian consecration. The conversions of Justin Martyr, Origen, Constantine, Francis of Assisi, Luther, Wesley, Bunyan, and Fox have transformed other men and made Christian history. The desert broodings of Mohammed changed his life and fired the world with a new religious zeal. Ramakrishna (1834-86) experienced a Hindu conversion that brought new life to an ancient religion, while Gandhi, in our time, has converted himself and others to a powerful movement of nonviolent reform.

Conversion means turning around and changing the course of life. One may turn in many directions, as from irreligion to religion, from one religion to another, from formal to vital experience, or from religion to no religion. To make a right-about-face, reversing the direction from one way of life to another, is a radical matter. If one has been going vigorously in one direction, a sudden reversal may be a violent shock. Riding a passenger train when the brakes are suddenly applied, one may be thrown out of his seat as cars are switched in the opposite direction. Just so conversion may be an upsetting experience. On the other hand, there need be no shock if the process is gradual and steady.

Conversion experiences may be as varied as life itself, in the multiple ways that life has of reorienting and regenerating its energies. A new birth is a major change in life, whether sudden and dramatic or quiet and inconspicuous. The crisis type of conversion has drawn attention because it is conspicuous, yet a gradual development may accomplish the same results. The essential mark of conversion is the completeness of the transformation. Social change may come to a nation by revolution or evolution. England turned from monarchy to democracy quite as thoroughly as France, yet gradually, without guillotines or violent revolution. So an individual may be as completely changed by gradual growth as by a sudden crisis. Minor adjustments may not be recognized as conversion, yet enough of them may eventually transform life entirely. [15]

The type of conversion is influenced by social expectation. There are styles of conversion, as there are of worship and theology. A theology of crisis produces experiences of crisis. If a man is convicted of original sin and total depravity, if he is taught to fear the terrors of an angry God, fiery hell, and eternal damnation, his conversion is likely to be as dramatic as a brand plucked from the burning. Puritan theology may be seen vividly at work in the revivals and conversions of John Bunyan, David Brainerd, and Jonathan Edwards, taking men by storm and sweeping them into the mass movements of that time.[16] Evangelical denominations have stressed the emotional crisis more than Catholic, Lutheran, and Anglican churches, which seek by confirmation to approve the gradual growth of religious education. Yet in the twentieth century these evangelical churches have emphasized education and continuous growth more than they did in the last century, when revivals and camp meetings were the popular style.

Changing styles of conversion are evident in successive studies during the past fifty years. The average age of conversion has been appearing three or four years earlier than before, as shown in the table at the top of page 100.

What types of experience are most prevalent in conversion? Starbuck, in 1899, found the most prominent preconversion experiences (in descending order) to be depression and pensive sadness, calling on God, restless anxiety and uncertainty, sense of sin, loss of sleep or appetite, feeling of estrangement from God,

---

[15] F. S. Hickman, *Introduction to the Psychology of Religion* (New York: The Abingdon Press, 1926), pp. 215-20, proposes to call the lesser adaptations religious adjustments, reserving the term "conversion" for a sudden revolution. In general use, however, conversion may be either gradual or sudden if it results in a major change of life.

[16] Pratt, *The Religious Consciousness*, pp. 140-56, traces this development and observes that theologians by their teachings have induced a "largely artificial form of experience."

AGE OF CONVERSION [17]

Studies	Date	Number of Cases	Average Age
Starbuck	1899	1,265	16.4
Coe	1900	1,784	16.4
Hall	1904	4,054	16.6
Athearn	1922	6,194	14.6
Clark	1929	2,174	12.7

desire for a better life, doubt and questing, earnest seriousness, weeping, and nervousness.[18] He found the following motives leading to conversion: social pressure and urging, the following out of a moral idea, remorse for sin, fear of death or hell, example or imitation, response to teaching, self-regarding motives, and altruistic motives. Central factors in conversion experiences he noted as spontaneous awakening, forgiveness, public confession, sense of oneness, self-surrender, determination, and divine aid. Emotions following conversion, as listed by Starbuck, are joy, peace, acceptance and oneness with God or Christ, happiness, bodily lightness, weeping or shouting, partial disappointment, relief, struggle and sense of responsibility, load lifted from body or heart, and subdued calmness. Conversion was a crucial and necessary experience to that generation.

E. T. Clark, in his questionnaire study thirty years later, classified three types of religious awakening: (*a*) definite crisis (in emotions and attitudes), (*b*) emotional stimulus, (less intense, no special change, but some event recalled as stimulus to awaken religious consciousness), and (*c*) gradual awakening (religious

[17] Starbuck, *The Psychology of Religion*; Coe, *The Psychology of Religion*; Hall, *Adolescence*; Athearn *et. al*, *Indiana Survey of Religious Education*; Clark, *The Psychology of Religious Awakening*. Note also Conklin, *The Psychology of Religious Adjustment*, pp. 108-20.

[18] *Op. cit.*, p. 63.

life flows on like a stream, enlarging and growing, striking no obstructions and forming no cataracts). In contrast to the emotional
crises prevalent in Starbuck's study, he finds the crisis type far
outweighed by the tendency of gradual growth.

The more radical awakenings of crisis tend to occur about the
age of seventeen—which coincides with earlier reports of Starbuck
and Hall. But when religion develops as a gradual process, the
awakening comes as early as twelve years. If the process is inter-
rupted or resisted at this age, it is then deferred about five years
and requires an emotional crisis to overcome obstructions. The
later the conversion comes, the more intense and revolutionary
it is, for the changes are more drastic and difficult. The sterner
theology of the past discouraged gradual growth by denying that
religious capacities exist. Today the sterner theology is declining,
as Clark finds that only 10 per cent of his group seem to have
heard of it, while the majority think of a God of love and forgiveness. The relation of theology to type of conversion is indicated in the following table:

THEOLOGY RELATED TO TYPE OF RELIGIOUS AWAKENING [19]

Group	No. of Cases	Definite Crisis	Emotional Stimulus	Gradual Growth
Total	2,174	6.7%	34.7%	66.1%
Stern Theology	176	34.6	34.7	30.7
Confirmation	133	2.2	5.5	92.3
Above 40 years	81	35.8	30.9	33.3

Viewed in perspective, conversion is an incident in the process
of religious growth. Without continuous growth before and after
the climax, conversion is unreal and futile. With the preparation
of previous development and the continuation of later progress,

[19] Clark, *op. cit.*, p. 87.

it may be decisive for the whole life. The timing of a crisis may be incidental but the growing through time is essential. A sudden conversion may speed up the developing process, and yet normally contain the same steps of progress. These steps move in a sequence of three periods: preparation, climax, and continuation. The climax may rise to a sharp peak of contrast standing like a Great Divide between two epochs of life. It may be marked by a quiet moment of decision on a fairly even pathway of advance. Or religious growth may consist in a series of decisions and rededications that carries forward a lifelong purpose to a worthy goal. Decisive as one hour of dedication may be, it is the constant renewal of personal devotion that holds continuing significance.

The following statement is fairly typical of young people today. Their conversions are not violent crises in which they struggle against evil and finally renounce the world, the flesh, and the devil once for all. The conversion is one of a series of decisions in a continuous process of religious growth. This does not minimize, but rather magnifies, the act of conversion, because the growing religious experience confirms and supports the progress.

When I was six years old, I went forward in a revival meeting that was being held in a tabernacle under the auspices of our church. As I look back, I can see that I barely realized at that time the general significance of the Christian life, although that decision has had a deep meaning in my Christian life. I knew that my actions indicated that I intended to follow Jesus and be good. My conversion was not limited to that experience nor to any other one but was more a growth than a sudden change. What transformation was made at this early experience was not sudden nor unexpected but the result of the religious influences of home and church from my birth. Since that time my religious life has likewise been a gradual growth, more or less steady, with high spots interspersed. I cannot mark my conversion down to a definite time, because it did not all happen at once.

There have been quite a few of these high points, some coming during a religious service but others when I have been alone in my room or out

among the trees and the hills. I can classify only part of them. Included
are the experiences through which I came to decide that I must enter into
some type of religious service. Others have come when everything looked
dark and I had to ask myself the true value of the religion that I professed.
Such an experience came to me when I turned to God to lift me out of
my sorrow and despair after the death of my mother. Then I had one
of the most meaningful religious experiences of my life. Other high points
have been brought about when all was joyful and everything seemed to be
truly working together for good. I have had not only a second blessing
but many blessings through which I have been drawn nearer to God and
have received new meanings of him and added power to do the work
before me.

What are the psychological causes of conversion? De Sanctis [20]
separates physiological from psychic causes, noting that physiological conditions, such as puberty, fatigue, and disease, become significant only as they acquire psychic meanings. The psychic causes
may be either external or internal. External influences include the
effects of preaching and religious association, of reading and conversation, of disasters social and cosmic, of prophecies and portents.
Influential as these may be, it is the internal psychic causes that
finally determine the outcome of religious progress. Upon these
inner forces of religious experience psychologists have focused
attention.

a) *Innate tendencies* have been recognized from earliest psychological investigations. The fear, sex, and herd instincts came in for
their share of attention. The decline of interest in instinct (noted
in Chapter II) has discounted these theories. And yet there must
be motives at work in the dynamics of human nature. Emotions
of fear played no small part in revivals of the Puritans, though this
points to concern for values rather than instinct. The correlation
of conversion and adolescence has raised questions about sex factors
in religious development. If sex is viewed physiologically as a

[20] *Religious Conversion*, pp. 27-51.

glandular function or a blind instinct, it has little to offer. But if one looks at sex as all that constitutes manhood or womanhood, there is reason to see religious meaning in the unfolding experiences of adolescence. The gregarious tendencies may not reflect a herd instinct, but they do point to social participation that makes possible the social values of religious growth.

The most significant innate tendency is the power to grow— the mysterious processes by which potencies come out of the potential into the actual. Without these dynamic tendencies to grow in appreciation of values and organization of energies toward constant purposes, conversion would not occur. Innate capacities to develop enlarging interests are basic to all worthy advance.

b) *Conflict and release* appear in conversion, especially of the crisis type. The contrast between the ideal and the actual, the person one longs to be and the person one is, is a painful frustration. "In the light of the ideal we all stand condemned." The conviction of sin, the feeling of estrangement from God, the anxiety and distress before conversion, indicate the inner conflict and struggle for release. William James recognizes this situation in defining conversion as "the process, gradual or sudden, by which a self hitherto divided, and consciously wrong, inferior and unhappy, becomes unified and consciously right, superior and happy, in consequence of its firmer hold upon religious realities." [21]

His intimation that these processes of conflict and release arise from the unconscious forces of personality is taken up by psychoanalytic interpreters. They view these conflicts of desire as repressions that cause tensions until they break loose in some form of release. If this release is a false solution, it will be a neurotic evasion or domination by one desire, to the defeat of the total success of personality. A genuine conversion, however, is a true solution in which former conflicts are released into the harmony and unity of integrated personality.

[21] *Op. cit.,* p. 189.

Jung sees conversion as a reversal of tendency from introversion to extraversion or vice versa, a compensation in which balance of personality is restored. To Adler, conversion is the attainment of equillibrium whereby one moves from inferiority toward superiority. Psychotherapists seek to accomplish in their patients a release and integration equivalent to religious conversion. The results are not always as successful as religious conversion.[22]

c) *Recentering of interest, value, and purpose* is another characteristic of conversion. Hall and Starbuck emphasize this change of center in conversion. Hall [23] describes it as a change from autocentric to heterocentric life, in which the selfish individualism of childhood moves out to larger social concerns. To him, conversion is a process of socialization, which expands the range of activities and values. It may suggest Jung's view of conversion as a reversal from introversion to extraversion, though for Jung the conversion may turn in either direction. Starbuck [24] also finds an organization of life about a new center. Conversion is called a process of unselfing. No longer self-centered, the converted person feels closer to other persons, to nature, and to God. He is called out from himself into active sympathy with the world of other persons.

William James [25] finds a shifting of hot spots in consciousness as emotional excitement alters. To this new focus of interest one devotes attention, and the constellation of ideas and emotion becomes "the habitual center of his personal energy." Religious ideas and purposes, once peripheral, now take the central place in consciousness at the point from which the new aim is taken. De Sanctis sees conversion as a rebirth that recognizes psychic systems and substitutes new complexes for old ones as effective energy is transferred from one object to another.[26] Coe shows how conversion

[22] See H. C. Link, *The Return to Religion* (New York: The Macmillan Co., 1936), pp. 3-10.
[23] *Op. cit.*, II, 301-5.
[24] *Op. cit.*, p. 125.
[25] *Op. cit.*, pp. 195-96.
[26] *Op. cit.*, pp. 103-26.

changes the whole scale of values, until what was formerly desired is desired no more and what was neglected becomes the chief good: "Here the religious experience itself is a revaluation of values, a reconstruction of life's enterprise, a change in desire and in the ends of conduct." [27]

These psychological changes of religious conversion constitute the birth of a new self. When the prodigal son "came to himself," he was actually coming into his own for the first time. He thought he had come into his own when he asserted adolescent independence, demanded his inheritance, and went to a far country, with none to curb his rash desires. After many mistakes and bitter experiences he saw himself and his family in a new light. With this truer perspective he came to a new purpose, "I will arise and go to my father." Coming to himself was the first step in coming to his family.[28] Self-realization is not complete until it is also social realization. With new appreciations come new loyalties. Harmony within produces harmony without, an expansive devotion that creates new interpersonal relations with God and fellow men.

4. REVIVAL AND SURVIVAL

During the past century, Protestant Christianity has advanced on successive waves of revivals. No church calendar was complete without its stated times for special meetings. In frontier American life camp meetings brought people in buckboards and wagons from the whole countryside to get religion hilariously. At a later period tabernacles were constructed of rough lumber where the whole town was invited to come forward and receive revival blessings. The value of revivals in those times can scarcely be doubted. They met religious and social needs of the pioneers in ways that were native to their style of life.

There is question, however, of the value of such revivals today.

[27] *Op. cit.*, pp. 171, 222.

[28] Luke 15:11-32. Coe observes that the language of the parable is scientifically accurate.—*Ibid.*, p. 171.

Wieman [29] considers the traditional revival pattern artificial and ineffective today. It provided a needed stimulus for religious appreciations and loyalties. This could occur when men shared a common view of God, heaven, hell, and human destiny. Without this common cultural background conversion is not accepted today. In the scheme of modern life the revival customs of the past are hollow forms, lacking the appeal they once had. Generalizations are tempting, and this may overstate the case. Established churches now depend less upon traditional revival meetings for their religious progress. They rely on continuous religious education, dignified and artistic worship experience, personal counseling, intellectual and ethical interpretations, to carry forward the religious advance. At the same time tabernacle sects and old-fashioned revivals still thrive among the masses of folk who enjoy them.

A college senior, the daughter of a Methodist minister in the Midwest, was asked how she was indebted to revivals for her religious growth. Her home and church background were definitely evangelical, yet to her religious experience revivals meant very little. What to others was a serious matter was to her analytical mind, even at the age of ten, a circus.

My first experience in a revival meeting left very much the same effect as a good circus would have; for I was ten years old. In fact, it was so much like a circus that I find my childish reaction quite amusing. The tent was very large and we sat on planks which were separated by barrels. The ground was covered with sawdust, which was great fun to kick around, as I remember. Some were on their knees the entire evening, some stood, and I think there was "standing room only" in the Amen corner. They had a piano player who could have done justice to "St Louis Blues," and two saxophone players who outdid Cab Calloway's band. And to top it all, during the rendition of the sermon, the evangelist said he thought

[29] *Normative Psychology of Religion*, pp. 162-63. See also F. M. Davenport, *Primitive Traits in Religious Revivals* (New York: The Macmillan Co., 1905); S. G. Dimond, *The Psychology of the Methodist Revival* (London: Oxford University Press, 1926); W. W. Sweet, *Revivalism in America* (New York: Charles Scribner's Sons, 1944).

several of the town businessmen were "crooked," and that the Congregational minister wasn't fit to preach in a church. This kind of tickled the Methodists, but I guess most of the "Congos" walked out (they probably each wanted to be the first to tell their minister). Well, after the "Congos" left, everybody got into the spirit of the thing, and there was a lot of singing, praying, and amen-ing. These meetings lasted for two weeks, and I'm surprised the evangelist managed to save his life that long! After he left the town was split into three factions; and the Congregational minister was asked to leave. There still remains some ill feeling between the churches of the town.

Revivalism certainly isn't essential to my religious growth. In fact, I have such crazy ideas about it that, when I do go to one, I can't take it very seriously. It's very much like *Uncle Tom's Cabin*, which I once saw satirized—I never again could be very much overwhelmed by the story. When I read about little Eva dying and going to heaven, I see that hook coming down to lift her up.

I don't think it would be possible for me to have too much religion. At present I am striving for more, with no fear of becoming too religious.

It may be the style of revival that is out of date, not the revival itself. "Conversion of the worthy sort will always be needed in religious living." [30] There are some who contend that the gradual growth of religious education will entirely supplant the need of revivals. But this is a shallow view of human needs. The progress of persons or societies is seldom as straight and smooth as a newly paved cement highway on the Western plains. Curves of learning show plateaus; evolution advances by emerging levels; personal development has its ups and downs, its spurts and its lags; progress goes by fits and starts, zigzags, and spirals. Crises in growth will always occur. Major reorganizations of personality will be needed to fulfill normal health and growth. If the old styles of revival are no longer appropriate, it is high time new and better methods are found to encourage and renew religious growth. Secular movements present their appeal to awaken interest and command loyal-

[30] Wieman, *op. cit.*, p. 165.

ty. Shall religion hold interest and loyalty by less effective methods?

Without revival there is no survival. This law of life applies to religion. To continue living, religion must be refreshed and renewed in regular ways. If former methods of revival are inappropriate today, then religious people will need to find other methods that will be more effective. It would be folly to hold sacred any form or method that no longer serves its purpose effectively. In the days when automobiles were first replacing horses and buggies, flustered drivers were known to call out "Whoa!" when they wanted to stop the vehicle. The religious appeals that succeeded in one generation may be quite as ineffective if another generation has outgrown them.

The old-style revivals were native to the environment in which they arose. Meetings were held outdoors in tents or indoors in rough tabernacles because that was the best equipment available. When the committee of a modern city church votes to build a tabernacle for Sunday evening services, it is hankering for the good old horse-and-buggy days. Is a rough tabernacle more artistic, comfortable, or worshipful than a brick church with well-appointed furnishings? What can religious people do better in a tabernacle than in a church? Why should tabernacles appeal more to urban churchgoers than Gothic architecture? It's a matter of what each means to them. Gothic architecture and church symbols are more ancient than American nineteenth-century tabernacles with rough benches and sawdust floors. But some people remember the vivid revivals that occurred in tabernacles, and the association is meaningful to them. To others, who have had significant experiences in Gothic sanctuaries, the tabernacles or tent suggests the circus more than it suggests worship.

Each generation must find its own methods of living. Religious people may be victims of a social lag. Modern as we are in business, transportation, home equipment, telephone, dress, and medical services, we are apt to lag in other aspects of culture, such as religion. If religious methods are out of date they will be neglected as meaningless. Nothing kills religion more fatally than forgetting to grow. While religion holds eternal values of timeless significance, yet they are carried in containers that are dated by local customs. The forms of religion must change to bring vital meanings to each generation. To merit survival, religion must find methods of revival appropriate to contemporary needs.

It would be unwise to leap to the conclusion that what is old is necessarily out of date. The oldest styles may be the best styles, or the worst. Not the age of a method but its value in utility, beauty, and meaning is the decisive question. In seeking effective methods of religious revival it is well to consider what is psychologically sound. Waves of backsliding were natural reactions to emotional peaks artificially produced by fear or social pressure. People converted on the tide of crowd suggestion have found themselves incapable of ecstatic expectations in daily living, and consequently have felt they have lost the religion that swept them off their feet the night before. What methods will revive true religious growth?

Religious bodies used psychology long before psychology began to analyze religion. By intuition and experiment certain methods have been adopted because they meet religious needs. They do not belong to one sect or age, for they seem to have universal appeal. To list a few will suggest others: (a) telling stories of heroes; (b) tracing the causes and consequences of history; (c) singing songs that teach and inspire; (d) unison reciting, marching, or listening; (e) mutual appreciation of beauty and symbols; (f) group thinking stimulated by preaching and discussion; (g) appealing for decision and dedication of life; (h) presentation of divine command or call; (i) joining a religious group with initiation ceremonies; (j) religious tasks and prayers; (k) regular responsibility to carry with public recognition; (l) self-denial for the sake of larger, unselfish good. These activities contribute to religious awakening and education—not once, but over and again.

No single method of revival is enough; for each in itself is partial, and religion seeks the complete life by complete devotion. A true conversion takes all of a person and redirects the total life upon a new course. It holds the dramatic appeal of eternal destinies and divine imperatives. It offers a great adventure to lose all or win all, a decisive choice between good and evil. Religious education may seem trivial if it misses this dramatic appeal of great issues at stake. Gradual growth may seem futile unless one has a vision of the ultimate goal and makes definite progress thereto. The revival meeting put the crisis now, in this very hour, with eloquent contrast between the way of life and the way of death.

This sense of urgency religion can ill afford to forget. To achieve the new religious life, therefore, requires new birth. The regenerative powers of religion are deeper than conscious knowledge; they rise from dynamic, extraconscious resources of personality. They are larger than the individual and come through the interpersonal reactions of a social and creative universe. The mysteries of life and death, birth and rebirth, will not be plumbed by superficial answers. They are greater than our knowledge by as much as cosmic energies are greater than a half-pint cup in the hand of a child. To experiment with mysterious powers is the work of science and the devotion of religion. Each in its way will explore the possibilities open for larger life.

V

Prayer and Devotion

1. SPONTANEOUS PRAYER

Prayer is the natural language of religious experience. The native language of all life is a cry. As birds and animals cry out to express emotions and to signal to others, so the first language of every human person is a cry. We understand the cries of infants to mean hunger, loneliness, pain, or joy. For the same motives prayer is offered, as situations of need call forth these responses. Even as a sharp pain may come to vocal expression in a groan, or a startling surprise produce a cry of fear, so prayer is the inevitable outburst of emotional distress. Primitive men preface prayers with rudimentary sounds, as whistling, clicking, or wailing, which reveal pre-linguistic backgrounds. People of our day are likely in moments of stress to ejaculate "O God! Help Me!" as a spontaneous expression.

Friedrich Heiler is undoubtedly correct in taking this cry for help as the original form of prayer.[1] From the wordless cry wrenched from one in danger or distress, prayer expands to elaborate forms, phrases, and conventions. Whatever the form and however elaborate the foliation, the taproot of prayer is the elemental sense of need. In years of comfortable living some forget to pray; but if danger or anguish becomes urgent enough, most men pray irresistibly.[2]

Prayer is as natural as conversation. One turns to speak to a friend to communicate ideas and share experiences. And if no one is listening we talk to ourselves, subvocally. But prayer is not

[1] Heiler, *Prayer*, tr. S. McComb and J. E. Park (London: Oxford University Press [1919], 1932), p. 11.

[2] Note how many turn to prayer in calamity or crisis, as, for instance, on Invasion Day, June 6, 1944.

meant to be talking to one's self. Those who pray believe that they are addressing an Other, invisible but none the less real. The sense of a real Presence is the condition of prayer, in which the first person *I* speaks to the second person *Thou*. The exact nature of the Other may be unknown, but he is sought as a Person who can hear and help. Magic and science are mechanical operations with impersonal powers. Prayer is interpersonal, a person-to-person call asking for an answer. Dynamic tendencies to interact with other persons come naturally to expression in language and prayer.

If prayer is natural for some, is it for all? It seems to be the universal language of religion everywhere. From age to age and land to land, whether among primitive tribes or sophisticated church members, religious aspirations rise in prayer. If

> Prayer is the soul's sincere desire,
> Uttered or unexpressed,[3]

then we may agree that everyone has sincere desires. Yet many sincere desires are not offered to a Thou who is trusted to create and sustain values. If we take prayer as conversation with God, this excludes (*a*) those who do not believe in a God, (*b*) those who seek to evade God because of fear or guilt, and (*c*) those who feel no unmet needs or think prayer of no avail. There are many who do not often pray, yet there are few who never pray.[4]

When do people pray? A group of Minnesota young people of college age in 1933 reported praying in situations of wonder and admiration, fear, great responsibility, joy and contentment, need, temptation, and love. When asked what they prayed for they suggested the following subjects: physical needs (including food, health, and weather), protection, forgiveness of sin, guidance to know the way, strength to carry on, humility, security in God's

---

[3] James Montgomery (1771-1854), "What Is Prayer?"
[4] For a survey of prayer in various religions see *Encyclopaedia of Religion and Ethics,* X, 154-214. To observe the extensive use of prayer in other religions is to ask if the followers of any religion pray less than the average Christian.

presence, vision to see ahead, intercession for family and friends, gratitude for God's help, petition for God's compassion, power to endure hardships, to be used for God's will on earth, help to live better and avoid former mistakes, the purifying of heart and mind, peace of soul, courage to dare, greater faith that God is ever with us, greater confidence in mankind, ability to discern the value of life, ability to serve fellow men more effectively, the church and its leaders and members, the tempted, God's kingdom, and better world conditions.[5]

No psychology of prayer can overlook needs, for every prayer comes to focus upon a need. The range of human needs varies with the specific situations in which people find themselves, from the elemental physical needs for maintaining life to the more sophisticated needs listed by these young people. H. A. Murray defines a need, in line with his dynamic psychology as a force organizing personal action to improve a situation.[6] Whenever the tension of need is urgent enough, a person does something about it. He may think, fret, worry, weep, or curse; or he may act overtly by going somewhere, exploring, experimenting, inventing, working, or striving to control. He may appeal, persuade, argue, plead, bargain, or promise to co-operate with a person who seems able to help. The social appeal to an Other for help is in the direction of prayer.

There are many needs of which we are not conscious. One is not conscious of the need for air until deprived of it. Of most needs we are conscious only intermittently. Our need for food and water is recurrent with the rhythm of organic requirements; the need for security varies with the awareness of risk and danger. We become conscious of needs as we come to the margin of loss and gain in values. New needs may be created by education, or advertising, or observation of what others enjoy. The needs of our

---

[5] P. E. Johnson, "When College Students Pray," *Christian Advocate*, CIX (1934), 179.

[6] *Exploration in Personality*, p. 124. See p. 43 above for the exact quotation.

civilization have multiplied beyond all expectation with progress in science, technology, and economies of abundance.

Human prayers follow human needs. We pray only for the needs we are conscious of. The more urgent the need and the less adequate we feel, the surer we are to pray. If a need is trivial, it may not matter enough to pray; if we can meet the need independently, there may be little reason to call for help. So prayers rise and fall with the ebb and flow of conscious need. Does this mean that prayer is a confession of weakness? Relatively, yes; though it would be truer to say that it is a confession of inadequacy. Self-sufficiency is self-deception. No one is omnipotent; everyone has situations of need when he is inadequate.

It may be objected that this view turns one to prayer only as a last resort, when every other means has failed. The objection is accepted and sustained by the facts of human behavior. Most people pray intermittently, when special needs arise. Theirs is a faith that God helps those who help themselves. Why ask for help as long as one can help himself? Should not each person do his best to solve his own problems? The sturdy virtue of self-reliance seeks to go as far as possible without prayer. The time will come when needs overbalance adequacy; then, but not till then, do many resort to prayer.

We have described the practice of spontaneous prayer. It is impromptu, intermittent, and reserved for times of stress. This is the primitive and childlike use of prayer. But as men and women mature in the wisdom of experience, they see that spontaneous prayer is not enough. For the needs of life are persistent. One may live a hand-to-mouth existence without a thought beyond the next meal, but the risks and deprivations of life are too hazardous for a provident man. One may take no thought of his health until illness lays him low, but preventive medicine prepares to maintain health reserves before it is too late. To see and anticipate these needs is the most successful way of meeting them. Instead of waiting for emergencies to strike, the well-organized person plans and provides in advance to meet them more efficiently. Mature prayer is a preventive and sustaining procedure by which life may be held at higher levels of constant resourcefulness.

To understand this principle of larger spiritual preparedness is to move from spontaneous prayer to disciplined prayer. Instead of praying on the impulse of a mood, one may employ prayer to create the mood desired. Rather than use prayer as a last resort in desperate distraction, one may pray as a first resort to prevent distraction and come to difficult situations resourcefully. By frequent practice in the spiritual exercises of prayer, it is possible to develop powers and controls, attitudes and habits, that will prove more adequate to every situation. Those who desire the results enough will order and discipline the hours of every day to cultivate the inner resources of faithful devotion to a cause. Prayer in this way comes to be more than a "desire uttered or unexpressed," more than a cry or conversation. Prayer is then the conscious experience of harmony and co-operation with a Creator of Values.

2. METHODS OF DISCIPLINE

Those who are most devoted to prayer cultivate the inner life systematically. Like workmen who keep faithfully at a chosen task, or artists who know that excellence demands long hours of regular practice, or athletes who submit to rigorous training to be strong, they follow a schedule of daily spiritual exercise. Among those who make a business of prayer three religious vocations arise: the mystic, the prophet, and the priest. We may well study their methods.

The mystics are specialists in prayer. They have a passion for the Real, in the light of which other things are dark and unreal. Believing in the infinite value of spiritual reality, the mystics are ready to sacrifice material goods as worthless, and the appeals of the senses as deceptive illusion.[7] To them prayer is the highest

[7] J. H. Leuba, *The Psychology of Religious Mysticism* (New York: Harcourt, Brace & Co., 1925), pp. 137-55, finds sensual satisfactions present though not recognized as such by the mystics.

privilege and the deepest responsibility of life. In prayer they invest the working day, coming to prayer as a scientist to his laboratory, eager to discover reality, faithful to labor unsparingly, alert to improve methods of experiment and research.

The mystics of various religions—Hindu, Buddhist, Hebrew, Christian, and Moslem—have developed methods accepted as standard. From similar devotional experiences have come devotional exercises common to mystics everywhere.[8] These are often referred to as the "ladder of prayer" or the mystical ascent to God.[9] Four steps are noted, which may be described as awakening, purgation, meditation, and union.[10]

a) Awakening is the first step in religious progress. Experiences urging toward mysticism may be dissatisfactory human conditions, inner restlessness and conflict, hunger for a better state, vision of the splendor of a larger life, or a foretaste of ecstatic joy. It may be a conversion, or a vivid and compelling reawakening. Augustine decided. "I know nothing other than that the fleeting and falling should be spurned, the fixed and eternal sought after."[11] Pascal wrote. "From half-past ten to half-past twelve fire, joy, certainty."[12] Suso declared, "O my heart's joy, never shall my soul forget this hour."[13] A vivid, first-hand experience of spiritual value is essential.

b) Purgation is the negative path of renunciation. The logic of renunciation is that devotion to the mystical purpose requires purification. The natural life is distorted by carnal desires and material

---

[8] See Rudolf Otto, *Mysticism East and West*, tr. B. L. Bracey and R. C. Payne (New York: The Macmillan Co., 1932).

[9] Jeremy Taylor views prayer as an "ascent of the mind to God."—*The Rule and Exercise of Holy Living* (London, 1686), iv, 7.

[10] In the discussion of these steps I am indebted to Evelyn Underhill, *Mysticism* (New York: E. P. Dutton & Co., 1911); Hocking, *The Meaning of God in Human Experience*; James, *The Varieties of Religious Experience*; and Pratt, *The Religious Consciousness*.

[11] *The Soliloquies of St. Augustine*, tr. R. E. Cleveland (Boston: Little, Brown & Co., 1910), p. 8.

[12] From the *Memorial*, quoted in Underhill, op. cit., p. 228.

[13] *Leben und Schriften*, quoted in *ibid.*, p. 225.

values, a false universe of egocentricity. The earnest devotee seeks
to correct his perspective by clearing away whatever is not in
harmony with true reality. This detachment is represented by the
threefold monastic vow of poverty, chastity, and obedience. Morti-
fication is a self-discipline to break up the old selfish habits, aban-
don the comforts of least resistance, and take on a new spiritual
daring. The aim is to produce a definite vitality and efficiency
just as athletes do in the physical exercises of the gymnasium and
the field.

c) *Meditation* is voluntary concentration upon the object of
devotion. Recollection is used in the sense not of remembering but
of collecting the self together, narrowing attention to focus on
one aspect of reality—a word, name, or attribute of God, a verse
of scripture, or an incident in the life of Jesus. This leads to another stage of progress known as "orison," or quiet relaxation.
The struggle for concentration yields to surrender of the will to
God, a turning from doing to being. Orison is not the prayer of
petition, but a trustful waiting, a wordless communion, a silent
yearning of the soul, an opening of the spiritual eye to gaze upon
the glory of God. Contemplation is often named as another step
beyond meditation. It means self-forgetting attentiveness, an
illuminating act of the whole personality in devotion to God.

d) *Union* is the goal of mystical progress. A merging or absorption of self with the Absolute is sought by pantheists. An intimate
sense of personal fellowship with God is the aim of theists. Hypnotic states of ecstasy, rapture, and trance are welcomed by some;
depressive states of darkness and separation are endured by others
as emotional reactions of fatigue and relapse. Beyond these emotional extremes true mystics seek a transforming of character
that will become a permanent incarnation of the divine in the
human. "Not I, but Christ liveth in me," said Paul.[14] "My life
shall be real, because it is full of Thee," declared Augustine.[15] In

[14] Gal. 2:20.
[15] *Confessions* X. xxviii.

118

such complete devotion to the divine cause there comes a consciousness of sharing, divine strength, freedom, and serenity. A person so dedicated and inspired becomes a radiating center of spiritual vitality and goodness to others.

Prophets are also men of prayer. They are fully as devoted to the religious cause as the mystics, but they follow another discipline. The mystic is regulated by the aim of self-control, while the prophet is directed by the aim of social action. The mystic is an individual who turns to God in private devotions; "so must the single soul be allowed its own single love." [16] The prophet is devoted to social welfare and identifies himself with the common life of his people.[17] He broods with God over the evils of his time and cries out the divine message of repentance and reform. The urgency of social needs possesses the prophet until he can bear it no longer, and he is compelled to throw his life recklessly into courageous action with God to serve others.

Heiler strikingly contrasts mystical and prophetic prayer.[18] Although mystics may also be prophets and vice versa, greater clarity is gained by noting the emphasis of each. Prophetic prayer arises in concrete need and comes to a vigorous emotional expression. Mysticism is calm, aesthetic contemplation, but prophecy is stormy in emotion and urgent in ethical demands. It takes the form of ardent petition and intercession for others by eloquent persuasion. Abraham pleading with God to save Sodom argues persuasively, "Wilt thou also destroy the righteous with the wicked?" and, "Shall not the Judge of all the earth do right?" [19] Prophetic prayer freely confesses sin and unworthiness.

[16] *The Essence of Plotinus*, ed. G. H. Turnbull (New York: Oxford University Press, 1934), p. 96. The social implications of this are also stated by Plotinus: "This does not make the man unfriendly or harsh; giving freely to his intimates of all he has to give, he will be the best of friends by his very union with Divine Mind."—*Ibid.*, p. 37.

[17] Note Moses, praying God to forgive his people, ". . . and if not, blot me, I pray thee, out of thy book which thou hast written."—Exod. 32:32.

[18] *Op. cit.*, 135-285. See also Hocking, *op. cit.*, pp. 485-514.

[19] Gen. 18:23, 25.

The yearning for vision of God is not an experience for the prophet himself, but one to share with his people. "The Lord God hath spoken, who can but prophesy." [20] The practical social emphasis is evident in the prayer of Jesus for his disciples, "For their sakes I sanctify myself, that they also might be sanctified through the truth, . . . that the love wherewith thou hast loved me may be in them." [21] Francis of Assisi felt it was a great shame when he found anyone poorer than he, and prayed for grace to love more truly. The prophet therefore is disciplined by his keen sense of need, his responsiveness to God's revelation, and his devotion to social religious progress.

The priests are also men of prayer. They take up prayer as a religious vocation and work faithfully at the task of praying. But their discipline is not the self-control of the mystic or the social action of the prophet. Priestly discipline is ritual. The life of prayer is regulated in the temple by tradition and authority. Spontaneous prayer is too chaotic and inexact for institutional use. Extempore prayer consequently yields to literary editing. Fluid expressions set into forms that become norms. The present experience is subject to the authority of the past with its cumulative traditions and meanings. In this discipline priests feel obliged to be correct, to utter their prayers in good style, according to the established proprieties. So develops a priestly liturgy for public prayer and a breviary for daily offices.

Each of these disciplines has its psychological value. Priestly prayer is rich in traditional symbols, aware of historical continuities, precise in well-ordered expression, effective in literary and dramatic power, solemn in dignity, and impressive in social resonance. Priestly prayer gathers up the experience of the group and distills its essence into a fragrant expression. But repetition may result in sterile, hollow formality. Then prophetic revolt breaks forth as a cleansing moral imperative.

[20] Amos 3:8.
[21] John 17:19, 26.

I hate, I despise your feast days, and I will not smell in your solemn assemblies. . . . Take thou away from me the noise of thy songs; for I will not hear the melody of thy viols. But let justice run down as waters, and righteousness as a mighty stream.[22]

And when social service grows weary or reforms are lost in failure and despair, the sources of spiritual vitality may be renewed in the transforming mystical experience of communion with God. Each discipline supplements the others in kindling anew the flame of devotion.

3. Psychological Effects

Spontaneous prayer arises from urgent need. Disciplined prayer anticipates needs and seeks dynamic resources to fulfill them. What needs can prayer meet? How effective is prayer for any purpose? Work achieves visible results. By appropriate action one can walk a mile, build a house, or bake a loaf of bread. What does prayer accomplish? Can prayer transport, build, or bake? Prayer is no substitute for action; neither is intelligence, trust, or kindness. But action may fail for lack of intelligence, persons are ill for lack of trust, and poverty is unrelieved without kindness. Not all action is constructive; not all work is successful. Mere busyness is futile if one does the wrong thing. What can work accomplish without foresight, skill, and co-operation?

Success is a delicate balance of many factors. Every value achieved is a product of insight and action, appreciation and constructive labor, desire and effort toward fulfillment, organization and social co-operation. The achievements of prayer result from its proper use. Prayer does not work as a substitute for a steel chisel or the wing of an airplane. It does not replace muscular action in walking, or faithful study in meeting an examination. These are not the proper uses of prayer. But prayer may help to calm the nerves when one is using a chisel in bone surgery, or bringing the plane to a landing. Prayer may guide one in choosing

---

[22] Amos 5:21-24.

a destination to walk toward, and strengthen one's purpose to prepare thoroughly for the examination.

In the psychological realm of motivation, the effects of prayer can be observed. This is the field where the operation of prayer seems most appropriate. The inner life of tensions and desires, stresses and problems, is the dynamic area of spiritual energies. What are the psychological effects of prayer?

a) *Awareness of needs and realities.* As prayer arises from needs, so needs become clearer in praying. The realities of life are faced with One who knows all; self-deception is laid aside and deeper honesty opens truer understanding.

b) *Confession and harmonious adjustment.* To confess needs, failures, and anxieties is a purging emotional catharsis. In the prayer of confession one may find assurance of forgiveness and harmonious adjustment to a larger, interpersonal destiny.

c) *Trust and relaxation.* Prayer in faith and hope releases tensions, brings peace of mind, disposes of worry and fear, undergirds insecurity with basic confidence.

d) *Perspective and clarification.* Prayer aims to see life steadily and whole in the perspective of God. As a cluttered desk is put in order, so in prayer confused experiences become coherent. Prayerful meditation solves problems and works out practical plans of action.

e) *Decision and dedication.* In this clarifying perspective goals come into view and purposes move toward them. Dedication of self to a cause relieves indecision and becomes an urgent motor set to effective action. Such a decision is a first step in unleashing powers to achieve progress.

f) *Renewal of emotional energy.* In the sense of meeting God one may have creative experiences of elation, inspiration, and expansion of emotional resources. Such experiences are euphoric and energizing.

g) *Social responsiveness.* The prayer experience of meeting God overcomes isolation and loneliness because we feel we are not alone.

There is moral support, courage, and virility in this feeling of social response. In praying for and with others one becomes socially sensitive to their needs and more ready to co-operate for the good of all.

h) *Joy, gratitude, and reconciliation*. Prayer affirms values, enlarges appreciation, and recognizes present good. These affirmations give a joyous undertone, awakening gratitude and reconciling one to sorrow and loss. Whatever comes, one is better prepared to meet it in this spirit.

i) *Loyalty and perseverance*. Prayer is an act of devotion and renewal. Loyalties are fostered by approving values and giving one's self in faithful devotion. Rededication in prayer develops persistence to carry on in the face of obstacles and fatigue.

j) *Integration of personality*. Amid the distraction and contradiction of many appeals, prayer focuses attention upon a supreme Object of loyalty. In the conflicts of ambivalent desires, prayer recollects the major purpose and unifies the energies along the channel of this dedication. Those who pray faithfully manifest a basic integrity that gives life poise and inner peace.

This list of psychological effects may appear to some an overstatement, but to those who have explored the resources of prayer it will seem an understatement. Not all praying is so effective, for prayer is often misused and misunderstood. Prayer is bound to fail, as is any other instrument taken out of its proper field and put to magical rather than experimental use. The prevalent neglect of prayer indicates the misunderstanding and misuse of it. The total value and influence of prayer is beyond our knowledge. But in the psychological functions listed above, prayer is well employed. Prayer with none of these results is futile. If prayer has even one of these effects it is well worth while. Rightly used, prayer may have enlarging effectiveness in the psychological needs of personality.

4. RELIGIOUS DEVOTION

The psychology of religious devotion is very perplexing. Why does a sincere person who wants to be religious find it so difficult? Man may be incurably religious, but he is just as persistently irreligious. The confessions of saints as well as the more conspicuous faults of sinners, bring a convincing weight of testimony. The earnest religious life never ceases to be a struggle against temptation and resistance. Whoever takes religion as an easy way of life has less than a complete devotion.

Psychological analysis may help to disclose the causes of difficulty in religious devotion. How is such devotion possible? What are the inner resistances that distract and defeat singleness of purpose? Religious devotion includes the following psychological processes: (*a*) interest in and attention to spiritual values; (*b*) conscious decision, choosing the way of life that offers these values; (*c*) identification of self with the religious cause; (*d*) renunciation of other interests that conflict and lead away from this devotion; (*e*) progressive integration of personality around God and His will for life.

If these five psychological factors are essential to religious devotion, what is it that so often prevents fulfillment of them? Personality is not one stream of energy flowing in one direction. Rather do we find many streams of energy playing upon each other in crosscurrents and counterforces that swirl around in all directions. Whatever unity we have is won against heavy odds. For personality is a dynamic unity of multiple and contradictory tendencies.

Each step in the progress of religious devotion is met with its own particular resistances. (*a*) Religious interest is rivaled by other interests, whose secular attractions appeal seductively to the senses. To concentrate upon any object, especially the invisible, intangible objects of religion, is to wage a battle against distraction. (*b*) Deciding for a religious goal means deciding against other goals that may seem even more delightful. To make any decision is to reject other possible goods and overrule other alternatives. (c) Identification with a religious cause will require detachment from other activities, yet without detachment from other persons. Selective attention and loyalty to religious values requires a high degree of self-control. (d) Renunciation may not be so difficult in the first enthusiasm of a great reaction. How to endure and re-enact that renunciation hour after hour is the lifelong test. (e) Progressive integration is easier said than done, for it involves the difficult art of taking each developing interest and obligation as it comes and reorganizing the shifting kaleidoscope of life into new unities of consecutive purpose. To follow any course consistently is a running combat with fading spans of attention, contrary desires, comfortable inertias, frequent doubts, and the surprising perplexities of constant readjustment.

To observe this in life, let us study the concrete situation of a student who asked for counsel. He was a capable young man of twenty-five years, the son of a minister, a graduate of a church-related college, recently married, completing his third year of graduate theological study, and serving a village church. His dilemma was a deep uncertainty about his vocation as a Christian minister. To explore these problems a series of seven interviews was held in the counselor's office. Excerpts from these interviews are submitted: [23]

Interview 1

Student. I'd like to be more stable emotionally. While in college I had a conflict over the ministry as a vocation, turning away from it, leading a double life as it were, until I came to accept it and integrate my life around that purpose. I felt, and my friends seemed to feel, that I had made the right choice. I looked forward to the theological school, but when I got there I was disappointed.

Counselor. Immediately?

S. No, the first semester was fine. I had inspiring teachers, and thought

[23] Such confidences are to be respected. The information is used here with permission of the student, whose kindness is gratefully acknowledged.

I was really interested in the subjects. The second semester I felt my interest slipping until I was quite unhappy.

C. How do you feel about it now?

S. Last evening my wife and I were going over the whole situation, considering whether to remain another year at our present church. She has been watching me this year, and concludes that I will never be happy in a small town. I need the stimulus of cultural variety, aesthetic interests, and intellectual people.

C. Since becoming pastor of this church, what is it doing to you?

S. It has made me feel it is not the place for me. There is a constant conflict between my church work and my studies. I long to give undivided attention to my studies. I'd like to work for a Ph.D. in psychology. My wife is working in a university environment and will be happier in that life.

C. What has marriage done for your emotional life?

S. Perfect harmony. Minor differences and anxieties at first, but we have outgrown them. We are a good deal alike; we enjoy the same interests, and share everything mutually.

C. Marriage is a mutual adjustment, including her interests as well as your own.

S. Yes, and she is all for the Ph.D. in psychology. For that is where our mutual interests lie.

C. I wonder if your unhappiness has been caused by detachment. During the college years of conflict you sought satisfaction in a cynical aloofness.

S. That's right. My critical attitude stands in the way of my whole-hearted acceptance of anything.

C. It keeps you from identifying your self heartily with any situation. Do you stand off even while you are preaching and think, "Is that the way I look?"

S. That is what I have been doing. Not all of me has been participating. Some of me is looking the rest of me over with cynical rejection.

C. Has marriage pulled you out of that? Putting your whole self into it means identifying yourself with your beloved.

S. Right after our engagement there were three days when we could

126

not see each other and I worried a lot. Then I decided that love was an adventure of trust, and I would trust her love completely.

C. There will come testing times.

S. But there is a way to prepare for the tests of the future. And that is to enjoy to the utmost the present.

C. Exactly. To take the present as the great opportunity, and identify one's self with the present adventure, instead of deferring to a receding future that never arrives.

S. It is good to see the pattern of life's meaning coming to focus in the present opportunity. What do you think of our plans?

C. That is a question for the next hour. Shall we meet next week at the same time?

S. Yes.

Interview 2

C. What would you like to talk about today?

S. The problem of detachment we talked about seems to be the essential problem.

C. You experimented with it this week?

S. I spent time enough to prepare the sermon well, and gave it with complete absorption in what I was doing. I have tried to identify myself with each situation at hand, no matter how trivial. It goes better that way.

C. That's good.

S. The next problem is the vocation. One thing that sort of holds me back on graduate work is a little feeling of fear tugging at my heart. I'm certain I can do the work. The question is the *will*. Will I organize my life, sacrifice the comforts and cynical luxuries, to be completely wrapped up in it?

C. That is the decisive question. Only you can decide. It has to be decided every day.

S. I can see the necessity of making a choice with complete trust in God and myself. But the need and the fulfillment are two different things.

C. Is it because you know yourself too well or not well enough?

S. The first reaction might be, too well; but a more profound insight is that I don't know myself well enough.

C. So it is a matter of discovering and developing a deeper purpose.

S. In these moments of trying to be frank with myself I think it is this problem. . . . I fear that I will regress to a disintegrated life of distracted interests. I'd like to unify them.

C. It can be done. It's a matter of purpose. Devotion of love to wife and of life to God are threads of purpose.

S. Do you observe that the solution of a personal problem enables one to solve his other life problems?

C. Your question is vague.

S. In the identification of myself with this moment, will I be able to re-create such experiences and attain future goals?

C. No decision lasts forever. Every choice has to be reaffirmed at every step of progress.

S. And yet I feel that, until recently, no matter what I have done, I have had no real inspiration for it. On the other hand, if I can throw off this habit, I believe I can go into any number of things and make a success of them.

C. Well, you are doing some fundamental thinking.

Interview 3

C. How is it going this week?

S. Better to a certain extent. When shaving, or doing a routine task, my mind leaps ahead to a multitude of things that need to be done. I find that by concentrating on shaving I can do it in half the time, and it brings me out of that drowsy feeling. Also, thinking ahead restlessly must use up energy in anxieties.

C. You have found a way to correct distraction.

S. One thing I have wondered is if I am getting at causes or symptoms.

C. What do you think?

S. I really don't know, to be honest with you. But I think I am getting at causes. The result would indicate that I am. It helps to talk with someone. You need a stimulus to get the mind working. I haven't thought about these things until now. As we sit here, they come spontaneously. Looking at the picture now, it seems to me the heart of my trouble was that I needed to be ministered to more than the people to whom I was ministering.

C. Why have you felt that way?

S. The whole problem of detachment is what I mean. Because I wasn't happy in this distraught state I made excuses why I did not fit into the ministry. In religious terms, I was serving men rather than God, seeking other things than the true spirit of Jesus. With that contradiction I couldn't preach to my people.

C. Do you care to say what these other things were?

S. Things of the world, money, pleasant home, food, the plain desire to be economically secure. My wife wanted me to be happy as I wished her to be, so together we sought another vocation to escape from these problems with unattractive people, and find a more satisfactory environment. Now that I have faced these basic problems of identification and distraction, my vocational maladjustment has largely disappeared.

C. Has your wife made a readjustment at the same time with you?

S. I don't know. I was thinking of that just before you asked it. She might prefer to be a professor's wife with more economic security. It's so hard to make ends meet on twelve hundred dollars. I don't think professors are much better off.

C. I wondered when you would find that out. You now feel that you prefer the ministry?

S. Yes, I do. At this hour. A year from now it may be different. The basic step will be to renew the religious development I lost when I dropped away. So this week I have been meditating, and faithfully following a devotional plan. Not to blossom out one day and retreat the next, but to make steady progress.

C. If you can do that you are going to succeed.

Interview 4

C. What have you learned this week?

S. That simply laying out a plan of action, such as concentrating on each unit of work, is not sufficient?

C. What more do you find is needed?

S. After you work out certain techniques, you need to have the sense of power to use them.

C. What, in your case, seems to make the fluctuations that affect this sense of power?

S. The sense of power is difficult to control directly. But I find meditation and prayer a helpful resource.

C. Do you get an instant result from prayer and meditation?

S. When I first began I didn't, but I have been using this past week silent communion cards as an experiment?

C. What do you observe as results?

S. The first half of the week not very much result, partially by not putting enough into it; but the last half I had amazing results. It almost seemed like a miracle.

C. How so?

S. Well, I used the simple technique of going to a definite place here in the building; for instance, I go to the laundry room as the most homely part of the whole school. I don't go to the chapel because it would be a false surrounding. I go to a place where anyone might have to work. But no one is there, usually, and I choose a theme and meditate in silent communion.[24]

C. Yes.

S. The effect is immediately apparent in a changed attitude—a feeling of confidence, hope, security, and realization that I am not alone. It helps me to face the immediate task and free my mind of doubts concerning the future. It opens up my mind to all those infinite possibilities of growth. One feels completely renewed.

C. How long do these effects seem to last?

S. They vary. Oh, three or four hours; sometimes it tends to diminish as one becomes engulfed in his work. Some days I find it necessary to have more than others. Yesterday I had eight sessions. Day before, five.

C. How long do you spend in each session?

S. About four minutes. I've been able to concentrate much better.

C. Do you feel any different in the presence of different people?

S. It depends upon my spiritual vitality, the amount of energy I have at the time.

C. Can you specify?

S. If I have had silent communion I am able to control my reactions to various situations, to try to love and understand personalities who, in more uninspired moments, would tend to irritate me. Naturally I have greater affection for my wife and intimate friends.

[24] Following suggestions given by L. L. Dunnington, in *Handles of Power* (New York and Nashville: Abingdon-Cokesbury Press, 1942).

C. You find, then, that frequent renewal keeps you from going into fatigue and depression.

S. Yes, it's more than rest. It's creative rest.

Interview 5

S. I believe I have insights this week that change the entire picture. I think it will be of value to get them out in the open.

C. Yes, I believe it will.

S. An emotional situation which I had forgotten and refused to face is probably the cause, or a main cause, of my tensions.

(The student here related an experience of his boyhood.)

S. It was a tremendous shock. I thought I had committed a terrible sin. This, accompanied with a feeling of guilt which I could share with no one, made me miserable and unhappy. I attempted to forget intentionally and deliberately, but the shock, fear, and guilt remained.

C. Yes, that would be hard to take.

S. The entire experience, largely because of ignorance, was magnified beyond due proportions.

C. Did you outgrow the feeling of guilt?

S. Well, yes, I did. But it must have affected me unconsciously. I was valedictorian in high school. But my last semester in high school I had increasing difficulty with my school work.

C. School work?

S. Yes, mainly memory work, anything taking concentration. This was about the same time that I was achieving satisfaction in my social relationships.

C. What do you think brought it on?

S. I think it was this repression, resulting in inability to concentrate. I just couldn't study; I went to the library, but couldn't study.

C. And this has brought insight to the current problem?

S. Yes, it has. It shows me why I have found difficulty in accepting myself.

C. You mean that the early guilt experience created a division within you, and one part of you was hating or fearing the other part.

S. Yes. I refused frankly to face the issue, and so I evaded it.

C. Now that you are facing it, what does it mean to you?

S. It means that I must realize that my nature is not evil, that I must cease dodging it, accept it, live with it, and realize it as nothing to be ashamed of.

C. Yes, that would be part of it.

Interview 6

C. Where shall we start today? Have you had any insights?

S. I don't know. A few, I guess. . . . The main insight is that personality integration is quite a complicated affair. There seem to be no simple rules.

C. What brought that to your attention?

S. The fact that I haven't attained any panacea.

C. Does this mean that the old problems recur?

S. Yes, it's progress and regression.

C. There are ups and downs.

S. They are natural, in a sense inevitable. But I tend to have a certain division in my personality that is unreliable and unpredictable.

C. Does this seem discouraging?

S. The discouraging part comes from the fumbling of little things, a certain indecision and procrastination, which seems to be deeply ingrained.

C. I know what you mean.

S. Sometimes I jump on my bicycle and ride gaily away without any inhibitions; other times, when I see the doctor ride by in his Buick, I feel foolish and stupid riding down to the square on a bicycle as a minister of the flock. I have a feeling of the little boy who wears the only pair of knickers to school.

C. You have moments of self-pity when you see others forging ahead and gaining advantages that do not come to you.

S. Sometimes, yes. (Pause.) The feeling comes and goes. It has not bothered me the past two years, until I married.

C. Do you see any relation there?

S. It wouldn't be wise to draw a hasty conclusion, but since last June the problem has been evident. That is, as long as I was single and without responsibilities, the actual life of the pastor did not bother me.

C. What background does your wife come from?

S. Rather secular background for the most part. One which puts the emphasis on things. It's quite predominant in our society, for that matter.

C. Had she already entered a career?

S. Yes, she turned down a three-thousand-dollar job with maintenance last spring.

C. Have you had occasion to talk over these matters since marriage?

S. In a general way.

C. Do you see any problems here?

S. Dimly, perhaps. Many of my anxieties and frustrations regarding the future originate from marriage responsibilities. The marital experience also has served to stir up past repressions and conflicts which had not been properly solved. The best course would be to face it frankly with my wife.

C. Her family and the general society standard of values is secular, and you feel that your success is being judged on a secular basis by her family and society in general. This rouses in you the ambivalent desire to make good in secular ways that society will honor and approve. Without intending to do so, and without either of you regretting your decision to marry, you are fighting temptations toward what you have renounced.

S. You think then it is a case of deciding what we want most?

C. That is involved in the process of growth. Your suggestion of facing it together is wise, I believe. When shall we meet next week?

Interview 7

The student presented a written summary of progress:

Immediately following the last interview I went to a room where it was quiet and I could be with myself alone. There I saw what I had been doing, living with anxieties and self-pity, racing away from the present moment, and escaping the responsibility of facing myself in the living hour. Suddenly I realized I didn't *have* to do this. I asked myself, Why all this rush to do this and this? Why not just stop and see where I am going and why?

Therein I found an amazing source of freshness. It was as if a heavy burden had been lifted from me. And I had the inner spirit to have a frank talk with my wife upon the future in the parsonage.

She has considered the situation and realizes what it means in hardship and privations. She is more than willing to meet them. Her only concern has been about me and my seeming indifference to my call. We have reached a new understanding and bond of unity.

While this has by no means solved all of my problems, it has provided a beginning. I can see goals again. Life is more meaningful. People are becoming increasingly valuable. In fact, I am re-estimating my whole conception of religion. Above all, I have to keep coming again and again to the thought that we have creative power and divine aid to improve habits.

C. This looks like the turning point, doesn't it?

S. I certainly hope so.

C. For a while it seemed baffling, but now you feel that you truly understand the causes of this problem.

S. Yes, I do. It's a question of being true to myself and God, with faith and love, hope and courage; not engaging in self-pity or enjoying my anxieties, but finding higher forces and satisfactions. Facing present reality seems to be my greatest need.

C. And you now feel that your wife understands and shares completely your purposes and ideals.

S. Yes, she does. As completely as possible she realizes and shares the point of view, the values, the necessary sacrifices, and the deeper joys which come from the consecrated life in the parsonage.

C. She is therefore able to reinforce your best impulses and deepest devotions. Do you pray together?

S. Yes.

C. How often?

S. Every morning before breakfast and occasionally evenings when we go to bed at the same time.

C. And you find strength and satisfaction in talking and praying together.

S. Yes, we do. Have you any other suggestions?

C. You have worked these problems out by putting your insights immediately to work. How much better than secretly cherishing or wrestling with desires and fears is this open sharing of them together. And you each have a door of access to God for confession and renewal of energy and devotion.

S. Thank you. I appreciate these conversations that helped to make the progress possible.

Conclusion

What do we learn from this young man about the psychological forces that obstruct religious devotion? The following causes seem to have a part in blocking the integration which he seeks:

1. The sense of guilt, arising from a misunderstood experience in boyhood, set up an inner division by causing him to fear and reject himself.

2. The loneliness, which came from his isolation and inability to share his fears or gain truer understanding from others, made him feel different and detached.

3. The effort to escape painful experiences led to repression of these conflicts and the persistence of an inner division that frustrated the unity of personality.

4. The stern ideals of his family and church called forth his admiration; yet, in contrast to that code, desires were cherished though not approved, constituting a resistance within him.

5. To break the deadlock of conflicting interests he sought to justify the ways of the world by a cynical revolt against the restraining ideals. When this failed to satisfy, he chose a religious vocation and sought to renounce the world.

6. But criticism and doubts swung him into a dead center again, where he felt detached from former enthusiasm and questioned former decisions.

7. While he was not yet integrated himself, marriage presented new interests of sex, home and equipment, income and security, wife's career and secular success, prestige and cultural advantages, to be fitted into the pattern of life.

8. Seeking for solutions, he considered a way of escape into university teaching. But his commitment to the ministry did not yield, and he fluctuated in alternating rejection and acceptance.

9. Nervous tensions from indecision and conflict brought fatigue and unhappiness, inability to concentrate or do his best, and a general sense of futility.

What means did he find to resolve these conflicts and bring unity out of his distraction? The following resources proved helpful:

1. Opportunity to confess his difficulties and gain emotional release came by talking it over with a counselor. Secret reservations were disposed of in open discussion.

2. Insights into the history and present nature of resistance within suggested new attitudes and methods of integration.

3. Conversations with his wife led to mutual understanding and agreement upon the goal of life. This achieved more complete unity of purpose and devotion.

4. Experiments in concentration showed him how to identify himself more adequately with each situation, to give himself more heartily and enjoy being at his best.

5. Practice of silent communion brought renewal of purpose, energy, and harmony within and with others.

6. Rededication of self to God proved necessary every day. Old decisions need to be renewed, former purposes reaffirmed, affections revived, to restore the losses of time and change.

7. Faithful action will create faith. Devotion therefore requires action, and active work achieves a growing devotion. Accepting each responsibility as a privilege was the antidote for habits of evasion.

8. A forgiving spirit was needed, with good sense not to demand impossible perfection, and the good humor to accept the faults of others and the errors of one's self graciously. Self-pity and condemnation will have to give place to approval and inner reconciliation.

9. His final conclusion was to redeem the present opportunity by taking each experience as a new adventure. If he will do this, and to the extent that he does achieve religious values in each moment, he will find the joy of true devotion.

A life of devotion is difficult for a variety of reasons, inner and outer. The environment presents a multitude of distracting stimuli, and, at the same time, the organism presents a complexity of conflicting desires. How to integrate these changing crosscurrents of interests baffles the best of us, more so now than ever before in history. Our age has come to a crisis that none deny yet few comprehend. Pitirim Sorokin gives a profound analysis of our social situation, showing the inflation and bankruptcy of our sensate culture.[25] Sensory desires conflict with ideational, yet they need to complement each other in a larger and more creative culture. Creative culture is an interpersonal achievement, requiring personal choice of the worthiest goals and mutual devotion to a Supreme Goal. To clarify choice and renew faithful devotion, to revive culture and have new life, calls for the regenerative powers of religion. Of all methods and powers of regeneration none is more creative than prayer. For prayer is the heart of aspiration and devotion, as devotion is the creative source of rebirth.

[25] *The Crisis of Our Age* (New York: E. P. Dutton & Co., 1941).

VI

Worship

1. THE SEARCH FOR GOD

a) Hindu Worship. At the Ramakrishna Chapel of the Hindu Vedanta Society, Deerfield Street, Boston, Massachusetts, a service of worship was conducted December 18, 1943, by Swami Akhilananda. The altar of carved mahogany is dedicated to God, identified by the Sanskrit character *Om,* and bears the motto: "Truth is One, men call it by various names." Candles were burning, and the altar was surrounded by a profuse array of flowers, fruits, and emblems for use in ceremonies.

The swami entered, removed his shoes, and seated himself beside the altar, legs crossed, hands folded, eyes closed in silent prayer. Then, following the prescribed ritual, and employing the appropriate Hindu words, chants, gestures, and implements, he enacted the earnest drama of the human spirit in search of God. The service proceeded for two hours in the following order:

1. Consecration of the room.
2. Invocation, asking the blessings of the different aspects of God, fingering the beads of a rosary, and bowing with folded hands.
3. Prayer:
    "May Thou be installed in the hearts of all devotees.
    May Thou be the Source of their knowledge.
    May Thy Divine Love be with them.
    We are worshiping Thee that thy eternal glory may be with all, that all beings may be illumined and led to Thy realization."
4. Removal of evil influences from the room with flowers, rice, and mustard seed; drawing a line of light around the worshiper as well as the devotees; clapping and snapping fingers around his head.
5. Consecration of water for worship, with gestures, prayers, and blessings.

6. Purification of the prayer rug, with prayers and a flower.

7. Purification of flowers and other emblems of worship, including eight large silver trays of various fruits, milk, honey, and holy water from the Ganges River.

8. Transformation of the constituent parts of the body. Then transformation of the whole body, by awakening latent Divine power, through different gestures and prayers.

9. *Pranayama*, or rhythmic breathing through alternate nostrils.

10. Awakening all the mystic centers of the body by praying, chanting, and touching these parts of the body.

11. Installation of the Deity within the worshiper, bowing to the floor, praying aloud, and placing a flower in the hair at the center of the head.

12. *Pranayama* (rhythmic breathing).

13. Worship of the different aspects of God: Creative, Preservative, Destructive, Masculine, and Feminine; different powers and incarnations including Christ, Buddha, Krishna, and others with five offerings: perfume, flowers, incense, light, and food.

14. *Dhyana*, or meditation in silence—body poised, eyes closed, mind focused in concentration.

15. Mental worship with the particles and chemicals of the body, mind, and emotions of love, patience, devotion, etc.

16. Purification of another receptacle of water.

17. *Dhyana* (meditation).

18. Worship of the particular Aspect of God for the day—the Divine Mother, with offerings of flowers, milk, honey, water, use of bell, relics, mystic circles with incense, kneeling, and chanting.

19. Special worship of other Holy Personalities, incarnations as above. Members of congregation offering flowers to Christ, Ramakrishna, and the Holy Mother. Reading from the Gospel of John, chapter 1.

20. Surrender of the fruit of worship to God.

21. Benediction: a prayer for peace, harmony, joy, and bliss in the world.

b) *Hebrew Worship.* On Saturday morning, June 3, 1944, the psychology of religion class from Boston University visited the

Sabbath service at Temple Israel.[1] In contrast to the elaborate symbolism of the Hindu worship this service was simplified to accent the naturalness of communion with God. The marble pulpit was decorated only with two stars of David and two palm branches. Large seven-branch candlesticks at either side upheld electric candles. The ark directly behind the pulpit was concealed by sliding doors bearing the star of David. Marble pillars stood at either side, and the eternal flame was burning above. The choir loft with organ and musicians was concealed by a plush curtain. Members of the congregation were provided with prayer books and hymnals, to participate at the direction of the rabbi in the following order of worship:

1. Invocation.
2. Hymn.
3. Prayers in Hebrew and English by the rabbi and congregation.
4. Chants by the cantor.
5. Responsive readings from the Psalter.
6. Hymn.
7. Prayers in Hebrew and English by the rabbi and congregation.
8. Prayers before the ark.
9. Presentation of the scroll (Torah) from the ark with blessings.
10. Reading from the Torah, or sacred law, by a thirteen-year-old boy (the confirmand) and his teacher in the religious school.
11. Prophetic reading and interpretation of a chapter in Jeremiah by the boy to be confirmed, followed by his pledge to uphold the faith.
12. Prayer on replacing the Torah in the ark.
13. Confirmation of the boy by the rabbi, welcoming him into the membership of the temple, and eloquently charging him to be loyal to God.
14. Sermon by the rabbi on "Life."
15. Prayer for the sick, the refugees, and the suffering, for the nation

---

[1] Commonwealth Avenue, Boston, Mass., Joshua L. Liebman, rabbi. A class of fifty-eight boys and girls had been confirmed the preceding Sunday. Rabbi David B. Alpert conducted the service June 3.

and the victory of democracy, for all peoples and the brotherhood of man.

16. Prayer for the eternal welfare of the dead and the comfort of the mourners.

17. Benediction in Hebrew.

18. Organ postlude.

c) *Roman Catholic Worship.* Sunday morning, July 30, 1944, four masses were celebrated in the Corpus Christi Church, Auburndale, Massachusetts, by the pastor, John B. Condon and his assistant, Thomas Grogan. The people assembled in reverent spirit, genuflecting toward the altar before entering the pew, and then kneeling to pray silently, guided by the rosary or the missal. The Mass was conducted in Latin, to be followed by the congregation either in Latin or English, with appropriate responses. The theme of the Ninth Sunday after Pentecost, "Thou hast not known the time of thy visitation," was the need to profit by the lessons of history. The priest was attired in green vestments, the seasonal symbol of hope, carried a veiled chalice, and was accompanied by two altar boys.

1. Mass began at the foot of the altar (pure white, holding the crucifix, with kneeling angelic figures, white candles, the tabernacle, and altar cards), as the priest made the sign of the cross, saying "In the name of the Father and of the Son and of the Holy Ghost. Amen. I will go into the altar of God. To God who giveth joy to my youth." Confessing and asking forgiveness, the priest ascended to the altar.

2. Introit (to enter), a psalm signifying entrance to the presence of God, read by the celebrant from the Epistle (right) side of the altar.

3. The Kyrie, "Lord, have mercy upon us," followed by the Gloria.

4. Prayer of invocation and thanksgiving.

5. Epistle, I Corinthians 10.

6. Gradual (*gradus* step from where it was formerly sung), Psalm 8.

7. Preparation for Gospel (at middle of altar): "The Lord be in my heart and on my lips, that I may worthily and becomingly announce his Gospel. Amen." (Signing forehead to understand it, lips to declare it, and heart to love it.)

8. Gospel, Luke 19. (People standing.) Priest read from the Gospel side of the altar, then kissed the sacred page and prayed: "May our sins be blotted out by the words of the Gospel."

9. Creed (Nicene, composed A.D. 325). Priest then faced the people. "The Lord be with you." The people responded, "And with thy spirit."

10. Sermon and announcements from the pulpit.

11. Offertory, Psalm 17. Collection received by ushers from the people. Priest uncovered the chalice.

12. Offerings of Bread and Wine. Priest lifted the bread on the paten with prayers, adding water to wine, bowing before altar. Then he blessed the bread and wine, washed his fingers, kissed the altar, and turned to the people, who responded, "May the Lord receive this sacrifice at thy hands, to the praise and glory of His Name, to our own benefit, and to that of all His Holy Church. Amen."

13. Secret (from Latin for "separated"), a petition for acceptance of gifts now separated from secular use.

14. The Preface, a hymn of praise and thanksgiving to exalt the mind for sacred actions.

15. The Canon (Greek word for rule or standard), six prayers of remembrance and four prayers of offering, half before and half after the Consecration.

16. Consecration of Bread and Wine. Priest genuflecting, elevated the Host, then the Chalice. Bell rang thrice for each event. Prayers.

17. Communion. Priest received Sacred Host and Precious Blood, and distributed wafer to each of the faithful who knelt at the altar rail. Prayers and responses. Priest closed tabernacle, and rinsed Chalice with wine for purification.

18. Communion Verse and Response.

19. Postcommunion Prayer: "May this heavenly Sacrament be to us, O Lord, a renewal of both mind and body, so that as we perform this act of worship we may also feel its effect."

20. Final Blessing: "May Almighty God bless you, Father, Son, and Holy Ghost. Amen."
21. The Last Gospel. (People standing.) John 1.
22. Prayers after Mass. Addressed to Mary, God, St. Michael, and concluding responsively:

> "Most sacred Heart of Jesus,
> Have mercy on us."

d) Protestant Worship. Sunday morning worship in the Copley Methodist Church,[2] June 4, 1944, may well represent another design in the human search for God. The movement of worship is clearly marked in four stages of advance, as definite as altar stairs ascending to the Living Presence. Not content to remain in the sanctuary as a sheltered place, the worship culminates in a dedication of life to go forth in service to the world. The order of service is a unity of contrast and response, a dynamic motive of progress to a goal.

I. Adoration of God

1. Quiet. (Let the people be in devout meditation.)
2. Organ Prelude, "Prayer."
3. Processional Hymn, "Ancient of Days."
4. Call to Worship (by the minister).
5. Invocation (by the minister).
6. Sanctus (the people uniting): "Therefore with angels and archangels, and with all the company of heaven, we laud and magnify thy glorious name, evermore praising thee, and saying": Choir: "Holy, holy, holy, Lord God of hosts, heaven and earth are full of thy glory. Glory be to thee, O Lord most high!"

II. Confession of Sin

7. Prayer of Confession (the people uniting): "Almighty and most merciful Father, we have erred and strayed from thy ways like lost sheep. We have followed too much the devices and desires

---

[2] Exeter Street, Boston, Mass., Fred Winslow Adams and Morris J. Morgan, ministers. Mr. Morgan conducted the service June 4.

of our own hearts. We have offended against thy holy laws. We have left undone those things which we ought to have done, and we have done those things which we ought not to have done. But thou, O Lord, have mercy upon us. Spare thou those, O God, who confess their faults. Restore thou those who are penitent, according to thy promises declared unto mankind in Christ Jesus our Lord. And grant, O most merciful Father, for his sake, that we may hereafter live a godly, righteous, and sober life; to the glory of thy holy name. Amen."

8. Choral Response, "The Lord is in his holy temple."
9. The Sacrament of Silence. Relaxation of body, mind, and spirit. Listen for the Voice of God.
10. Angelus Bells.
11. Words of Assurance (by the minister).
12. Word of Forgiveness (by the minister).
13. The Lord's Prayer.

III. Affirmation of Faith

14. Message in Song, "O rest in the Lord."
15. Psalter, "An Unfaltering Trust," responsive reading.
16. Gloria Patri.
17. First Lesson, "The Lord's Promise," Jeremiah 29:12-13.
18. Second Lesson, "The Comforting Spirit," John 14:15-25.
19. Call to Prayer:

    Minister: The Lord be with you.

    Choir: And with thy spirit.

    Minister: Let us pray. O Lord, show thy mercy upon us.

    Choir: And grant us thy salvation.

    Minister: O God, make clean our hearts within us.

    Choir: And take not thy Holy Spirit from us.

20. Collect for Peace (all uniting): "Our God and Father, whose rule is over men and nation; bless the President of the United States and all those associated with him in authority, and grant that our country may take her rightful place in the council of nations, in securing righteousness and freedom for mankind, and in forging and maintaining a peace that shall be just, merciful, and enduring

for the welfare of the whole world; through Jesus Christ our Lord. Amen."

21. Silent Intercession, for those in service.
22. Prayer of Communion. Choral Response.

IV. *Dedication of Life*

23. The Offertory, Presentation, and Doxology.
24. Hymn, "There's a Wideness in God's Mercy."
25. Sermon, "With You Always."
26. Recessional Hymn, "Are Ye Able?"
27. Silence (the people bowed in prayerful dedication).
28. Benediction. Choral Response.
29. Organ Postlude, "Grand Choeur."

These orders of worship come from three religions, each one rich in centuries of experience and tradition. Each one is unique in the features, symbols, and beliefs that constitute its distinctive life. Yet all manifest significant traits in common. The dominant motif in every religion is the search for God as the Creator and Sustainer of Values. A sense of supreme value pervades the entire process, and with this an earnest determination to lay aside the unreal for the real, the transient for the eternal good. Physical objects are not despised; they are consecrated as a bridge to the spiritual. Natural values are not denied, but blessed as means to intrinsic divine value. Human efforts are not neglected, but are dedicated to the service of God and man.

These four contemporary journeys Godward may serve to introduce us to the ways of worship. We may be mystified by the forms and symbols of worship until we discover the increasing purpose that underlies and runs through them. To discover this direction is to understand the heart of worship and see the devotion that overflows in artistry of many radiant expressions. To explore the motives and methods of worship is to enter more deeply into the psychology of religious experience.

2. FORMS AND SYMBOLS

Worship has an eventful history. The word is Anglo-Saxon in origin, but the experience belongs to every people. A contraction of "worth-ship," it refers to value. Worship is reverence for the Author of values. In practice, worship consists of acts designed to establish a better relationship with the Sustainer of desired values. Men may not agree in their conceptions of who and what this Power is, nor in the methods and devices by which a better relationship is to be established; but most of them do unite in the earnest desire to secure values by some reverent means. Magic and science attempt to secure values by mechanical means, understanding natural laws, and controlling impersonal forces. In contrast to these mechanical methods, religion seeks values by personal appeal and social co-operation.

Forms of worship present a variety of mysterious activities. The mystery is essential to the adventure, for worship seeks to cope with the deepest mysteries of life and death. The ultimate fate of values is ever shrouded in mystery, and worshipers stand in awe of the controlling Power that dispenses life and death, good and evil.[3] Yet every act of worship has a meaning, if one is initiated to its secret. The outsider is often baffled because he does not understand what the action means to the actors. To understand worship one must be a worshiper. Appreciation is the essence of understanding, for only as we sense the worth can we comprehend the meaning.

To observe every worshiping group from primitive tribe to city cathedral is not possible for any one student. If we are to view these many forms in perspective, we must rely upon the reports of others who describe what they have seen. A survey of worship in action will show the following forms:

[3] Strickland finds in all forms of worship implications of the Divine as (a) superhuman power and wisdom, (b) goodness, (c) mystery and (d) control of destinies of men. The entire chapter nine, "The Nature of Worship," of *Psychology of Religious Experience* well repays reading.

a) *The dance and procession* may be solemn in magnificent pageantry, or exciting in ecstatic frenzy. Dances are employed religiously by American Indians, the Negroid peoples, whirling dervishes of Semitic tradition, and Hindu worshipers of Siva and Kali. They dramatize tradition, prepare for expeditions, or induce excitement felt as divine possession. Processions are more evident in religious ceremonies. A gold effigy of Osiris was daily presented to the setting sun, taken for a ceremonial voyage, or carried around the walls of Memphis. In the New Year festival of Babylon, images of gods arrived from other temples, as Anu from Erech and Enlil from Nippur, "to take the hands of the great Lord, Marduk." [4] Processions appear in the festivities of Greek mystery cults, Jewish pilgrimages to the temple, and Moslem pilgrimages to Mecca. In these, and in Christian church worship, they signify approaching the Divine Presence, progressing toward the religious goal.

b) *Invocation* is the calling of a superior being to be present. It may be a vocal salutation, as an opening request in a worship ceremony; or the invitation may be extended in artistic representation of the deity and in religious symbols. Sketches and paintings of religious objects have been discovered in paleolithic caves of France, Spain, and Algeria.[5] Sand painting and totem portrayal survive among American Indians; the modeling and carving of images has wide religious use. Judaic, Christian, and Moslem spiritual worship has prohibited images, and turned to architecture rich in symbols and eloquent in religious meaning. Altars, pyramids and obelisks, minarets and mosques, Gothic arches and lofty spires, are invitations to meet God.

c) *Dramatic ritual* seeks to enact the enterprises that provide values for the group. In hunting or combat the desired results are

---

[4] *Myth and Ritual*, ed. S. H. Hooke (London: Oxford Univeristy Press, 1933), pp. 19-24.

[5] See H. L. Friess and H. W. Schneider, *Religion in Various Cultures* (New York: Henry Holt & Co., 1932), pp. 9-32.

dramatized to induce success. Agricultural ceremonies enact planting and fertility, rain-making, harvesting, and threshing. Myths and legends are dramatized to revive heroic exploits and honor the ancestral spirits. A ritual pattern in Egypt and Asia dramatized the death, resurrection, combat with enemies, sacred marriage, and triumph of the god. Candle burning to signify the divine presence, incense to indicate the rising spirit of prayer, sacrifice, and dedication are dramatic elements prevalent in many religions. The Roman Catholic Mass is a dramatic portrayal of the sacrificial work of Christ.

d) *Sacred music,* vocal and instrumental, is widely used in worship. Rhythmic beating of tom-toms and vocal chants are used by Africans and Amerindians. Wooden drums are used in the intonation of Buddhist scriptures. Temple bells are as common in China, India, and Japan as church bells in Europe and America, calling the faithful to worship and the deity to listen. The Hopi Indians conduct a flute ceremony with prayers and offerings for nine days. Psalms and laments have been sung in Hebrew worship from the time of the Exodus. The chorus had a prominent part in the Greek tragedies, celebrating religious mythology. Christian choral music has developed stirring harmonies that, with congregational singing, express the emotions of modern worship.

e) *Prayer* is an act of worship that takes many forms. Mechanical devices, such as prayer wheels, placing prayers in wells, waves, fires, and so forth, are little more than incantations. Repetition of sacred names, ejaculations, and ecstatic cries may have earnest appeal of urgent need and sincere devotion. Fixation of attention by posture, closed eyes, controlled gaze, or rosary seeks to avoid distraction and concentrate wholly upon the divine good. Prayers may be called out in a loud voice to attract the deity, or brought to a vigil of silence to create intimate communion. Prayer is the heart of worship. Without divine visitation and communion, worship is not complete.

f) *Sacrifice* has been practiced in the worship of most religions.

The Hebrews offered the first fruits of the harvest and flock in gratitude for divine blessings. The Vedic Aryans poured melted butter on the fire; Romans made a libation of wine; Brahmins offered horse sacrifices; followers of Mithra sacrificed a bull. Human sacrifices were offered by the Aztecs and Maoris. Offerings express gratitude or petition, expiate sin, dedicate for sacramental use, seal vows and covenants. To Christians, the crucifixion of Jesus is a vicarious sacrifice for the sins of the world, reconciling God and man. Feasts are historically associated with sacrifices. The Jewish Passover and the Christian sacrament of Holy Communion (Eucharist) are feasts to re-create spiritual life.

g) *Confession and purification* recognize the evils of life and seek to dispose of them. Primitive evils may be contagious powers to quarantine by taboo or magic. With the rise of conscience evils become sins to be expiated. Lustrations are widely used by Japanese, Egyptians, Greeks, Hindus, and others for purification. The Christian rite of baptism is in the purifying tradition. Fire is a purifying energy among Celts, Romans, and Persians. Heaping sins of the people upon a scapegoat driven into the wilderness (Hebrews) or upon boats sent out to sea (Japanese) is another purifying ceremony. Navajo chant practices for the removing of evil and illness require an elaborate use of prayer sticks, plumed wands, paddles, snake sticks, ashes, powder, feathers, jewels, reeds, mush offerings, arrows, whistles, bullroarers, flints, clubs, chant tokens, rattles, and medicines.[6] Confession of sin brings the purification to a higher level of repentance, forgiveness, and renewal.

h) *Recitation* forms a natural part of worship. No people is without traditions cherished as a unique heritage. The reciting of these traditions is significant for the instruction of the young and for the interpretation of customs and events. Frazer considers mythology to be the philosophy of primitive man, attempting to answer the mysterious questions of creation, nature, life, and

[6] See Clyde Kluckhohn and L. C. Wyman, "An Introduction to Navajo Chant Practice," *Memoirs of the American Anthropological Association*, LIII (1940).

destiny.[7] Every mature religion has its bible to preserve the words of life, the true teachings and history of the faith. Sacred scriptures are accepted as divine revelation, to be heeded and followed by all who profess the faith. Professing the faith brings the creed to a lofty place in worship, as the affirmation and avowal of the faithful. The synagogue service of the Jews opens with the Shema, and calls upon laymen to come forward and read from the Torah. Moslems listen with rapt attention to the reciting of the Koran. Christian worship gives a large place to reading and preaching from the Bible. By meditating upon the inspired word, sacred traditions are enshrined in living personalities, and come to new birth through the labors of many minds.

Divergent as these forms of worship appear, they converge into a clear pattern of unity. Coming from every time and place of human habitation, these varieties of aspiration have a common center. If the psychological motive of each form is followed, they will all point to God, as Sustainer of Values. It is evident from a study of religious experience that worship is a reverent outreach of the human spirit toward what is believed to be a Savior of cherished values.

3. WHY WORSHIP?

To understand an act of worship, one must explore what it means to the worshiper. Why does he worship? What does he seek? How does he feel about it? Each form and symbol has a history in the tradition of the group. Every worshiping attitude and aspiration has a purpose reaching out to some desired goal. Special acts carry specific meanings, to be understood by participation and interpretation. From these cultic events, general trends broaden out into universal principles of worship: procession, invocation, dramatization, music, prayer, sacrifice, purification, and recitation.

To ask why men worship in these ways is to open the question of motivation. What moves such different people to do such simi-

[7] *Myths of the Origin of Fire* (London: Macmillan & Co., 1930).

lar things? Evidently there are universal needs that urge their claim to be satisfied in typical ways. Human needs we have seen to be dynamic tensions arising from organic and psychic urges tending goalward. Many needs are unconscious, yet on the way to conscious awareness pain from within and suggestion from without bring them to attention. Interpersonal activity sharpens the focus of these needs and develops methods for meeting them. The social acts of worship are methods of expressing and seeking satisfaction for vital needs. A psychological analysis of worship activities should clarify these motives:

a) *Approaching* is the motive evident in religious processions. Why do religious persons want to approach objects of worship? Curiosity, wonder, fascination, are interests that motivate approach. Insects and animals are lured by bright colors, moving objects, attractive odors, and the like. Symbols used in worship may also attract by sensual appeal, yet there are deeper motives that draw men to an invisible presence. Rudolf Otto [8] describes this as the appeal of a tremendous mystery arousing awe before the overpowering majesty, fascination in the solemn beauty, and rapture in the vital urgency of divine energy. These exciting emotional responses are directed to a Wholly Other not easy to approach yet earnestly desired, unapproachable yet inescapable. Fear and hope mingle in approaching a powerful Mystery who is thought to control the values of life. Trust and affection are stronger motives of approach, and draw creatures to creator, as children to parents, for comfort and confidence. It is natural to approach with assurance one who is expected to save desired values.

b) *Recognizing* is the motive of invocation. Approaching leads to recognition, as when two men study each other first as strangers, then, seeing the identity of a friend, smile, nod, and speak. So the worshiper in approaching a divine Person gives a salutation as a sign of recognition. Invocations are offered in terms of address, to

---

[8] *The Idea of the Holy*, pp. 12-41. See Section 4, "Religious Emotion," in Chapter II above.

announce arrival and open communication. There is no worship without recognition of One who is worthy of worship, near enough to exchange greetings. Whatever the sign of this presence, the meaning is clearly to recognize a potential Savior and seek a mutual response.

c) *Anticipating* is a mood of expectation native to worship. "Religion is anticipated attainment." [9] Not content with life as it is, worshipers hope to reach a better condition. To realize this, religious ceremonies dramatize attainments, as planting and harvesting festivals, or rising from the dead. Worship focuses attention upon the values so dramatically that it becomes a powerful incentive to their attainment. The function of ritual is to anticipate goals, to arouse zealous purposes, and to enact the efforts needed to achieve them. Such religious action is neither isolated nor mechanical, but co-operative and interpersonal. Worship approaches a recognized deity by persuasion, appealing for aid, seeking guidance and strength, offering to work together for mutual welfare. Anticipation is essential to realization.

d) *Praising* is a rapturous expression of gratitude that follows recognition and anticipation of worth. To recognize divine beauty, truth, and goodness is to admire a glorious splendor. Adoration is the outreach of admiration toward the perfection one desires yet falls short of. Holding joyous attention upon God as the ideal to emulate is an elevating experience that sublimates the petty impulses of life to nobler harmonies. To anticipate these gains is to believe them genuine, already in the process of attainment. For such progress one feels gratitude and turns to thanksgiving. Praise may thus move from the Giver to the gifts received in gratitude, returning again to express appreciation to the Giver in a constant round of rejoicing. These notes of praise and rejoicing find wings in hymn and poetry. Sacred music rises to melody and harmony in expressing this delight, as a fountain overflows irrepressibly.

e) *Asking* is what prayer means to the average person. Worship

[9] Hocking, *The Meaning of God in Human Experience*, p. 31.

is more than asking, but it cannot be less. Asking may seem natural to children, but it has important prerequisites. No one asks until he wants and knows what he wants. Again, no one asks except where personal relationships invite the expectation of a kindly response. Knowing how, when, and whom to ask is a basic question for everyone. Not to ask indicates false pride and mock independence. Worship is an attitude of humility in which one acknowledges dependence upon greater powers and faith in their kindness and mercy. In this attitude it is as appropriate to ask for future goods as to give thanks for past ones. Asking is an expression of courtesy, not to command or demand, not to receive dumbly, but to offer petitions in deference and trust.

f) *Offering* is the act of giving some valued thing to another. This is a motive in the sacrifices which have taken so many forms in the history of religion. But why do people give to One who seems to have everything without lack? Evidently because giving is itself a value. There may be uses for gifts in a religious cause, as giving for missions or to feed the starving. But greater than any gift is the act of giving itself. The religious meaning of giving is dedication of life to God. When it is voluntary, as the free offering of life for others, it becomes a holy deed of complete devotion. "Greater love hath no man than this, that a man lay down his life for his friends."[10] No worship is complete without a genuine offering in this sense, to carry the devotion from emotion to consecrated action. Such an offering has objective value and influence beyond the individual as a causative energy.

g) *Renewing* is one of the elemental needs of life, because of fatigue, error, guilt, and conflict. Distressed by depletions of energy, mistakes, quarrels, sins, and frustrations, we need to be renewed. Worship is a means of grace by which to restore broken spirits. Rites of purification give symbolic cleansing to cancel evils and heal diseases. In the temple vision of Isaiah the holiness of

[10] John 15:13.

God made his own guilt unbearable until his lips were cleansed with a live coal from the altar.[11] Standing in the divine presence makes this need acute and demands purgation to renew life to purity and power. Until one is cleansed and energized, he is not fit for the religious life and mission. He will need to return again and again to worship, to renew the vows and power of heroic living. For renewal is a constant need and worship a constant opportunity.

b) Affirming is a constructive act of rejoicing in the truth. No mere dumb assent is worship, but a creative assertion of what makes life most worth living. To recite a creed is to declare a faith with conviction, as a code to live by and die for. To read scripture is to discover new insights and recover lost treasure. It is easy to forget, and even the greatest experiences fade in time. Only renewed insights survive. To Wordsworth poetry arises from "emotion recollected in tranquillity." Dean Sperry points out that remembered emotion may be more significant than emotion first felt. He finds worship an "occasion for that recollection in tranquillity by which we possess ourselves permanently of the certitudes which have been ours."[12] The great affirmations bear reaffirming, for instead of wearing out they gain in meaning as we grow in understanding.

We have noted that all forms and motives in worship point to a central object of devotion known as God. The verbs expressing these motives are active, transitive verbs. Worship is an act moving out to an object. A worshiper is not passive, neither is he content to talk to himself in autosuggestion. He is reaching out to a Helper who is above himself, who has what he lacks, and who may fulfill what he needs. Worshiping is approaching God, recognizing God, anticipating God, praising God, asking of God, offering to God, renewing from God, affirming God. God is the object of every act of worship. Men may not agree as to what God is, nor be

[11] Isa. 6:1-9.
[12] *Reality in Worship* (New York: The Macmillan Co., 1925), pp. 194-96.

able to prove that he is; but in worship they believe they are addressing a real Being, who is good enough and great enough to respond.

True worship, therefore, has objective reference. J. B. Pratt [13] has distinguished between subjective and objective worship. Objective worship aims to affect or communicate with the Deity; subjective worship seeks to influence the worshiper. From historical and contemporary practices he shows how the objective worship, as in the Catholic Mass, turns from man to God. Cathedrals are constructed and ceremonies conducted for God, not for the congregation, who may be unable to see, hear, or understand the words intoned in a foreign language as the priest faces the altar and addresses God who is the Host. Subjective worship in ancient Buddhism or modern humanism ignores God, as too unreal or impersonal to hear prayer, and performs rituals for the human effect. Much of Protestant worship is subjective in aim, placing a pulpit at the center, reading and preaching, singing and enjoying harmonies, to create a mood and instruct the congregation.

In conclusion Pratt shows that subjective worship is self-defeating. If the churchgoer understands that public ceremonies are put on as a show to make a psychological impression on him, he will not be deeply impressed. He may be entertained and edified, but more as a passive spectator than as an earnest participant. Eventually he will come to distrust the sincerity of the performance staged for his benefit. For if nothing objectively real happens at church, his attendance will become a matter of convenience, mood, and impulse, subject to the relative interest of competing attractions. Lack of reality is a cause of indifference toward church worship.

We may go a step further, to ask whether this subjective aim without objective reference is worship at all? If worship is reverence for the Creator of Values, then activities which ignore God fall short of the essence of worship. A visit to a prominent human-

[13] *The Religious Consciousness*, pp. 290-309.

ist society will be instructive.[14] The "Sunday Morning Meeting"—not designated divine worship—was held in a theater. The service opened with organ preludes and continued with a hymn by Rudyard Kipling addressed to the "Spirit of Truth." Instead of Scripture the leader read a passage from the dean of an Eastern university. In place of prayer he gave an "Aspiration on the Rising Generation," followed by organ response and instrumentation by a string trio: The second hymn was addressed to the congregation:

> Who will say the world is dying?
> Who will say our prime is past?
> Sparks of good, within us, lying,
> Flash, and will flash to the last.
> Still the race of hero spirits
> Pass the lamp from hand to hand,
> And the growing light of knowledge
> Casts its rays o'er every land.

In place of the sermon came an address, "What Happens to a College Student's Religion?" showing how the study of sciences makes God improbable and unnecessary. This was followed by an "Offertory" played by the string trio, during which the collection was taken, offered not to God but to the society to defray expenses of the meeting. The final hymn was a poem "Youth," by Robert Bridges.

There was no benediction, but instead "Closing Words" by the leader, followed by an organ postlude. Mottoes headed the pages of the calendar with the sentiments: "Enlightened Reason Our Guide in Religion," "Mental Freedom Our Method in Religion," "Human Service Our Aim in Religion." The first page declared: "We cannot fathom the Infinite. It is enough for us to love and serve humanity."

This was an hour well spent, for the address was eloquent, the

[14] The First Unitarian Society, 1526 Harmon Place, Minneapolis, Minn., John H. Dietrich, minister. The service attended was held in the Garrick Theater, February 10, 1929.

thoughts read were noble, the music was delightful. But was it worship? There was no prayer, no recognition of God, no confession, offering, or dedication to God. To affirm human values is good; but the deeper needs of life, conscious and unconscious, cry out for higher resources. Worship is that deepest of hungers seeking cosmic harmony and co-operation. The health-giving whole-making power of worship is a creative source of new life.

4. THE ART OF WORSHIP

Worship is a fine art. It is the highest of all arts in aim, for it seeks to reach divine perfection. It is the broadest of all, employing every art—architecture, painting, sculpture, stained glass, rhythm, music, literature, drama, speech—in the creative syntheses of worship. It is the deepest of all arts in significance, portraying the adventure of the human soul, the dramatic issue of man's eternal destiny. It is the most difficult of all arts, requiring insight to true values and skill in presenting their infinite mysteries. It is often a neglected art, for many do not comprehend its meaning or learn how to progress in its difficult attainments.

Worship is a journey. It is a quest for real beauty, the beauty that is objective and enduring, the beauty of God the altogether lovely. It seeks to incarnate the beauty of holiness, human life possessed of divine beauty. It hopes to achieve the elevation of spirit from the sordid to the sublime. We have spoken of religion as the human search for divine good. Worship is the highway of this search. It is a search for the highest values, the eternal good beyond our limitations and frustrations.

There is room and need for both objective and subjective aims in worship. Yet Pratt is correct in maintaining that objective worship achieves the best subjective effects. To meet Reality in the eventful experiences of adoration, prayer, and dedication renews the worshiper. If one cannot believe or find an objective Companion, the problem of worship is baffling. Humanists meet to affirm their beliefs or aspirations toward enlarging human values.

By honest sharing and noble utterance they give social support to the values essential to human service and progress. To hear but the echo of one's own voice is reassuring to that extent. Yet for those who can worship a God who they feel responds the effects are very different. They taste the joy of communion with the Creator of Values, in whose presence is fulfillment and peace. "Our hearts are restless till they find rest in Thee," said Augustine. Worship is an ardent preference for the highest perfection in beauty, goodness, and reality. It is therefore a pilgrimage from this world to another, from human to divine values, from man to God.

Worship follows a rhythm. Seeking and finding, asking and receiving, calling and answering, indicate the responsive action and reaction of man and the Energy he calls God. Worship is the response of man to the invitation of God and the response of God to the petition of man. In this way an order of worship is to be understood. Beneath these responses flows a deeper rhythm, the rising tide of worship's flood from lower to higher levels, the progressive movement of devotion to heights of spiritual communion. Hindu and Hebrew prayers reveal this undeniable outreach and upreach for the divine.

> From the unreal lead me to the real.
> From darkness lead me to light.
> From death to Immortality.[15]

Out of the depths have I cried unto thee, O Lord.

Lord, hear my voice; let thine ears be attentive to the voice of my supplications. . . .

My soul waiteth for the Lord more than they that watch for the morning. . . .[16]

The arts of worship are devoted to reaching God. Each religious group has its characteristic way of conducting worship. The ritual

[15] *Brihadaranyaka*, I, iii, 28.
[16] Ps. 130.

arts of Protestant Christianity have a long history, rising from primitive Hebrew cults to priestly rites of temple and synagogue, through centuries of Greek and Roman Catholicism, then diverging into spontaneous evangelical expression. Rediscovering the deep emotional power and unity of Christian tradition, modern churches are reviving neglected arts of worship. Orders and contents of worship are constructed to provide better vehicles in the contemporary search for God. What are the psychological effects of such worship?

The Prelude covers the noisy feet, greetings, and whisperings of the incoming congregation. This may overcome the confusion of assembling by a larger volume of sound, or add to the confusion by such competition. With proper education and reverence, it ought to accomplish far more than it does. It may give preparation for worship by creating an atmosphere of harmony and repose, recalling from confusion to meditation, and suggesting reverence that elevates the spirit to awareness of sublime beauty.

The Processional and Recessional provide a formal opening and closing for the service. Processionals, as noted above are dramatic invitations to advance into the presence of God. Too often they are mere parades, arousing trivial curiosity of onlookers, who miss the deeper significance of divine approach. To be genuine, as Sperry advises,[17] the choir should avoid unnecessary detours, moving from a natural point of departure directly toward the altar. Processionals should represent man's journey to God, an urgent forward march that lingers not, nor wanders, but moves onward to a definite goal. A congregation that joins in the processional hymn with understanding is advancing into the holy Presence.

Invocations and Calls to Worship offer salutations to God and invitations to worship him. They declare that

> God is in his holy temple,
> Let all the earth keep silence before him.

[17] *Op. cit.,* pp. 219-20.

This is the summons to attention, but it often fails to arrest the wandering mind, or to arouse the inert who sit in absent-minded apathy. Indifference has many causes—weariness from standing and singing, stupor of Sunday relaxation, lack of understanding and realization of what the summons means, negligence and unwilliness to believe, or the spectator attitude of letting the minister do it. Yet these invitations are opportunities to recognize the solemn privilege of meeting God.

The Hymn is a glorious invention to express praise, rejoicing in gratitude, purpose, faith, and consecration. Yet hymns often fail, for a variety of reasons—weak sentiment or uncongenial ideas, lyrics no better than nursery rhymes, music feeble in melody and weak in harmony, unfamiliarity and unwillingness to venture the unknown, dragging tempo that grows weary unto drowsiness, jerky time or breathless racing without expression, careless attention, singing absent-mindedly without comprehension, a reluctant spirit that begrudges the effort and prefers not to participate. Most people can learn to enjoy singing and, as they share enthusiasm, become unified into one body. Objective hymns addressed to God express religious devotion.

The Creed has long held an honored place in Christian worship, but fails in our time by doubts and mental reservations. It is often mumbled unwillingly or defiled by the dishonesty of saying what one does not actually believe. If that is the situation, why not remove the Apostles' Creed from the service of worship? Some churches do and substitute a modern affirmation of faith. But this breaks continuity with the historic church, rejecting the "faith of our fathers." There is value in confessing to God and the congregation the faith that binds us to our common cause. Yet language may become archaic, and theology antiquated, unless reinterpreted. Creeds need to grow with the expanding faith of believers through honest thinking, constant education, and rebirth of religious experience.

Collects and Responses interweave united prayers through the service, impelling the rhythm of intercourse with God. Short prayers known to the people and repeated in unison are social experiences of high meaning when participation is genuine. They may be disturbed by the mechanics of reading if they are not familiar, or rendered meaningless by unconscious repetition if they are too familar. The Lord's Prayer is the model of Christian prayer, but familiarity breeds inattention. The earnest worshiper who unites with friends in such prayer renews the devotion of religious living. Choral responses and litanies are very effective. Music gives wings to prayer and creates a sense of nearness to invisible glories. Audible affirmations, responses, and amens add the weight of personal testimony.

The Responsive Reading is traditionally drawn from the Hebrew Psalter, whose cadences have a natural antiphonal structure. There is no greater devotional literature than the Psalms, though they are marred by imprecations on enemies and need to be edited. As they are read in Protestant services, there is likely to be an artificial separation between pastor and people, uncertainty about timing or phrasing, or a listless attitude that is unresponsive. If the choir should read with the minister, or the congregation divide and answer antiphonally, the responses would have better balance. Unison reading brings social participation, resonance, and interpersonal co-operation.

The Gloria and Doxology give stirring expression to emotions of gratitude and praise when sung with good spirit and in time. When the time lags or the mind wanders they become an unwelcome burden. Musicians mislead worship when they make it subjective in aim to entertain the people. Anthems offered to God in reverent adoration become a religious service, vicariously expressing the emotions of the entire congregation.

The Scripture Lesson is significant as a religious meditation guiding thought to spiritual verities. It fails when carelessly selected, poorly read, or taken as a preaching device to lecture the people. When it is memorized or read dramatically with exaggerated emphasis, the personality of the reader may crowd out the Scripture, which is better able to bring its own message. A reader who is absorbed in the message to the point of forgetting himself becomes a voice for the utterance of its truth. The Bible has held a central place in Christian worship as the authority of divine revelation. Modernism, though freed of literalism, cannot afford to discount the value of the Word of God in worship.

The Pastoral Prayer is a difficult and strategic opportunity. It may fail by poverty of ideational and emotional content, repetition of language, overlength, unreality, self-consciousness, audience consciousness, or detachment from vital needs of the people. Extempore prayers may wander far or settle into ruts of well-worn phrases. Yet to read prayers is often to miss the sense of direct address to God. Here, if anywhere, worship needs to be objective in seeking to meet and commune with God. One who is equally aware of the divine Presence and of human dependence is in the prayer mood. To voice the needs of men and the desire of God to meet those needs, to sense the bewilderment of men and the urgency of God's redemptive purpose, is a high priestly privilege.

The Offering is beset with distractions of noisy plates and the maneuvers of ushers, fumbling for small change, worry and resentment about giving, or giving because others are watching to see what one gives. "The gift without the giver is bare," as Lowell has said. Yet it may be the climax of the whole service if one makes it an offering of self in dedication to God. The historic devotion of sacrifice comes to focus here, where the worshiper brings forward to the altar his sacrificial gift to offer his best to God. A genuine offering has the emotional release of surrender and the votive act of dedicating one's all as a living sacrifice.

The Sermon is exaggerated in many Protestant services, absorbing the chief interest of the preacher, who neglects everything else to prepare it, and of the congregation, who scamper indifferently over the "opening exercises." Placing the pulpit in the center of a lecture platform and judging a minister solely by his pulpit style may distort the perspective of objective worship. When a minister trains the spotlight on himself as the main show, he yields to the subtle temptation of the ego to appeal to popularity. He is then on the way to saying what the people want to hear rather than the prophetic truth as fearlessly as Amos uttered divine commands. No matter how frenzied the oratory or soothing the words that comfort the people in careless ways, the pulpit has betrayed its function. But a preacher dedicated to proclaiming the will of God to a people aware of his nearness has a true mission to fulfill. The sermon is an influential part of Protestant worship for prophetic vision, ethical insight, challenge to heroic action, and commission to Christian service.

The Benediction has repose easily lost in closing the service and hastening to other pursuits. The Recessional may suggest an anticlimax of fading voices and vanishing realities. To counteract these distractions, the congregation should be seated for an interlude of silence, to recall and confirm the sense of God's abiding presence. In these final moments of quiet before dismissal, the value of the whole service may be summed up in perspective. Then from the poised moment of rededication the Benediction sends the worshiper forth to do God's will, keenly aware that his guiding and sustaining presence will abide evermore, "even unto the end of the world." [18]

5. Learning to Worship

If worship is an art, it must be learned, for no art is a native condition. Every art consists of skills learned to improve original nature. A naïve sense of wonder, awe, and reverence may be a natural response, but it does not become worship until one learns how to approach God and realize the joy of his presence.

Can the art of worship be taught? There is no reason to doubt that either children or adults can learn to worship. It is true that

[18] Matt. 28:20.

worship is the most subtle of the fine arts. Worship is directed to an invisible Person whose revelations are not audible to the ear. For this reason visible symbols and audible sounds are used to make vivid experiences mutually shared. The forms of worship described above are employed to unite in experience all who participate. One learns to worship by worshiping, as any art is best learned in practice.

Forms and methods of worship can be taught verbally to instruct the understanding. But the deeper emotional responses of worship are not achieved in that way. The motivating advances of purpose, devotion, dedication, and co-operation are dynamic interpersonal acts. They are learned by contagious attitudes of reverence observed in others, by melodies and harmonies, by chants and responses, by familiar settings and symbols rich in funded meanings, by memories of former experiences and hopes that echo unforgettable expectations. The sharing of these emotions and meanings, the active participation in group responsiveness, awaken religious attitudes and motivate religious actions.

It is possible to worship anywhere, but it is not so natural in some places as others. Some do not worship unless the setting is conducive to it. Thresholds of stimuli keep one semiconscious of surroundings constantly. Church architecture with arches and symbols may be eloquent in traditional meaning, but these elements will divert and distract unless they converge upon a worship center to draw the attention of the worshipers to religious focus. A quiet hush of expectancy prepares for worship. To eliminate noise, distractions, or whispering, and withhold late comers, will establish habits of reverence upon coming into the sanctuary. Music is a powerful creator of atmosphere, as skillful lighting may also be. The leader's voice needs to be modulated by an inner spirit of quiet, repose, and reverence. If these contributing factors are brought into harmony, the mood may be right for worship. For atmosphere is a social product that arises from persons mutually aware of a significant reality.

Learning to worship is an artistic creation compounded of interest, practice, and understanding. Without interest there would be no practice, without practice no experience, and without experience no understanding. Worship values are increased by the wise use of these factors. Alvin T. Maberry [19] prepared two types of worship services, one with symbols and one without, which were presented twenty-eight times to seven different congregations of young people. The value of symbols in worship was convincingly shown. At the beginning of a service without symbols there was noise and confusion, talking and shifting of chairs. Upon entering the symbol service, with a worship center of cross, crown, picture of Jesus, and candles, the subjects became markedly quiet—conversation ceased, chairs were not shuffled, and the attention was good even before the call to worship. Fifty-eight of seventy questioned, 74.6 per cent, said this was because the setting was so worshipful, peaceful, prayerful, beautiful, churchlike. Nonparticipation (not singing, praying, or reading) in all items of the service without symbols was 18.4 per cent, in contrast to 8.18 per cent in the service with symbols. Nonattention (gazing about, fidgeting, manipulating hands, etc.) in the service without symbols was 24.55 per cent in contrast to 7.37 per cent in the service with symbols. Attention and participation was three times better in the service with symbols, indicating how symbols aid in learning to worship.

No one can communicate what he has not. If the leader does not sense God's presence, it is quite unlikely that the congregation will. It is the sense of the Divine Presence that makes an ordinary man a religious leader. In so far as he loses the sense of the Divine he becomes hollow, artificial, and futile. Constant daily prayer is the best psychological preparation for public worship. Then worship becomes a crescendo of religious sharing, arising from

[19] *Psychology of Religious Symbolism,* an M.A. thesis, Syracuse University (unpublished), 1939.

genuine inner experience. The deeper subconscious attitudes of religious faith and hope are basic causes and effects of worship. When such attitudes permeate the whole personality, there is calm courage for the sharp demands of crisis or for the dull routine of drudgery.

VII

The Psychology of Belief

1. PSYCHOLOGICAL CONDITIONS OF BELIEF

The psychological study of belief is to be clearly distinguished from the logical question of validity. Logic treats belief as true or false. It is a normative study of standards and methods for judging what constitutes valid belief.[1] Important as the question of truth is, it is not the problem of this chapter. We are concerned rather to investigate the nature of religious belief. What do people believe? What causes belief and doubt? What are the interpersonal effects of religious belief?

There seems to be a natural tendency to believe. Everyone is a believer. Not all persons believe the same things, but everyone believes something. Why do we believe some ideas and not others? How do we come to believe at all? The conditions of belief may be classified as sociological and psychological. While they overlap and interact, it will be well to consider the tendencies to believe from these two points of view.

Sociological conditions include all belief-making influences that come from association in social groups. The behavior of other persons suggests deeds and words to imitate. Attitudes of belief associated with deeds and words become contagious. We do as others do, feel as others feel, and think as others think because we desire to share a common life and become a part of the social group. By repetition customs and traditions arise, having the authority of group sanction—when so many believe, there must be something to it. If the wisest and best believe, there is qualitative as well as quantitative sanction, and we tend to believe on the

---

[1] For logical studies of religion see E. S. Brightman, *A Philosophy of Religion;* D. C. Macintosh, *The Problem of Religious Knowledge* (New York: Harper & Bros., 1940); D. E. Trueblood, *The Logic of Belief* (New York: Harper & Bros., 1942).

authority of prestige as well as numbers. "Each generation starts in believing what its predecessors believed, and a faith once thoroughly grounded is not easily disturbed." [2] Customs are social habits that become incorporated into the very life of individuals who enact them. Such believing attitudes become a frame of reference accepted as established, not to be questioned but defended as the stability and order by which we carry on. But we are so largely unconscious of the basic assumptions of belief that we take them for granted without question or defense.

Psychological conditions of belief appear in these social influences of suggestion and imitation. Why do we imitate others? Imitation occurs in stimulus-response situations. When interest directs attention to other persons, the whole organism responds in exploratory motor efforts to reproduce the observed event. [3] Note the tendency in spectators at a football game to reproduce the efforts of the players by incipient muscular tensions. Believing is a social attitude that responds in this way to the persistent stimuli of others' belief. A man standing on a street corner looking up stimulates others to look up also, for he acts as though he believes there is something up there worth looking at. It is natural to believe what others believe, and most of our beliefs are socially conditioned.

It has been customary to refer to man as a rational animal (*homo sapiens*). In this the ancient Greeks held man in higher opinion than do contemporary psychologists, who reason that man is essentially unreasonable. The paradox of this view lies in the use of reason to deny reason by addressing the reasonableness of others. But the intention is to rely upon sensible experience by appealing to the facts. On this ground who will deny that much of human behavior is motivated by irrational desires and fears?

[2] J. B. Pratt, *The Religious Consciousness*, p. 85.
[3] E. S. Ames, *The Psychology of Religious Experience*, pp. 303-6, treats this ideo-motor tendency as instinctive. But neuromuscular tensions, as we observe them, are goal-seeking tensions of interest. The term "ideo-motor," as he uses it, contradicts instinct by relating the motor activity to conscious ideation, equivalent to interest.

The persons we know best are not altogether rational or irrational but somewhat of both. And so it is with our beliefs; they arise from a mingling of rational and irrational tendencies.

The subrational roots of belief are deeply involved in the interests and needs, desires and aversions, ends and means, of living.[4] Psychological analyses have often tracked religious belief down to irrational deceptions of the unconscious: (*a*) Interest in God is called a manifestation of the "father complex," indicating a childish fixation that should normally be outgrown. It is viewed as a form of nostalgia, a pathetic homesickness for the parental care of infancy. (*b*) Religious hopes are taken as overcompensation for inferiority and ego frustration. Religious satisfaction is an opiate to which the weak become addicted in trying to dull the pain of a tragic existence. (*c*) Petition to God is considered a projection of the burden of dismay and dependence upon the Everlasting Arms. In God we trust for credit in lieu of cash. (*d*) Religious belief is called "wish-thinking" or "thobbing," luxuriating in the phantasies of believing what one wants to believe. Faith is suggestibility under the hypnotic effect of soft music and stained-glass windows, or under the social pressure of herd conformity.

There is much to learn from these psychological descriptions. Devious as they are, the mind of man is not less so. The amazing intricacy of behavior may well demand such elaborate explorations. Human nature can be fully as irrational and deceptive as psychology finds it. And the fact is that atheists have the same human nature that theists have. They also are infected by irrationality, sentimentality, and evasion. Their beliefs are subject to the same distortions of prejudice and desire. For atheism is, by every test, as much a belief as theism, and it is evidently quite as incapable of escaping the waves of emotion that beat upon beliefs.

First, atheism may be motivated by jealous revolt. There is a

[4] See P. E. Johnson, "Psychoanalyzing the Atheist," *The Christian Century*, LIII (1936), 292-94.

Greek legend of the young man Oedipus, who in a quarrel hurled his father off a mountain pass, married his mother, and became king upon his father's throne. Freud holds this rivalry and revolt typical of modern family conflicts. Now if theism may be traced to the father complex, it is quite as logical to trace atheism to the Oedipus complex, a jealous desire to overthrow and supplant the father. Rival affections and jealous conflicts displace loyalty to God. Many a son who falls into filial disagreement casts off his father's God in revolt against his father. In wider extension this attitude becomes a generalized revolt against all authority. "Down with God!" shout revolutionary leaders in Mexico, for God is a symbol of the traditional authorities they are out to destroy. The Russian Orthodox Church had so identified God with the imperialism which held the people in bondage that God must be assassinated with the Czar. Revolts against God occur where oppression weighs the heaviest, where God is on the side of the imperial armies and exploiting classes. Organized party atheism is everywhere associated with revolution against tyrannical authority, a contest in the struggle of power.

A second motivation in atheism is egotism. Freud finds in personality a basic reservoir of psychic energy, the "Id," which ever strives to gratify desire. It is unmoral, illogical, and inconsistent— a blind yet ceaseless striving for self-satisfaction. Adler regards the basic urge of personality as the ego striving for power. We have seen how atheism is related to the struggle for power. It is further involved in the urge for ego satisfaction. Nietzsche, denied military ambitions, turned his energy to literary conquests. His bitter attacks on Christianity as "slave morality" attempt compensation for an inferiority complex. In *Thus Spake Zarathustra* he offers the confession: "That I may reveal my heart entirely to you, my friends: if there were gods, how could I endure it to be no god? Therefore there are no gods." [5] Obviously the conclusion

[5] Pt. II, Discourse xxiv.

of this inference is not logical, but psychological—a conclusion to gratify the ego, not the canons of the syllogism. Thus may atheism become a sop to the ego, an escape from inferiority to inflated superiority. H. L. Mencken strikes a pose of superiority when he heaps scorn upon the "yokels of the Bible belt." Shaw strokes his ego by satirizing *The Adventures of the Black Girl in Her Search for God*. God is sacrificed upon the altar of conceit.

A third motive is projection. Projection is a device for avoiding condemnation by placing blame upon others. Primitive tribes have been known to vent resentment upon their gods of clay or wood by hacking them to pieces in a frenzy of wrath. It is no longer good taste to chastise gods or children with corporal punishment. We now refine our instruments of torture and resort to tongue lashings. Projection is a ready way of evading moral responsibility. If God made me, then he is responsible for my misdeeds. Or it may be more convenient to dispense with God entirely— remove God and immortality, and there is nothing to fear in this world or the next. Dostoevski reflects this outcome of the nineteenth-century atheism in *The Brothers Karamazov*. Ivan returns from his university studies and reports that if there is no God, anything is lawful, even cannibalism. His reckless brother Dmitri pounces upon the idea and takes advantage of this lawlessness to murder his father. Again the atheistic argument follows psychological labyrinths of irrational impulses rather than logical patterns of unbiased reason.

A fourth observation is that atheists rationalize. Rationalization is the victory of desire over reason. Belief in God is often pointed to as a conspicuous example of such wishful thinking. The same ax falls at the root of atheistic beliefs, which parade arguments in support of petulant desires. If theists emphasize meaning and value in the universe, atheists are often as anxious to accent the evil and insignificant. If the idealist rationalizes his desire for beauty and harmony, the realist surely rationalizes his preference for discord and ugliness. There is an oddly prevalent desire to have the worst of possible worlds. The style of "sweetness and light" was sentimental, but no wider of the mark than the mood of bitterness and darkness. The ardor with which cynics smash the idols of theistic hope approaches sadistic delight. Rationalization flourishes in the soil of credulity. The same credulity produces both the Pollyanna and the Scrooge. A Pollyanna is begging to believe the best; a Scrooge is begging to believe the worst. The appetite for cosmic scandal is quite as insatiable as the avid nose of the neighborhood gossipmonger. The chronic iconoclast traffics with the same cargo on a larger scale of paranoiac operation. Schopenhauer slept with pistols under his pillow because he distrusted his fellow men; he brooded over the hopeless evils of life because he distrusted the Will of the World. In both respects he suffered delusions of persecution. Atheism is a dogma that flourishes in emotional attitudes.

Where does reason enter this believing and doubting process? John Dewey contends that we do not think until we have to.[6] When life flows along smoothly there is no occasion to think until some obstacle or problem demands solution and wakens consciousness to employ ideas as tools to serve life needs. But reason does not oversleep so long as that. Daydreaming uses imaginative reason in autistic thinking. Subconscious motives work with clever reasons to gain their desires. Reason is not a separate faculty, standing aloof as a *deus ex machina* until called to meet a crisis. Some degree of reasoning is present in all conscious experience that relates fleeting impressions into meaning. There is no sharp line of demarcation between experience and reason, for reason is the coherent sense of experience. We believe not entirely by reason but never without an aspect of reasonableness. The subrational roots noted above already merge into complexes of coherent experience, from which reason stems and eventually blossoms into inferences, syllogisms, and theologies.

[6] John Dewey, *How We Think* (Boston: D. C. Heath & Co., 1910).

Reason serves a double function in belief, critical and constructive. When contradictions appear, critical suspicions arise and demand more careful scrutiny. Looking out of a train window after dark, one may mistake the station until a familiar landmark contradicts his belief and calls for a hasty re-examination before the train carries him beyond his destination. The constructive function draws data together into a coherent pattern of meaning worthy of belief. Critical and constructive efforts follow no rigid sequence, but intermingle in continuous efforts to make sense out of multiple impressions. The critical function is to guard against deception and falsehood. The constructive function is to develop standards of true validity and organize beliefs to form a coherent system.

2. THE PROBLEM OF DOUBT

Doubt is a problem. It is a painful perplexity that puzzles and worries the mind. As a negative denial of accepted belief, doubt revolts against authority, betraying and deserting established tradition. Skeptical unrest may have symptoms of acute distress, insecurity, lack of confidence, mingled with feelings of guilt. Persistent attitudes of doubt may come to moods of indifference or despair which defeat constructive action and prevent creative achievement.

For these reasons doubt is often feared and opposed. A religious editor recalls a Sunday-school teacher who said to him as a boy, "You have no right to doubt." David Nyvall, in a tract on *Doubt and How to Overcome It* (c.1930), declares that doubt is always an ill, and refers to critical discerning as defeating the highest purpose of life, suggesting that there is a blind faith the better for its blindness. But if doubt is an ill, it is not cured by fearful suppression.

Is doubt always an evil? The fact is that doubt performs a useful function. It arouses critical intelligence from "dogmatic slumber" as Kant demonstrated in his three great critiques.[7] It questions hollow assumption and challenges smug hypocrisy. It demands honest investigation, exposes error, and urges correction. It stimulates discussion and exchange of opinion, which foster progress in truth-seeking. Studies in superstition are instructive at this point. Without doubt superstition proliferates in rank jungles of error, confusion, and ignorant fear. Systematic doubting prunes out these errors and gives truth room to grow. The scientific obligation of psychology is to employ critical processes in thoroughgoing investigation.

American psychologists have made numerous investigations of superstition, defined as unfounded belief. Typical lists of superstitions are presented for judgment to students of different age, sex, and background to discover what factors are related to such unfounded beliefs. E. E. Emme [8] reviewed such studies and found the following implications:

1. Superstitious belief declines with age and education. High-school students are more credulous than college students; junior students are more credulous than high-school seniors.
2. Women appear to be more superstitious than men. This is evident in various studies, regardless of the age of the subjects. Rural children are more credulous than urban children.
3. Specific instruction reduces superstitious belief. General instruction in science does not seem to have this effect, but specific teaching is effective.
4. Sources of belief vary. Home, friends, observation, educational sources (books, newspapers, school, church) are important influences.
5. The more intelligent are less superstitious. They have fewer superstitions and are better able to reduce their prejudices.

Professor Emme then proceeded to study ninety-six Morningside College students by tests, instruction, interviews, and correla-

[7] Immanuel Kant, *Critique of Pure Reason*, B785; *Critique of Practical Reason; Critique of Judgment.*

[8] "Modification and Origin of Superstition Among 96 College Students," *The Journal of Psychology*, X (1940), 279-91.

tions in reference to a list of forty-seven superstitions. Twenty-four of these students had zero superstition scores. The ten most superstitious students had scores at the outset varying from fourteen to nineteen statements. Specific instruction reduced their scores to a range of one to six. The total mean average score was reduced from 2.96 to .67. Parents were found to be the primary factor in motivating belief or disbelief. Other factors were friends, courses, and reading. Negative correlations between intelligence and superstition were −.421 before the study and −.471 after the study.

Religion has often been condemned as superstition. It is evident that superstitious beliefs have accumulated around every area of human experience, including religion. Practices of government, war, trade, agriculture, birth, death, disease, health, and so forth, have in every culture operated through a maze of popular superstitions. Religion has had its share—and more, perhaps, by virtue of its devotion to supernatural and invisible powers. But in all fairness it should be recorded that religion is also a vigorous corrector of superstitions. Even as astronomy has shaken off the superstitions of astrology and chemistry the superstitions of alchemy, so the higher religions have battled steadily against error and superstition.

Sturdy faith welcomes doubt, as democracy welcomes freedom of speech, as judicial bodies welcome minority opinions, as scientists welcome revolutionary discoveries, as true religion welcomes prophetic denunciations for the sake of truth. Doubt, well employed, is essential to growing faith and true progress. "The doubt that a man confronts purifies his faith from error. . . . For honest doubt is a new aspect of truth standing at the door and knocking, seeking a place in the system of rational experience." [9]

The problem of doubt is how to doubt intelligently rather than blindly, for blind doubt is quite as superstitious as blind faith. Open-minded doubt is more eager to learn than to win arguments

[9] Henry Jones, *A Faith That Enquires* (New York: The Macmillan Co., 1922), pp. 9-10.

or defend prejudices. Honest doubt is fearless self-criticism that dissolves indifference and cynicism. Intelligent doubt concedes a belief to be affirmed as the counterpart of denial, and persists in seeking truth to affirm.

3. Religious Beliefs

The variety and extent of religious beliefs is boundless. Agreement in beliefs has social causes, as the authority of tradition and the contagion of custom shape beliefs to conformity. Similar needs and experiences suggest parallel interpretations. Yet beliefs are diverging today. Freedom to think and speak for one's self encourages individual opinion and independent judgment. The Protestant denominations in their democratic tendencies have encouraged differences, in contrast to the conformity of Catholic authority. As sciences gather new facts and social change moves along there is persistent demand to revise beliefs. Thinkers follow promising tangents and reach divergent conclusions. As each pursues his clues in search of truth, the seekers fan out widely over the fields open to exploration. The more ardently and thoroughly each hypothesis is investigated, the more likely are these co-operative enterprises to be fruitful.

What religious beliefs do contemporary Americans hold? Many surveys have been made in recent years. J. Dudycha[10] reports a study of the religious beliefs of students in six Midwestern church-related colleges in 1930. A questionnaire of religious concepts was submitted to 852 freshmen before they had attended their first classes. The same questionnaire was submitted to 305 seniors the same year to see how their beliefs differed from those of the freshmen. Comparing the beliefs declared by the freshmen with those of the seniors one finds the decline in beliefs is evident in every item but one. The seniors show lesser belief in every doctrine except immortality. The decrease varies from 3 per cent less

[10] "Religious Beliefs of College Students," *Journal of Applied Psychology* XVII (1933), 585-602.

belief in the existence of God to 38 per cent less belief in the creation of the world in six days. The least variation occurs in the doctrines generally considered most fundamental in Christian theology, as the doctrine of the existence of God. Freshman beliefs vary from 96 to 53 per cent, while senior beliefs vary from 93 to 15 per cent; the widest variance appears in questions of heaven and hell, angels and devils, creation and final judgment.

Grouped by denominations, the Catholics, Lutherans, and United Presbyterians led with 78-79 per cent average implicit belief; the Baptists and Presbyterians averaged 67-69 per cent; the Methodists and miscellaneous 59-62 per cent; the Congregationalists 50 per cent; and those of no denomination 40 per cent. The preference for pleasant over unpleasant beliefs is indicated— believing more in heaven than hell, more in angels than devils, more in immortality than a day of judgment, more in forgiveness of sin than reality of sin.

Another study of even more significance is the survey conducted by G. H. Betts of the beliefs of seven hundred Protestant ministers.[11] With the assistance of a dozen or more theologians a list of fifty-six questions was prepared referring to items most prominent in Protestant creeds. Five degrees of belief were indicated: (a) positive certainty, (b) moderate certainty, (c) undecided, (d) moderate disbelief, and (e) positive disbelief. The inquiry was sent to 1,309 ministers in service representing twenty denominations in the vicinity of Chicago, of whom 500 returned replies; and to students in five theological schools of three denominations, of whom 200 replied. Classification of returns by denominations shows marked degrees of conservative and liberal belief in accommodation to modern scientific thought. For instance, on the question of miracles 98 per cent of the Lutherans believe, in contrast to Evangelicals, 73 per cent; Episcopalians, 67 per cent; Baptists,

[11] *The Beliefs of 700 Ministers* (New York: The Abingdon Press, 1929).

64 per cent; Presbyterians, 57 per cent; Methodists, 55 per cent; and Congregationalists, 43 per cent.

An interesting comparison is shown between the liberal and skeptical trend of younger ministers, as represented in theological students, and the beliefs of older ministers. The students accept far fewer of the traditional religious beliefs than the older ministers. The average proportion of ministers expressing belief on the fifty-six items is 67 per cent; students, 39 per cent. For ministers the average of disbelief is 27 per cent; for the students, 49 per cent. For ministers the average declaring uncertainty is 6 per cent; for the students 12 per cent. All accept the existence of God, but only 44 per cent of the students accept the doctrine of the Trinity, against 80 per cent of ministers. The Genesis account of creation is taken literally by only 5 per cent of the students, against 47 per cent of the ministers. The idea of evolution is questioned by only 8 per cent of the students, but denied by 33 per cent of the ministers. Only 9 per cent of the students believe in the devil, against 60 per cent of the ministers, while only 11 per cent of the students think of hell as an actual place against 53 per cent of the ministers. While 89 per cent of the students believe in life after death, 69 per cent deny the resurrection of the body against 33 per cent denial of the ministers.

Recognizing a psychological need for beliefs, Betts is concerned about the meaning of this situation for religious education. With the widely diverging beliefs of Protestant ministers, how can children know what to believe? There is little hope of teaching a uniform creed believed by all. Democratic freedom to think and let think encourages differences of opinion. The memorizing of verbal forms with little meaning or emotional conviction is largely futile anyhow, for belief does not arise in this way. Belief is more successful when it comes as a personal discovery. What ministers and teachers have discovered and encourage youth to discover for themselves will be vital and workable.

Is there any common body of religious beliefs on which these ministers agree that may serve as a credo of minimum essentials for the Christian faith? There are eleven items of belief from the original list of fifty-six on which three fourths of the seven hundred ministers and students agree: [12]

1. There is a supreme being; God exists (100 per cent).
3. God is omnipotent (80 per cent).
4. God's relation to man is that of Father (98 per cent).
8. God controls the universe through his personal presence and power (82 per cent).
13. God is a being with personal attributes, complete and perfect in all moral qualities (90 per cent).
27. Jesus while on earth was subject to temptation as other men (97 per cent).
28. Jesus met his problems and difficulties using only those powers and resources available to all men (76 per cent).
29. Jesus lived on earth without sin (87 per cent).
39. Life continues after death (95 per cent).
48. Forgiveness of sin is essential to a right relationship with God (96 per cent).
52. God operates on human lives through the agency and person of the Holy Spirit (91 per cent).

This creed states the essence of the Christian faith. It gives God as Father, perfect in moral qualities, with power to effect his good purpose in the world. It shows Jesus on earth meeting his temptations and problems without sin by resources available to all men. It provides for a future life and declares forgiveness essential to a right relation with God. Three basic areas of religious experience and co-operation are recognized: God, the universe, and man's destiny. A simplified creed would focus on essentials and provide common ground for belief. It would therefore tend to unite religious bodies and meet the psychological need for religious belief with freedom for individual differences in detail. If beliefs are

[12] *Ibid.*, p. 63.

taken not as static ends in themselves, but as dynamic instruments for the development of true experience and social action, they may serve as a practical working faith. Rather than face backward to unchanging traditions, growing belief faces forward to present realities.

4. Ideas of God

It is evident that religious beliefs are subject to change. Beliefs are modified by developing experiences of the individual and by social conditions in a world where nothing stands still. Churches have employed the authority of apostolic succession, inerrant Scripture, and infallible judgment to resist the forces of change. But, even so, variations occur and new views alter the religious perspective. Within social patterns of belief individuals show even more flexibility in private reservations and personal opinions. Social change is speeding up in our mobile civilization, and religious beliefs are not impervious to these new viewpoints. The divergence in beliefs of older and younger ministers as well as between college freshmen and seniors, indicates such change.

J. H. Leuba has sampled the religious beliefs of American scientists in two surveys, conducted in 1914 and 1933.[13] In 1914 he submitted questionnaires on God and immortality to 1,000 scientists listed in *American Men of Science* in two groups of 500 each, selected at random from 5,500 names. In 1933 he sent the same questionnaire to a sampled number of 23,000 scientists [14] listed in the 1933 edition of *American Men of Science,* supplemented by lists of the American Sociological Society (1931) and the 1933 yearbook of the American Psychological Association. Replies came from at least 75 per cent of selected scientists, classified in four fields: physicists (concerned with inanimate matter), biologists

---

[13] *The Belief in God and Immortality* (New York: Sherman French & Co., 1916; Chicago: Open Court, 1921) and "Religious Beliefs of American Scientists," *Harper's Magazine,* CLXIX (1934), 291-300.

[14] Leuba does not give the exact number of these scientists to whom the questionnaire was sent in 1933. The number of sociologists was 157 and psychologists 164.

(concerned with living matter), sociologists, and psychologists. These were further classified as greater scientists (starred as eminent by a poll of their fellow scientists), and lesser scientists. Each scientist was asked to check one of the following three statements on God:

1. I believe in a God to whom one can pray in the expectation of receiving an answer. By "answer" I mean more than the natural, subjective, psychological effect of prayer.
2. I do not believe in God as defined above.
3. I have no definite belief regarding this question.

A statistical comparison of the believers in God among these scientists in 1914 and 1933 is shown as follows:

THE BELIEVERS IN GOD

	Lesser Scientists		Greater Scientists	
	1914	1933	1914	1933
Physicists	50%	43%	34%	17%
Biologists	39	31	17	12
Sociologists	29	30	19	13
Psychologists	32	13	13	12

Leuba has conducted his surveys with a commendable effort to be objective and accurate. His figures seem to indicate (*a*) that scientists tend more to disbelief than to belief in God; (*b*) that greater scientists believe less than the lesser scientists; and (*c*) that belief in God is generally declining among scientists in these nineteen years. This is a good demonstration of scientific method in the study of religious belief. No one can deny the facts presented or fail to be impressed by the trends revealed. But there are dangers of hasty generalization in statistical surveys that need careful scrutiny before coming to final conclusions.

First, one must not confuse these scientists with all scientists. While Leuba employed his sampling method with care to have a random selection that would be representative, the fact is that we do not know what the other scientists would have said. The number not consulted is obviously much greater than those consulted; and approximately 25 per cent of those questioned did not reply. Some replied to protest that the three statements were inadequate to define their position. The inductive leap from some to all, or even to others not examined, is notably hazardous. This is a general difficulty affecting all scientific induction and should not be forgotten in this study.

Second, one must not mistake this definition of God for any or all belief in God. Ideas of God are so variously understood that no single view of God could be acceptable to all believers in God. In this case the definition of God is so obviously narrow and unscientific as to exclude scientists in particular from belief. By ruling out "natural, subjective, and psychological effect of prayer" Leuba defines God as a being who works externally and magically by setting aside natural laws. Scientists who believe in a God working in nature through uniform laws and subjective experiences have no choice but to reject Leuba's definition of God and be counted as disbelievers. Yet they may be earnest believers in a God who employs lawful means.

Third, the apparent decline of belief among greater and more recent scientists is probably influenced by the phrasing of the questionnaire. A statement of belief that is antiscientific will force a disjunction between such religious belief and science. The more devoted one is to science the more surely will he defend his scientific system of beliefs when challenged by antiscientific statements. Furthermore it should be noted that surveys of public opinion are important factors in influencing opinion as shown in the use of the Gallup Poll in recent political contests. The published returns of Leuba's survey in 1914 evidently influenced the furtherance of reported trends in 1933. When students of science find that scientists disbelieve, and that greater scientists are greater doubters, they are naturally impressed. The prestige of scientific authority may overshadow religious authority in our time. The separation of education from religion and the preponderance of time which children and youth spend in secular schools joins with the prestige of teachers and the wonders of science to give scientific belief a favored position.

Fourth, it should be evident that the questionnaire confuses the existence of God with the effects of prayer. One may believe in God without subscribing to the kind of prayer that sets aside natural processes. It might be argued that God is not the decisive issue of the question, but rather what one believes about prayer and miracles. At this point it is interesting to note that only 21 per cent of the theological students and 64 per cent of the ministers whom Betts surveyed believed that prayer has the power to change conditions in nature such as drought. Yet 58 per cent of the students and 83 per cent of the ministers believe that prayer for others directly affects their lives. With the variation of belief on a redefinition of prayer it is evident that subtle distinctions make a wide difference in statistical returns. Though narrow in one sense, Leuba's statement is too complex to be selective at the point of the existence of God. Other issues latent in the statement are: (*a*) How does God hear prayer? (*b*) How does God answer prayer? (*c*) What is supernatural? (*d*) Why are subjective effects discounted? (*e*) Are psychological processes impervious to God's influence?

In defense of this definition Leuba says, "That is the God worshiped in every branch of religion. In the absence of belief in a God who hears and sympathizes with man, who under certain conditions answers his prayers, traditional worship could not go on." [15]

But there is enough loose play in this statement for it likewise to be ambiguous. We may believe that God sympathizes without answering in ways defined, or we may hold that worship need not

[15] "Religious Beliefs . . . ," *Harper's,* p. 292.

be traditional. The net is much too large to separate worshipers of God from nonworshipers. To assume that scientists do not believe in God because they reject a given formula, or do not pray because they expect a different kind of answer, is not exactly clarifying.

A more refined instrument for measuring belief in God was employed by Daniel Katz and F. H. Allport in studying students' attitudes at Syracuse University.[16] A scale of seven steps was devised to distinguish different concepts of God, and 1,321 liberal arts students were asked to select the statement most nearly representing their beliefs. Only the first of the seven items could possibly agree with Leuba's definition of God, and this was acceptable to just 21 per cent of the students. Yet only 4.7 per cent of the students (items 6 and 7) denied belief in God.

Factors influencing changes in students' religious belief were: teaching in certain courses, 72.4 per cent; contacts with fellow students, 46.2 per cent; general process of becoming more mature, 37.5 per cent; reading outside of courses, 29.7 per cent; personal influence of professors in courses, 21 per cent; other influences outside of college life, 19.7 per cent; religious services in churches of the city, 6.7 per cent. These changes in religious belief were accompanied by a new and satisfying philosophy of life for 62.4 per cent of the students, though of these 38.4 per cent said that certain doubts remained.

A. H. MacLean has published a valuable study of what children think of God.[17] Interviews were held with seventy-five Protestant children eight years of age or younger living in New York City. The following responses were given by the children:

God is like a man with long white robes. He looks very kind.
God is an old man and has long white whiskers all over his face.

[16] *Students' Attitudes* (Syracuse, N. Y.: The Craftsman Press, 1931), pp. 257-318.
[17] *The Idea of God in Protestant Religious Education* (New York: Teachers College, Columbia University, 1930).

I just can't tell.

God is a spirit and can get into places without being seen.

God is like a spirit—like that part of you which goes to heaven when you die.

God is a very good man.

God is nature.

God is a man with power who uses his power in the right way.

God is quite different from man. He has power to create things.

God is a powerful doctor.

God has a different spirit from us. Mamma told me so.

God is a spirit. He doesn't really live, but gives you thoughts to do things to help people.

God is as big as a cloud. He wears a long dress and a blackish beard.

Mamma has a picture of God. He has hair down to his shoulders. He is old.

God has a smiling face.

God is like us.

God is like a fairy.

God is a young man.

God is a king—the greatest king of all.

God has a head.

God is the same as Jesus.

Nobody ever saw God.

General trends appear from these responses. Forty per cent think of God as a man with flesh and bones and whiskers; 20 per cent think of him as a spirit, ghost, or fairy; 25 per cent refer to his kindness or goodness, and 12 per cent to his power.

In response to the question: Where do you think God is? the majority said that God is away up in the sky, or in Heaven. Many others said that God is everywhere, and 27 per cent that he is near us all the time. "God is down inside of me," "God is in our hearts."

Four hundred and forty-three intermediate children (ages 9 to 14) in New York Protestant church schools were given a true-false test of 218 statements concerning God. Grouping these scores by deciles, MacLean gives the following summary of the children's beliefs.

Over 90 per cent of the children believe that God is omniscient; that he is changeless in nature; that in character he most resembles a loving father or mother, or the man Jesus; that He is present everywhere; that the addressing of prayers to Him is primarily useful in quest of moral guidance; that God's love is universally extended to mankind; that He will forgive even murder; that He protects children at night and supplies man's every physical need; that He loves all classes and races, even our enemies; that He desires us to help the underprivileged share advantages; that war should be speedily terminated; and that we should believe all the Bible says about God.

Between 80 and 90 per cent of the children believe that God is a wonderful person—He is three persons in one; He could make the sun stop and go back the other way if He wished; He lives in Heaven and will supply anything we ask; He will not grant every wish, but only what we need; He is found in the call of duty and ethical relations; He reveals Himself in blossom and sunshine; He provides a Heaven for the faithful; He has made laws we must discover and obey; He created the world and life in six days; Adam and Eve brought disaster on mankind, but God is redeeming us; He asks us to work for a world free of poverty and privation; He wants us to participate in war only when our cause is just and every peace effort has failed.

Between 70 and 80 per cent of the children believe that God has a face, hands, and feet like a man; no one really knows what God is like; God answers prayers in doing only what we cannot do ourselves; He reveals Himself through dreams, miracles, inspired men, storms, earthquakes; He uses natural forces in punishment of wrong doing; He needs human co-operation in His work of mercy and redemption; He will save a man from drowning even if he cannot swim a stroke; He desires songs of praises, church membership, and unquestioning obedience to parents; to participate in war under any circumstances is against His will; He wants us to go to war whenever our government asks us to; only those will go to heaven who believe in Jesus; it is Jesus' exemplary life that saves from sin; Jesus rose from the grave, and will come to the world again.

From 60 to 70 per cent agree that no one knows where God is; the Bibles of Chinese and Buddhists contain some knowledge about God; angels bring word from Him; He dictated the Bible to some of his followers; no one would be sick or meet with disaster if he had faith enough in the Father; God will not save the good from accidents any more than the wicked; He is responsible for only the good that is done in the world; He planned all things from the beginning; He created woman from man's rib; He will give the sinner a chance to redeem himself after death; He will send some to Hell; Jesus possesses unlimited power.

Wider disagreements appear in the group of replies from 40 to 60 per cent. God is not like a person at all; He cannot make men good unless they desire to be good; He lives especially in church buildings; He is up in the sky; to know Him one must join the Christian church; scientists can tell us something about Him; He appeared in material form to men but does not now; He created life in the world by slow degrees developing from lower to higher forms; He will not do anything for us that we cannot do for ourselves; God will slay by lightning a man who cursed Him; He will someday come to the world to destroy it; He asks us to love Him more than we do people and animals; the cross of Jesus is essential to salvation; it is hard to understand the saving mystery of the cross and the miracles of Jesus; the nativity stories are make-believe; Jesus was God's son as Lincoln and other good men are; Jesus was God himself.[18]

The contradictions in these ideas of God indicate something of the confusion that arises in this area of knowledge. The items of highest agreement (above 90 per cent) are quite consistent except for the last one, believing all the Bible says about God. For the Bible says contradictory things about God, and may be considered one of the sources of the confusion. The statements in the deciles of 40 to 80 per cent approval show wider disagreements and more striking contradictions. There are good reasons why agreement on the questions of God is difficult.

If God is an invisible being, he is not directly observable to the

[18] Condensed from *ibid.*, pp. 106-9.

senses of all. Each person has to interpret and infer what God is like from his own experience.

Imagination weaves the visual context of knowledge. When sense objects are not present we imagine them as we have seen them. When we have not seen an object we use imagination to portray it. God is portrayed in whatever imagery best seems to suggest his attributes—as the spacious sky for omnipresence, or the kindly face that indicates fatherly love.

Picture thinking is vivid but misleading in giving form to the formless. The crude anthropomorphic pictures of God soon become inadequate to a thinking mind. For concepts of God expand so that no picture frame is able to contain the greater vision. The pictures of God are a delight to childhood but a limitation to maturity.

Theologians then turn to word thinking to convey the larger meaning of deity. Words are also symbols, but more flexible and less limiting than the spatial forms of pictures. The attributes of God may be defined in abstract and unlimited terms as far as thought can reach, even beyond present experience. Creeds sculpture God in language, to view his nature and describe his traits in the subtle distinctions of speculative thought. Yet this linguistic art has its dangers too, for it may substitute words for reality, or cling to symbols as unreal as the pictures.

It is evident that no one can think without content of some kind. The media of words, images, and relations are essential to whatever knowledge we have. If they are not taken as final, they may sharpen concepts by debate and mutual criticism. Each thinker may wrestle with the glory of God and discover for himself a conviction of personal experience. And together seekers for God have learned much from social experience, from scientific experiment and systematic philosophy.

Awareness of God is a total experience, a perspective of all impressions together. Robert Browning portrays this multiple revelation of God in Pippa's song:

> The year's at the spring
> The day's at the morn;
> Morning's at seven;
> The hillside's dew-pearled;
> The lark's on the wing;
> The snail's on the thorn:
> God's in his heaven—
> All's right with the world.

No single impression, but all impressions in a perspective of beauty and harmony mean God to this singer. It is the total intuition that "all's right with the world" that brings the conviction, "God's in his heaven." All things taken together yield a unity, order, and purpose that one understands to mean God.

Such experiences arise from intersensory perception, the participation of many sense modalities in a single perceptual experience. Most perceptual experience is intersensory, a product of co-operating sensitivities and relations in judgments of meaning. Perceptions of space and time require perspectives of here and there, of now and then. The scientific labor of constructing hypotheses and generalizing data into universal laws is similar to awareness of God. Belief in a system of orderly nature follows psychological processes equivalent to belief in God. Both employ total experience of many clues to reach a perspective of what it all means. Theist and atheist are both employing the same psychological powers to attain a universal integration of empirical evidence.[19]

Different views of God and the universe are not a scandal of confusion, but a richness of supplementation. No finite mind can comprehend the infinite range of truth and reality. Every honest view of what appears real is a contribution to our growing understanding of truth. Truth is enlarged and verified by interpersonal sharing and testing of fragmentary insights. If revelation comes

---

[19] See P. E. Johnson, "The Illusion of Religion," *The Journal of Religion*, XII (1932), 333-40, and "The Inductive Approach to God," *The Journal of Philosophy*, XXXVIII (1941), 375-81.

from God, that is also interpersonal. What appear as contradictions at the moment may in the progress of expanding discovery become complementary. Paradoxes should not be scorned as false but valued as pregnant suggestions to deliver new truth.

Personal experiences have emotional depth. Vital knowledge of God is personal experience. Pictures and words about God may be borrowed from others, yet they are poor substitutes for experience of one's own. Forms and symbols are convenient to pick up and pass along, but often prove counterfeit without the ring of of reality. Yet personal experiences need to be enlarged and corrected by interpersonal discoveries, thinking together and seeing together what reality means. Pratt tells of a man who described God as a kind of oblong blur.[20] He had rejected the anthropomorphic pictures of childhood and put nothing in their place. He had also neglected the means of grace and growth—religious education and social participation in a stimulating religious community. Reality is too large for lonely individuals to comprehend. Truth seekers wisely form associations, schools, and churches to provide the interpersonal activity that makes education a social achievement.

5. FUNCTIONS OF FAITH

Faith is more than belief. The terms may be synonymous in current language, but psychological analysis shows a deep distinction. Strickland recognizes this distinction when, describing faith in God, he says, "We accept and believe truths but we trust persons."[21] Faith may include belief, but it is a larger experience than intellectual assent. It is not confined to one aspect of personality, but is rather an attitude of personality as a whole.

Belief is judgment. Faith is devotion of total personality in loyal assurance. Belief may be less than knowledge, but faith is more. "Faith is reason grown courageous." The dynamic quality of faith

[20] *The Religious Consciousness*, p. 200.
[21] *Psychology of Religious Experience*, p. 152.

is indicated in a volitional activity of purpose, loyalty, and steadfastness. Regardless of contrary evidence, opposition, or suffering, one may continue to give unswerving loyalty. This is the meaning of faithfulness—an act of willing and persevering devotion. The emotional quality of faith is indicated in a basic confidence and security that gives one assurance. In this sense faith is the opposite of fear, anxiety, and uncertainty. Without emotional security there is no relaxation, but tension, distress, and instability. Assurance is the firm emotional undertone that enables one to have steady nerves and calm poise in the face of danger or confusion.

Wieman gives a clarifying analysis of the use of belief in art, science, and religion. Art seeks to quicken vivid awareness of reality. Science seeks true knowledge about reality. But religious faith is a belief in the reality one lives by. Such faith uses belief to guide one's living so that the reality can enter more fully into all of one's activities. A belief is a faith not merely when it is accepted as true but when it determines what one shall live for and shapes the way of living.

A faith is a transforming and activating belief. Faith is belief controlling the viscera. It is belief become dynamic, functioning in life. It is belief which gives direction to a dominant loyalty. It is belief which gives us access to what we love and honor most. Religious faith is a belief which organizes and integrates our activities and hidden impulses, and connects them with an ongoing movement of life which reaches higher than we have yet explored.[22]

For this reason religious beliefs are more difficult to correct and criticize. They have grown into one's life and permeate one's whole manner of living. As the very existence of the family rests upon mutual love and faith in the beloved, so the entire manner of living is involved in religious faith. It is natural to identify faithfulness with unchanged beliefs. If a person is devoted to a religion he

[22] H. N. and R. W. Wieman, *Normative Psychology of Religion*, p. 127.

may come to hold his religious beliefs with all the tenacious force of his personality. In this way men become dogmatic and intolerant, defending beliefs against all evidence and critical attack as a matter of personal honor. In this mood of passionate devotion religious people may unknowingly support error and give their lives to a false cause. Religion is then discredited as falsehood by blind determination of its followers to be true to uncritical beliefs.

Static beliefs need to become dynamic, ready to change as new perspectives show the way to larger faith. They need to be tested and pruned by a loyalty too alert to accept a belief as true without inspection. Untested beliefs shut us out from true reality as Wieman shows:

They prevent us from seeking further.
They impair intellectual integrity by dividing loyalty.
They divert us from the most urgent and genuine problems of life.
They dazzle and befuddle us with a false mirage.
They cause disintegration of personality and make religion unstable.
They promote bigotry, persecution, and superstition.
They imprison the imagination.

On the other hand, beliefs that are constantly tested by observation and reason direct us toward reality in the following ways:

They keep us reaching out for more truth.
They make religion more vital and practical.
They make religion indestructible.
They unify religious devotion about that which is tested.
They make religion constructive rather than defensive.
They enable us to combine tolerance with zeal.
They make error a means to truth as a problem to solve.
They keep us true to the ancient faith of seeking and finding.
They make us critically conservative of the ancient heritage.[63]

In conclusion, we may note that faith has five productive functions making for human progress:

[63] Condensed from *ibid.*, pp. 125-26.

First, faith explores the unknown. It is customary to exalt the daring of explorers, who leave the comforts of settled and familiar backgrounds to venture forth into the unknown. Deeper understanding shows that this daring stems from faith, the fundamental trait of such personalities. Columbus persisted beyond his contemporaries because he had more faith. Galileo invented the telescope and challenged the authority of astronomical tradition by faith in his hypothesis. Lincoln challenged slavery and Wilson international discord by larger faith in freedom, peace, and justice. Faith in the undiscovered impels its discovery.

Second, trust creates values. Faith sees the invisible and forsees the not yet attained. Truth advances in every field by this power of the mind to see the invisible. Mathematicians construct laws and scientists fling out universal systems from their confidence in reason and the orderliness of reality. Business credit structures arise from mutual confidence in the intangible values of economic exchange. Governments maintain law and order by public confidence in mutual welfare. Civilization is the sum total of human values achieved by co-operation, mutual appreciation, and trust.

Third, creeds unite believers. This is a paradox, for creeds have also divided men into rival sects and denominations. But underlying the surface tensions of division are the deeper unities of common faith. Every social unity and co-operation rises from common beliefs. If we did not believe in the same values, we would not work together for them. If we did not trust each other, we would not dwell in peace and harmony as largely as we do. Creeds are not only religious; they are also political, economic, social, and scientific. But religious creeds are higher in cosmic perspective, and deeper in the tide of eternal destinies.

Fourth, assurance releases tensions. Tensions arise in seeking and striving to reach goals. These are dynamic springs of constructive achievement. Other tensions, such as fears and anxieties, are paralyzing and thwarting. These are destructive of peace, poise, and efficiency. They may become obsessive fixations or neurotic compulsions, leading to nervous disorders and mental diseases. There is no cure for these functional disorders short of faith. Without faith every other effort fails. Faith is an antidote, the specific condition essential to relaxation and to facilitation of normal functions.

Fifth, faithful devotion integrates personality. Devotion to a cause becomes a major purpose that gathers up all the energies of life and channels them into unified expression. Distractions of scattered interests and conflicts of contrary desires are integrated into whole-souled devotion. Faith in a religious way of life makes it worth every effort and sacrifice. Such faith in religious values transforms all values in reference to its standards. Actions are judged by their service to the religious cause. Desires are rejected or approved as they meet the requirements of the religious life. A center has been found whereby every impulse may be oriented in the direction of unselfish love and service. Nothing so integrates personality as faithful devotion to a cause, and no cause demands more faithfulness than a religious mission led by eternal imperatives.

VIII

Religious Behavior

1. UNCONSCIOUS MOTIVATION

Behavior is overt. What persons do in public is open to observation. Actions have objective effects in the space-time world that can be noted and described. But motives are covert. Why persons do what they do is their own business, not open to public observation. They belong to the secrets of private life, well kept and closely guarded by their owners. Motives may be hidden even from the one who obeys them. And yet without knowing these motives behavior cannot be understood.

The term "motive" is derived from the Latin *movere*, meaning "to move." It is related to "emotion"—derived from the Latin *e + movere*, "to move out" or "stir up." Motivation is therefore the process of arousing energies of personality leading to action. To understand religious behavior we need to investigate its motivation, that is, what causes people to act as they do, and what goals they move toward. "Any psychology that treats *motives* is called a dynamic psychology." [1] It goes beyond description of what to a bolder search for why. Various concepts have been employed: instincts, propensity, impulse, urge, drive, need, interest, desire, attitude, sentiment—each claiming to explain why we act as we do.

An older rational psychology may have viewed all human behaviour as directed by conscious choices. But motives are unconscious as well as conscious. The age of reason is yielding to a more comprehensive view of the complex forces, conscious and unconscious, that incite and inhibit action. And so intricate are the complexities of human nature that the chief danger in all interpretations is over-simplification. It might appear simple to

[1] Allport, *Personality: A Psychological Interpretation*, p. 192.

195

distinguish "conscious" from "unconscious," so obvious are the symptoms. Yet few words are used with less clarity than these.

J. G. Miller in a recent study [2] finds sixteen meanings of "unconscious" in current psychological writings. These meanings of "unconscious" as applied to an individual are:

1. Inanimate or subhuman.
2. Absent-minded, daydreaming, anesthetized, unresponsive to stimulation.
3. Not mental.
4. Undiscriminating.
5. Conditioned, acting sheerly on the basis of conditioning.
6. Unsensing: (a) stimuli not reaching organism; (b) inadequate stimuli affecting organism; (c) sensory tract incapable of conveying stimuli (d) subliminal stimuli affecting organism; (e) stimuli not reaching cortex (or the seat of "awareness" of the nervous system).
7. Unnoticing or unattending.
8. Insightless, lacking insight in the sense used by the *Gestalt* school of psychologists.
9. Unremembering.
10. Acting instinctively, behaving on an unlearned basis.
11. Unrecognizing.
12. Acting involuntarily.
13. Unable to communicate.
14. Ignoring.
15. Psychoanalytic meaning.
16. Unaware of discrimination.

Of all these views the most influential in our generation are the psychoanalytic interpretations of Freud and his associates. Sigmund Freud (1856–1939), physician and professor at University of Vienna, diagnosed nervous disorders by analysis of the emotional history of the patient.[3] Originally psychoanalysis re-

[2] *Unconsciousness* (New York: John Wiley & Sons, 1942), pp. 22-43.
[3] *The Basic Writings of Sigmund Freud*, ed. A. A. Brill (New York: Random House, Inc., 1938).

ferred to certain therapeutic methods; later it became a systematic theory of unconscious psychic processes in dynamic interplay of urging and checking forces.

The psychic life, according to Freud, is divided into unconscious, preconscious, and conscious activities. The "Unconscious" (Ucs) he considered to be the larger part of mental life, never conscious or else repressed from consciousness. Unconscious traits consist of nonmoral and asocial cravings of ego and sexuality, infantile and painful memories repressed as unacceptable to conscious standards. The "Preconscious" (Pcs) was his name for that part of the psychic life which may at any time become conscious. It consists of verbalized material, nearer consciousness and more accessible to voluntary control. The "Conscious" (Cs) is that fragmentary and fleeting part of the mental life of which the individual is aware at any moment. It consists of transitory impressions and ideas that are relatively less significant, Freud believed, in determining behavior.

More recently Freud offered another triple division of the mental life to classify the forces of personality: (*a*) The "Id" is the source of instinctive energy in each individual. It is the unconscious reservoir of the "libido" (psychic sex energy), aiming to gratify the pleasure principle and avoid pain. It is unmoral and illogical, with no unity of purpose or sense of time. (*b*) The "Ego" is a coherent organization of mental processes derived from the Id by interaction with the external world. It is partly conscious and partly unconscious, seeking to regulate personality by repression and sublimation. It strives to be reasonable and moral, to mediate between the world and the Id by submitting the pleasure principle to the reality principle. It goes to sleep but exercises censorship on dreams; it condenses, symbolizes, and rationalizes asocial motives to make them appear more acceptable. (*c*) The "Super-Ego" is the conscience, representing the permanent influence of parents and society in modifying the Ego and the Id. It is largely unconscious and inaccessible to the conscious Ego, yet its chief function is criticism creating a sense of guilt. It constitutes the higher nature of man, the ideals of parents and teachers as absorbed by the individual.

The energy of personality accumulates in tensions and attachments ("cathexes"). Libidinal energy may concentrate in ego-cathexis, becoming narcissism, or affectionate regard for one's own body. It may concentrate on objects, object-cathexis, directing motor striving outward to some person or thing. It may concentrate in a phantasy-cathexis, directing the libido toward the inner world of imagination (introversion). Ego cravings are often in conflict with social standards. Confronted by the reality principle of social requirements, yet unwilling to surrender the pleasure principle of ego satisfaction, the personality seeks compromise solutions by such defense mechanisms as repression, regression, reaction-formation, isolation, undoing, projection, introjection, turning against the self, reversal, and sublimation. The most notorious of these defenses is repression, the unconscious disposal of painful memories and unacceptable wishes. Yet there is confusion among psychoanalysts as to what forces do the repressing. Among the agents accused of repression are the "Censor," the Ego, the ego ideal, the Super-Ego, the ego instincts, the death instinct, fear, anxiety, the pleasure-pain principle, guilt feelings, self-esteem, the master sentiment of self-regard, and the sex instinct.

When the libidinal urges are fixated or frustrated as neuroses they disturb the normal functioning of personality and require therapeutic treatment. Diagnostic methods included hypnosis (rejected later), dream analysis, free association, analysis of resistances, mistakes and forgetting, exploring childhood incidents and emotions, translation of symbolism, interpretation of social relations (Oedipus complex), and ambivalent desires. Psychoanalytic therapy includes catharsis by confession, insight by bringing the unconscious complexes to conscious attention, and transference and sublimation by finding more acceptable modes of expression.

The pioneer work of Freud has been a target for criticism. In the early violence of psychoanalytic controversy one was either Freudian or anti-Freudian. Followers of Freud were apt to claim (as did mystics of their noetic experiences) that no one could understand Freud unless he had been converted and believed the whole gospel. The unconverted who rejected the teachings of Freud were unfortunately suffering from repressions that resisted and distorted the truth. Yet many of his most able associates have parted from him on major issues and taken their independent ways.

Recently two trends have appeared. Followers of Freud are critically alert to sift the true from the false in his theories. They employ clinical and experimental data to reopen conclusions for reconsideration and verification. They are free to accept in part and follow only what meets the test of continued investigation. Again, the influence of Freud is steadily gaining in psychological, medical, and social sciences. The extent to which unconscious factors bear upon health, character, and motives is ever more widely recognized. The effects of repression are increasingly evident upon memory, behavior, and nervous problems. The difficulties of voluntary control over these inner forces are more truly appraised, permitting more tolerant and wiser guidance of youth.

A fair evaluation of Freudian psychology will recognize his great contributions even while modifying them in truer understanding of personality:

a) He has shown the deeper possibilities of unconscious motivation. But he separates conscious from unconscious in artificial dualism. He sets all psychic forces in rigid pairs of final and fatalistic opposition. In reality consciousness is a degree of more or less awareness, and the forces of life co-ordinate far more than they conflict.

b) He makes a systematic analysis of psychic causation. Every mental effect has a mental cause; natural science operates in psychology. But Freud's mechanistic determinism is reductive, as Jung points out.[4] It tends to reduce everything to its own principle, which is primitive instinct. This oversimplification underestimates the complexity of human nature. It misses the creative efforts of goal-seeking purpose and decisive choice.

c) The influence of childhood experiences is well emphasized. But the tendency to reduce present problems to infantile frustrations is overworked. To Freud the past controls the present. Little new happens after the age of five—only repetitions, fixations, and regressions. Is life so helpless and the present so unreal?

d) He takes a dynamic view of motives arising from emotional forces. But he reduces these drives to instincts of sex and death. The person is a passive victim of biological fatalism. The Ego is caught helplessly in the play of these conflicting forces. How can this be a truly dynamic psychology? Freud was a student of the pathological, and his view of the Ego is a neurotic one. Such an Ego is a phony self, as Horney says,[5] and not the real self of normal people who use judgment and will effectively.

e) Freud reveals the workings of neurotic anxiety. But he extends neurotic trends to all people indiscriminately, and overemphasizes the pathological aspects of life. He naïvely assumes cultural uniformity and seems to believe that what he found in Vienna is true everywhere. To him art, morality, religion, and civilization are the unstable product of neurotic motives.

f) He provides the basic methodological tools for psychotherapy. But his therapeutic goal is too negative in seeking freedom only from specific symptoms. A more positive goal is needed, that there may also be freedom to develop one's potentialities. A deeper personal change than Freud attempted is required to release the full powers of personality. Courage is needed to be one's self, and to take a larger part in interpersonal achievements. The individual is not

[4] *Psychological Types*, p. 577.
[5] *Self-Analysis* (New York: W. W. Norton & Co., 1942), p. 23. See also her *New Ways of Psychoanalysis* (Norton, 1939) for a thoroughgoing criticism.

forever set against society as an enemy to outwit; it is rather a sponsoring fellowship whose values are shared.

g) Freud seeks to free the person from repression and regression. But he fails to see how this requires the acceptance of responsibility. His method of authority and transference invites the patient to a dependent role, in which he transfers affection and responsibility to the physician. But no freedom is possible until a person accepts responsibility for himself and his own problems. Neither does Freud see the value of social responsibility. "Why should I love my neighbor?" This attitude of social irresponsibility Adler considered antisocial, and a serious threat to moral progress. The Freudian Unconscious relieves the individual of responsibility by causal determinism. But evading responsibility is the neurotic pattern and does not win the freedom desired.

h) Freud appears to reify abstract nouns into metaphysical realities. His constant use of Unconscious (with the capital *U*) seems to deify a mystery as the supreme power determining the destiny of helpless creatures. A negative concept is lifted to omnipotence as a substitute for God, and saves the individual from responsibility.[6] Freud's personifying of psychic forces is almost equivalent to devil-possession. Id, Ego, and Super-Ego struggle in plots and counterplots as rival demonic powers within the secret recesses of their victim. In dreams he refers to an anthropomorphic Censor as standing guard over wishes seeking expression. This treating of the concrete abstractly and the abstract as if it were concrete is obscure.

There are psychologists who challenge the introspective data so glibly drawn from unconscious depths. Freud's claims are not proved scientifically, but merely supported by illustration. He scorns statistics and experiment, gleaning his intuitions from private confessions, dreams, and mythology. There is reason to question the empirical basis of Freud's vast knowledge of "the un-

[6] See Otto Rank, *Will Therapy,* tr. J. Taft (New York: Alfred A. Knopf, 1936), p. 41.

knowable." His elaborate theories exceed the facts, and often control the data.

In spite of these aberrations the Freudian psychology is bringing a new understanding of personality. Modified and corrected by the significant work of Adler, Jung, Rank, Horney, Fromm, and other depth psychologists, it is influencing what man thinks of man. Religious psychology is coming to appreciate these viewpoints. Clinical training in hospitals is provided for theological students under the joint supervision of chaplains and psychiatrists. Doctors, psychologists, and clergymen are co-operating increasingly in clinics, institutions, and parishes to understand and help individuals adjust personality problems. Ministers are counseling persons of all ages more skillfully as they come to employ the insights of clinical psychology in pastoral care. Preaching and religious education become practically helpful in a deeper sense as the forces of unconscious motivation are better understood.[7]

Extravagant claims that a mysterious subconsciousness is the savior or the denier of religion are discounted by sober judgment. Psychologists today are more cautious than William James, who saw the subconscious as the open door where God approaches man in mystical experiences,[8] or Freudians who disposed of God as nothing but the irrational projection of a father complex.[9] Studies of unconscious motivation are proving a valuable resource for the psychological understanding of religious behavior, demonstrating:

1. The rise of religious impulses in the deepest needs of the psychic life.
2. The power of religious motives to influence action.
3. The importance and persistence of early religious experiences.

---

[7] See Rollo May, *The Art of Counseling* (New York and Nashville: Abingdon-Cokesbury Press, 1939), and K. R. Stolz, *The Church and Psychotherapy* (New York and Nashville: Abingdon-Cokesbury Press, 1943).

[8] *The Varieties of Religious Experience*, pp. 507-19.

[9] See *Totem and Taboo*, in *The Basic Writings of Sigmund Freud*, pp. 807-930; and Sigmund Freud, *Moses and Monotheism*, tr. K. Jones (New York: Alfred A. Knopf, 1939). Freud bases his theory on the doubtful assumption of a racial memory, biologically inherited, of a primeval father murdered and deified.

4. The value of symbolism in religious education and worship.
5. The need for wholesome attitudes and positive suggestion to maintain emotional stability.
6. The psychological advantages of prayer and meditation in achieving integration.
7. The need for confession, transference, and sublimation of repressed complexes.
8. The therapeutic value of faith and love.

2. RELIGIOUS CONDUCT

In this topic we come to the most practical problem of religious living. Religion may be respected for its noble ideals, long history, and impressive institutions. But does it work? How does religion affect conduct? Does religious instruction make children honest? Do chapel exercises in college make less cheating in examinations? Does church membership increase socal justice and economic equality? Can you tell a Christian, Hindu, or Moslem by the way he acts? The most urgent question asked of religious people is, What are you going to do about this? The crucial test of religion is the test of conduct. "One hour of justice is worth more than seventy years of prayer," said Mohammed. "He that would wait upon me, let him wait upon the sick brethren," said Buddha. "Inasmuch as ye have done it unto one of the least of these my brethren, ye have done it unto me," said Jesus. As the experimental test is to science, so is the test of conduct in demonstrating the genuineness of religion.

Conduct is voluntary behavior. This is the field of ethics, in which one is responsible for what he is able to control by conscious choice. It is the meeting point of ethics and religion, where one does good from religious motives, and religious motives produce good works. How shall we know what behavior is religious? Two answers are given: (*a*) "By their fruits ye shall know them." [10] This is the test of action, looking toward the ends or consequences

[10] Matt. 7:20.

to see what the effects are. Surely these are not to be ignored, but religious acts are confusing to behold. For what deed has not been done in the name of religion? The variety of religious acts is almost infinite and the contradictions are quite perplexing. Acts that are criminal in other circumstances—for example, murder, prostitution—may be sanctioned by religious authority. Or the same act—for example, giving alms—may be done for either religious or secular motives. So we turn to motives. (*b*) By their motives you shall know them. No act is meaningful until the motive is comprehended. Deeds of service may be grudgingly given under compulsion of slavery, or shrewdly offered for economic gain, or cleverly displayed for political power. In contrast to these, religious service is cheerfully volunteered for the sake of others to please God and satisfy ideal imperatives. It is the motive that makes the essential difference and governs the quality of the deed. And effects of conduct are different, likewise, because motives so direct them.

Religious motivation is that which incites to religious conduct. Religion has been defined as response to a Sustainer of Values. Whatever attitude recognizes a power able to control value is a religious motive in the general sense. Religion was again defined in a differential sense as personal co-operation with a trusted Creator of Values.[11] Whatever action aims to co-operate with a trusted Creator of Values is religious conduct. It is evident that religious conduct may be either ethical or unethical, whether judged by formal standards of intention or utilitarian standards of effect. It is further evident that the nature of religious conduct depends largely upon one's idea of God (Sustainer and Creator of Values), what his purposes are thought to be, and what he expects of mortals.

At primitive religious levels fear of punishment and hope of reward are conscious motives. Natural evils such as famine, flood,

[11] See Chapter I above.

barren womb, illness, misfortune, or failure in enterprise are seen as intended by angry spirits for spite or corrective punishment. If the deity is capricious, he must be appeased; if he is moral, then man must repent of his sins and mend his ways. Beyond the vicissitudes of this life loom the mysteries of death with prospects of torture in hell and reward in heaven.

Other motives that come to have enlarging appeal are social approval, ideal imperatives, and loving devotion. Social influences operate constantly in human relations by example and imitation. The tendency to follow the crowd and do as others do is almost irresistible. It is odd to be different and lonely to stand aloof; man hungers for the unity and solidarity of association. The Soviet Union has demonstrated the strength of social approval as greater than economic motive, while in other nations patriotic devotion is a cause for which men live and die. The approval of the religious community, whether primitive or modern, is always to be reckoned with.

And yet heroic nonconformists like Jesus, Socrates, Spinoza, and Luther will accept excommunication and death for an imperative ideal. They prove that ideal motives can outreach fear of punishment, hope of reward, or social approval. This sense of duty is conscience, no fractional part of the self, but the whole mind in the act of moral judgment.[12] Conscience has been taken as the voice of God, and again as the voice of the crowd. Yet the independent conscience is an inner authority, often revolting against the established codes and creeds of the crowd. In this way social, moral, and religious progress comes. Conscience is no wiser than its owner. Yet it is capable of growth through education. A growing conscience utilizes all the resources of social tradition and moral custom, the teaching of scripture, the advice of friends, the mis-

---

[12] See Johnson, *Who Are You?* pp. 39-63; and I. G. Whitchurch, *An Enlightened Conscience* (New York: Harper & Bros., 1941), pp. 141-43. Whitchurch says, "Conscience makes up an integral part of a whole personality. . . . It participates in the limitations and growing integrity of the self as a whole."

takes of the past, the lessons of history, the logic of events, and the revelations of divine purpose.

Is it possible for religion to be overconscientious? That depends upon the conscience. An ignorant, superstitious, fear-ridden conscience may be the undoing of a neurotic victim of anxiety. A misguided, intolerant, persecuting conscience can do great damage, as the history of inquisitions, witch-burning, and anti-Semitism shows. Conscience operates with high-voltage dynamics, not to be recklessly used. The power of human motives is potentially charged for good or evil, but we do not fail to employ electricity or conscience because they are dangerous.

Christianity is a religion of duty. This is the essential nature of any religion worth having. A religion or a life without obligation is most dangerous. It flies to emotional excesses and riotous passion. Immanuel Kant defined religion as "the recognition of all duties as divine commands." [13] Every valid experience has imperatives. The imperative in science is the demand for coherent truth. The imperative in religion is co-operation with divine commands for the sake of human values. Duty is the essence of abiding meaning and purpose in life. Pleasure is a tramp whose transient, fleeting experience is inherently unstable and dissatisfying in relation to the desired future or remembered past. Loyalty to a larger cause is the unifier of all values uniting the divided self, binding many selves into a community, and giving consistent direction to life.[14]

Loyalty followed wholeheartedly comes to the devotion of love. The duty which Kant advocated so rigorously was the antithesis of desire. There are situations in which duty conflicts with desire, but that is not the whole story; for the conscientious person desires to do his duty, and duties often coincide with desires. The eating of nourishing food is at once a duty and a pleasure. Love

[13] *Religion Within the Limits of Reason Alone*, tr. T. M. Greene and H. H. Hudson (Chicago: Open Court Publishing Co., 1934), p. 142. [German ed., 1793.]

[14] See Josiah Royce, *The Philosophy of Loyalty* (New York: The Macmillan Co., 1908), and P. E. Johnson, "Is Loyalty Enough?" *The Personalist*, XXV (1944), 144-53.

is the supreme example of desire merging with duty. The love of a mother for her child makes every care a delight. The love of a husband for his wife is a passion of desiring completely to fulfill his duty. Love of God rises to the height of devotion in a surrender of self-will to divine will and of selfish concerns to the good of others. Love has the power to awaken desire, making the unlovely lovable and devotion eternal. While duty may go stale, the creative emotional resources of love renew joy and purpose ever again. Religious conduct motivated by love holds true in faithful devotion otherwise impossible.

Every conscious motive comes to focus upon action. Fears and hopes point to acts of punishment and reward. Social approval is a mutual program of action agreed upon as desirable. Duties are imperatives, and love is devotion to serve a desirable cause. These and other motives intermingle in the complex network of interests, desires, and purposes. Purity of motive is often lauded as if superior to mixed motives. But all motives are mixed; the only purity is not simplicity but harmony of many co-ordinating motives in symphonic chords of ongoing purpose. Motives are interpersonal. They arise from and lead to social interaction.

Goals are the crucial factors in human motivation. If one sees nothing worth striving for, he will give up the effort. Motives strike out from desires. They are tensions goalward that release energies in direct action. But desires are not determined by innate instincts or mechanical chains of cosmic causation. At least we have no empirical knowledge of mysterious forces pushing from behind. What we know from experience is the pull of goals. We see objects of interest and want them. We feel needs for specific values and go after them. We face alternatives and choose this goal instead of that. There are surely limits to the range of choice. No one can have everything he wants. Yet within these limits we are consciously choosing all the time. No psychology can make sense of human behavior, or follow motives, without noting preferences and choices. Determinism is determination and destiny is destination. Conduct is directed by motives, and motives are controlled by goals at which we decide to aim. The final cause, as Aristotle saw, is purpose. However it may be in the world at large, this is psychologically true for persons and societies. We are what we are moving toward. Religious conduct is action along the line of religious purpose.

3. CHARACTER AND RELIGIOUS EDUCATION

For a century the hopes of mankind have been invested in education. In one country after another educational reforms have gained momentum until better education for all is the accepted goal. Education has been trusted as a panacea for illiteracy, ignorance, error, ill health, and most of the other ills of persons and society. Education has become a major business of local and national governments, whether democratic or totalitarian. Propaganda and advertising have so cleverly utilized educational facilities that whole populations believe what they are told. Human nature is viewed as pliable clay in the hands of educators, who can shape it as they choose for good or for diabolical ends.

When public education was established in the American way, there was general belief in the separation of church and state to avoid the control of either by the other. To avoid doctrinal controversies religion has largely been excluded from public schools, and character education has also been neglected in the emphasis on scientific methods and secular interests. To correct this oversight our generation has promoted religious education in churches and character education in recreational organizations such as the Y.M.C.A. and Y.W.C.A., Boy Scouts, Girl Scouts, Campfire Girls, clubs, camps, and such. Recently public schools have sought to co-operate by releasing one or two hours of school time a week for religious education, or by fostering character interests in extra-curricular activities.

How effective is this education in promoting character and religious values? Attempts have been made to appraise our current educational practices. The most notable of these investigations is the extensive work of the Character Education Inquiry, directed by Hugh Hartshorne and Mark A. May. With commendable thoroughness and scientific objectivity forty-one tests of deception were constructed and administered to eleven thousand school pupils, aged eight to sixteen, ranging from the fourth grade through high school. Three types of deception were tested: cheating, lying, and stealing. Concrete tasks provided twenty-two opportunities to cheat in classroom work, four in athletics, two in party games, and one in homework. Lying tests consisted of thirty-six questions in one case and ten in the other which could be answered falsely. Stealing tests offered two opportunities to steal money and one to steal articles.

Conclusions drawn from statistical treatment of the data are as follows: [5]

1. Older pupils are slightly more deceptive.
2. Sex seems to make no difference.
3. Honesty is positively related to intelligence.
4. Emotional instability is related to deception.
5. Physical condition seems to have no effect on deception.
6. Members of higher-income families show less deceit.
7. Those with better manners and cultural background show less deceit.
8. Deceit is associated with other home conditions, as parental discord, example, bad discipline, unsocial attitudes, poverty, and changing socio-economic status.
9. Religious affiliation shows no general differences not attributable to social and intellectual level.
10. Kinship means similarity.
11. Differences in school grade are not significant, except that retarded children cheat more.

[25] Hartshorne and May, *Studies in Deceit* (New York: The Macmillan Co., 1928), pp. 408-14. An exhaustive study by C. F. Chassell, *The Relation Between Morality and Intellect* (New York: Columbia University, 1935), incorporating the findings of 300 other studies, concludes that correlation in restricted groups is extremely variable, and as low as .10 to .39.

12. Those who get high marks in classes cheat slightly less.
13. Those who are good in deportment cheat less.
14. Associates are much alike in cheating.
15. Those who show greater resistance to suggestion cheat less.
16. Children who attend movies more often cheat more.
17. There is less cheating when teacher-pupil relations are cordial.
18. Students in progressive schools cheat less.
19. Those enrolled in Sunday school cheat less. But those who attend Sunday school regularly cheat as much as those who rarely or never attend.
20. Members of character organizations cheat as much as nonmembers.
21. Deceit is not a unified trait. Honesty is a specific function of specific situations.

The concomitants of deceit are, in order of importance: (*a*) classroom association; (*b*) general personal handicaps, as low intelligence, poor resistance to suggestion, emotional instability; (*c*) cultural and social limitations in the home background.

Implications of these studies in deceit are: (*a*) No child is dishonest by nature, but merely as a mode of adjustment. Upon this there is general agreement. (*b*) Urging honest behavior or discussing ideals of honesty has no necessary relation to honest conduct. Such methods are variable and overrated, yet discussion may prove an aid to desirable conduct. (*c*) Prevailing methods of teaching ideals do little good. This inference is taken from the low correlation between membership in character organizations and the practice of honesty. Those who attend Sunday school regularly make no better showing than those who do not. Better methods of education are urgently needed. (*d*) The specific situation holds large influence. Teaching vague generalities and abstract concepts is futile. Honesty in one situation (as telling mother the truth) may not transfer to another situation (as telling a policeman the truth about the speed of driving, or telling one's age correctly when it is disadvantageous to do so). Honesty in paying a debt to a friend may not transfer to returning over-change pennies from a stranger in a crowded store. Unless teaching comes to specific situations with effective motivation and practice, ideals are remote from actual conduct.

It would be hasty to conclude, however, that persons have no general traits or attitudes to carry over from one situation to another. Allport[16] shows the significance of traits in personality and replies cogently to Hartshorne, May, and other exponents of specificity: (*a*) Low correlations "prove only that children are not consistent *in the same way,* not that they are inconsistent with themselves." They do not all have the same trait, but each does have his own traits. (*b*) The research is based upon artificial ethical concepts—from the point of view of society rather than the actual mental organization of the individual. (*c*) Socialized traits are not to be found in younger children so much as in older persons who have assimilated prevalent ideals gradually through years of social adjustment. (*d*) While the coefficients of correlation are low, yet it is notable that they are positive, and that twenty-three of the tests intercorrelate $+.30$ on the average. Complex statistical results are inevitably ambiguous. From the same data Maller, one of the associates in the study, reports a general factor of character, "c," readiness to forgo immediate gain for the sake of remote but greater gain. (*e*) Conclusions naturally depend on methods used, and others using different methods may find consistent general traits of honesty and deceit.

The net outcome of such studies is to startle us awake to the need for clearer understanding of psychological principles and better methods in character and religious education. No one can blink away these facts or be complacent in the face of these studies, which conclude:

There is little evidence that effectively organized moral education has been taking place. There is abundant evidence, however, that children have been acquiring habits which are important for character. . . . What

[16] *Personality: A Psychological Interpretation,* pp. 248-58.

they are learning at present of self-control, as also of service and honesty, is largely a matter of accident. Anarchy in the leadership of moral education is not likely to produce order in the character of the child.[17]

Further investigation and experimentation are needed to develop a program that achieves desired results in religious and ethical conduct. Constructive suggestions may be taken from these studies in planning a more adequate education:

1. What is to be learned must be experienced.
2. What is to be experienced must be represented in the situations to which children are exposed.
3. These situations must be opportunities to pursue interests which lead to the conduct desired.
4. This conduct must be carried on in relation to the particular situations.
5. A common and potent factor in such situations is the established practice and code of the group.
6. Standards and ideals . . . must be tools rather than objects of aesthetic appreciation.
7. The achievement of specific standards, attitudes, and modes of conduct does not imply their integration. Integration is itself a specific achievement.[18]

Civilization has been described as a race between education and catastrophe. In this crucial hour of history the race appears frantic. Catastrophe has already overtaken millions of our contemporaries in war and revolution. The revolutionary surge of these events provides no time for leisurely consideration of distant reforms. It demands an immediate program of social reconstruction in which education will be related to clearly defined goals of social and personal attainment. And yet in the welter of emergency measures there is danger of losing true perspective and doing the wrong

[17] Hartshorne and Maller, *Studies in Service and Self-Control* (New York: The Macmillan Co., 1929), p. 453.
[18] *Ibid*, p. 454.

things too efficiently. In other desperate hours of history notable progress has been won by seeing clearly true goals and choosing the right methods to achieve them. Grundtvig in Denmark and Pestalozzi in Switzerland led their people in educational reforms that created a democratic society where it was possible to develop and share true values for all.

Within the next five years we will know whether religion will survive as a great dynamic power or become weak and an outcast in the catacombs of earth. It can survive only if it helps to build the better new world order which must come into being . . . years after this war.[19]

These are the words of Reinhold Schairer, an educator influential in prewar Germany, recently working with British and American committees on educational reconstruction. He finds the most urgent need of today to be a world-wide educational program whereby the human character essential to a better world order can be developed. An efficient system of education must be truly democratic in structure and aims, utilizing the resources of family, community, religion, state, and international organization to reconstruct society at large. Such an educational program, he reports, has already been started in the underground movements of occupied countries, where leadership is being tested in the crucibles of persecution and suffering. Hitlerism can be overcome only by a stronger movement of passionate convictions, clear-eyed vision, and educational organization to spread it throughout the earth. This movement Schairer finds in democracy, now tried out locally here and there, and needing to become world democracy as a way of abundant life for and by all peoples. To accomplish this an international charter of education is proposed, and an International Education Office to co-ordinate and implement the writing of textbooks, the conduct of schools, and the stimulating of human awakenings in every land.

[19] Reinhold Schairer, "Human Character and World Order," in *Christian Bases of World Order* (New York: Abingdon-Cokesbury Press, 1943), pp. 217-18.

4. SIN AND GUILT

What is sin? Is it a sin to break a promise or tell a lie? Is it a sin to break a traffic rule? Is it a sin to ignore the rights of others? Strictly speaking, sin is a religious problem. It is related to other offenses such as crime, immorality, and selfishness. To avoid confusion it is well to see these relations clearly. Crime is antilegal behavior, an offense against the civil law. Immorality is antimoral conduct, flouting the moral code of accepted ideals and customs. Selfishness is antisocial behavior, disregarding the good of one's fellow men. Sin is distinctly antireligious conduct, contrary to the order of religious values. Not all offenses are sins, nor all sins public offenses. Any selfish, immoral, or criminal act may be a sin, but not for social, moral, or legal reasons. To those who believe in a God of moral law, a sin is any act or attitude that violates the law of God.[20]

Does this mean that atheists are incapable of sin? Atheists may be unconscious of sin, yet their disbelief in God does not dispense with the realities of the situation. The cosmic realities are questions for philosophy and theology. Psychology is concerned with the consciousness of sin and guilt. Yet from the psychological standpoint it is evident that guilt does not always coincide with awareness of guilt. Ignorance of the law does not excuse one from the penalty in courts of justice. Nor does ignorance of natural laws save one from unforeseen consequences. An innocent child who has not heard of the law of gravitation does not escape the results of falling from a window to the pavement below. The human experience which psychology studies is engaged in causal relations with realities which affect the nature of that experience. Whatever we think about sin is therefore a product of experience and reality.

How do human ideas of sin arise? First of all, from personal

[20] "Sin is disloyalty to God," says Wieman, *Normative Psychology of Religion*, p. 148. See also A. C. Knudson, *The Doctrine of Redemption* (New York and Nashville: Abingdon Cokesbury Press, 1933), pp. 239-70.

experiments and their consequences. Life is a series of experiments in which every organism acts and observes reactions. Some acts bring favorable results; others bring unfavorable results. Adventures in tasting foods result in bitter or sweet flavors, satisfying nourishment or distressing poison. Social experiments in approaching, threatening, persuading, attacking, or aiding other persons produce results that are viewed as desirable or undesirable. By such trials and errors individuals come to distinguish good from evil consequences, as reactions to good or evil deeds. The good so demonstrated wins social approval.

At this point in experimental learning, a second factor is the sense of personal responsibility. After numerous causal experiments, every evil may be taken as the result of some act or failure to act. "What have I done to bring this evil upon me?" Seeking to find the causes of evils like sickness, misfortune, or defeat, one may find the cause in himself. To find one's self personally responsible for evil is to feel guilty. The fault may have been ritual neglect, or it may have been a moral failure to do what one knew to be right. In a religious sense this personal guilt is viewed as sin in offending divine purpose. "Against thee, thee only, have I sinned." [21]

A third factor in the awareness of sin is the recognition of free choice. Personal responsibility implies voluntary choice in which one may do either this or that. If one has no choice in the matter how can he be responsible? The Hebrew consciousness of sin arose from this sense of ethical freedom. Under the stirring preaching of the prophets and the zealous devotion of priests to the law of God all evil became moral evil. Every man was accounted free to choose good or evil; consequently every one was responsible for his own evils. If Job suffered, he must have sinned; if Israel prospered, God must have been pleased.

A fourth factor in the experience of sin is the feeling of neces-

[21] Ps. 51:4.

sity. The undeserved sufferings of Job and Prometheus, Socrates and Jesus, have the note of sincerity. They represent the unjust ills of mankind, struggling from age to age against cruel necessities. The Greeks call this inescapable destiny "fate"; the Hindus name it "karma." The doctrine of karma, as developed by Hindus and Buddhists, was a law of inheritance whereby the consequences of past deeds carry over from birth to rebirth on the wheel of existence. The Christian doctrine of original sin emphasizes this necessity by which evil besets every life from the first man to the latest child. The tendency of the person to error and evil is further complicated by social evils that infect and obstruct human progress.

The idea of sin reveals the level of religious development. Lack of awareness of sin indicates lack of religious experience. Dull response to religious values suggests lack of interest and appreciation. Primitive ideas of sin mistake the trivial for the significant. Taboos may be based on ignorance and superstition. Magic and ritual often take precedence over ethical considerations of justice and mercy. To fulfill higher religious laws Jesus and the prophets set aside ceremonial requirements. Later ideas of sin show moral awakening and better understanding of true values. A growing consciousness of sin means clearer insight and more intelligent devotion to ethical progress.

In our time the sense of sin appears to be declining, and many moderns welcome the decline. There are psychologists who consider the feeling of sin an abnormal, unhealthy, morbid condition. There are sociologists who regard fear of sin as a social lag where old taboos no longer apply to new conditions. There are religious modernists who look upon theologies of sin as medieval concepts, not pertinent today. The conclusion is that sin is our own bad thinking, worry and fret over a past already gone. They advocate forgetting it and insist we will be all right if we think we are.

The sense of guilt is a serious psychological problem. It is the accusative personal and interpersonal sense of failure. Under stress

216

of it neurotic patterns may develop—anxieties and fears, rejecting one's self, evasion of responsibility in projection and repression, or defensive attitudes of aggression and compulsion. The burden of guilt is hard to bear, and suffering minds are not easily relieved of these tensions. If guilt feelings become a threat to health, a disturbing factor in personality, would it not be better, we are asked, to give up the idea of sin? Why should religious teachers and preachers encourage this uncomfortable feeling of guilt? Five answers to this question need to be considered.

a) Guilt feeling is a normal psychological experience. It is one of the natural tensions between psychic energy and goal, even as interest, need, desire, purpose, hope, or affection.[22] All conative urges goalward face the risk of not reaching their goal. The sense of failure to reach a goal is equivalent to a sense of guilt. Life might be more comfortable without tensions of striving and failing, but the tensions keep us going in normal efforts to reach goals.

b) Guilt feeling is inherent in ethical progress. Ethical awareness is recognizing an ideal as imperative. Ethical progress is working and growing toward ideals. Without guilt as a feeling of personal failure, or as a sense of urgency to do better, there is no imperative progress. Admitting inadequacies is inseparable from striving more adequately.

c) Guilt feeling is conducive to progress in social welfare. The welfare of society depends upon the willingness of its members to work for each other. Social justice rests upon the responsibility of each for all and all for each. The sense of guilt is recognition of personal responsibility, the feeling of shame in not doing one's share, and the sense of obligation to maintain the rights of others. The best servant of society is the conscientious person who knows and cares enough to do his duty for the common good.

---

[22] "Guilt feeling is actually a positive, constructive emotion. It is a perception of the difference between what a thing is and what it ought to be."—Rollo May, *The Art of Counseling*, p. 70.

d) Sinless religion is deceptive. It deceives all who think it makes no difference what one believes or does. It brings confusion of truth and error, good and evil, not recognizing the distinction between values and disvalues. If religion is the search for divine good, it matters supremely whether one is achieving good or evil. With lack of concern about sin there is failure to define, to declare, and to realize values.[23] A false complacency of careless neutrality is the nadir of religious deception.

e) Sinless religion is destructive. Refusal to distinguish good from bad destroys moral distinctions and undermines all values. Without this sense of urgency religion becomes useless and worthless, without interest for or command over human life.

5. CONFESSION AND FORGIVENESS

The problem of sin is not yet untangled. Guilt feeling is a disturbing factor in personality; yet it is inherent in normal persons and societies, and it is essential to ethical progress and religious achievement of values. It is a painful blessing—dangerous to have and fatal to be without. Like electricity, it is a dynamic current whose high-tension potentiality is not foolproof. When properly used it has manifold advantages; when misused it may have serious complications. Electricity must have an outlet; if denied an outlet, it will force its way by burning or shattering all opposition. Guilt feeling is like that—when denied an outlet it creates havoc in the personality that resists it. Yet its dynamic power may create values when it finds outlets to constructive action.

Repentance is the first outlet for guilt feeling. This is not the same as remorse. "Remorse looks to the past with no feeling beyond

---

[23] "This is a tremendous truth: The sense of guilt is altogether wholesome and noble when it arises from the depth and breadth of a man's appreciation of values. It comes not from the poverty of life and its possibilities, but exactly from the opposite. It springs from the realization of what might be and ought to be."—Wieman, *op. cit.*, p. 155.

one of vain regret, repentance looks to the future with hope." [24] Remorse is a sense of hopeless frustration that adds to the fixation of guilt. Repentance is a change of heart, attitude, and purpose. It works from within outward, and so dissolves resistance from the very center of the guilt complex. To repent is to stop denying and evading the guilt, to give up the resistance that prevents the cure, and to admit freely the evil one has done. Acceptance of personal responsibility releases the neurotic tensions of evasive repression and defiant self-defense. Acceptance brings welcome relief in honesty that ends the uncertainty and indecision of conflicting impulses. Without this basic inner release of genuine repentance, of acceptance of the blame and desire for a new start, there can be no freedom from anxious remorse.

Confession is a second outlet for guilt feeling. As long as a sin is secret it must be concealed, repressed, and guarded. The neurotic tensions play around evasion and defense. Confession is therefore cathartic, purging and releasing the pent-up guilty tensions into open expression. To talk aloud is to expel and cast out evil, to deliver it into the keeping of others, whose hearing verifies and acknowledges the declaration. To talk with another about one's anxieties is to objectify them, to detach them from secret inner rootage and hold them out in public view as separate from the self who surrenders them. Confession is vital to religious health. It cures the spreading disease of disloyalty and dishonesty.[25] Confession of sin is a way of deliverance from sin.

Forgiveness is a third outlet for guilt feeling. Tensions of guilt arise in interpersonal relations. Crime produces guilt in reference to the civil body and its legal authorities. Selfishness and immorality infect with guilt one's social obligations. Sin impairs one's relationships to God and the value system that constitutes religion.

[24] W. B. Selbie, *The Psychology of Religion* (Oxford: Clarendon Press, 1924), p. 236.
[25] See Wieman, *op. cit.*, p. 156; C. T. Holman, *The Religion of a Healthy Mind* (New York: Round Table Press, Inc., 1939), p. 121; and C. G. Jung, *Modern Man in Search of a Soul* (New York: Harcourt, Brace & Co., 1934), p. 39.

In each of these relations the wrong needs to be righted in reference to others. And the guilt is not erased until the wrong is forgiven. Forgiveness is therefore a social achievement in restoring broken relations to harmony. Until another forgives, one is not at liberty to forgive himself. If he has done his best to win forgiveness, his conscience may be clear, but his social relations have not yet been restored. To the religious mind the final release from guilt is confession to God and forgiveness by God. When this cosmic harmony is attained, men may misjudge and persecute in vain; a deeper security of divine approval is able to withstand the surface ripples of hostile injustice.

Reparation is a fourth outlet for guilt feeling. No emotion is adequately expressed until it finds release in appropriate action. Reparation is the act of making amends for a wrong or injury. It is not to be confused with retaliation. To return evil for evil in revenge and reprisal, is a frequent outlet for emotions of injured pride and anger. But here is no cure for guilt, only additional wrongs to be forgiven. Two wrongs cannot make a right, or justice either; for reprisals are bound to add an extra punch for good measure, and getting even is impossible by this method. True reparation is a voluntary desire to overcome evil with good. The act of making restitution for injury is a demonstration of sincere repentance, a public confession of one's desire to right a wrong. It therefore carries emotions and decisions into effective action, overcoming the frustration of remorse and inertia with constructive repair.

From this analysis the conclusion is clear. The essence of religious co-operation is loyalty to the divine cause of creating and maintaining values. Sin, as disloyalty to God and true values, is the defeat of religious goals. The sense of guilt is admission of personal responsibility for failures and the feeling that something must be done to make them right. A clear view of goals, a sensitive conscience, an urgent desire to achieve values more adequately, are dynamic factors in religious, ethical, and social progress.

Guilt tensions are therefore crucial in human success. If they are ignored in careless indifference, the nerve of effort is paralyzed. If they are resisted by evasive and defensive attitudes, neurotic complications undermine efficiency. But if these guilt tensions are honestly faced and carried through to social reparation, they promote the health and wholeness of personality.

Religious behavior springs from conscious and unconscious motivation. Tensions of need and desire pull life toward goals. Guilt feeling arises in the sense of failure to attain such goals. Ideal values will become specific goals as education becomes more effective and attractive in concrete life situations. Confession and forgiveness, counseling and comradeship, are therapeutic values that arise in religious association.

IX

Normal Personality

1. What Is Normal?

Normality is the deep concern of all who desire true success in any human enterprise. For success is the achievement of true rather than false values. To know true from false values requires a standard. And standards are norms by which values are judged. Norm is a word derived from the Latin *norma,* meaning a "carpenter's square," "rule," "pattern"—which perhaps came from the Greek *gnorimos,* meaning "well known." A norm is therefore a recognized standard, and normal means agreeing with an accepted standard.

Everyone may desire normality, but not everyone knows what is normal. There is no little confusion and very little agreement upon standards of human value. The United States Bureau of Standards maintains authoritative standards of physical weights and measures. But psychical values are not standardized to the acceptance of all. Some people use one norm, some another. Language is deceptive to those who assume that one word means one thing. Words have multiple meanings. There are three current uses of the concept "normal."

The first use of normal is to indicate an *average* standard. In this sense the normal experience is the common one, the usual and customary, the prevalent and popular. The statistical norm is the average or mean between extremes. R. C. Cattell [1] finds psychological measurement of three kinds: (*a*) "normative," which makes the group the standard; (*b*) "ipsative," which takes the individual as the standard; and (*c*) "interactive," which standardizes the interaction of the individual and his environment. The

[1] "Psychological Measurement: Normative, Ipsative, Interactive," *Psychological Review,* LI (1944), 292-303.

first of these is normative in the sense of what is average for the group. Whatever differs from the average is abnormal, different, and, consequently, subject to suspicion or ridicule. In social comparison it is natural to feel different, but neurotics fear being different. In seeking to avoid difference they merge into the protective group to appear normal. Yet the neurotic fear of being different lacks the stability to be actually normal.

A second use of normal points to a standard of *efficiency*. A heart is normal when functioning well, a workman when he carries on his work with precision and productivity. Karen Horney defines a normal person as one who gets along efficiently in his daily responsibilities and whose handicaps do not interfere with his success.[2] This is the pragmatic standard of practical working success. It is widely employed in industry, business, the professions, health, and social welfare. This coincides with Cattell's third standard of interactive behavior. Efficiency is the interpersonal success of an individual in reference to his social environment. The interactive norm is dynamic, meaningful, and useful in prediction or adjustment.

A third use of normal refers to *ideal growth* or progress. Schools use this standard in classifying pupils into grades, and judging their success by progress up the educational ladder. A pupil is judged to be "retarded" or "accelerated" in school progress in relation to the grade level he is expected to reach at his age. The first mental tests (Binet-Simon) were constructed by grading tasks according to age and arriving at the intelligence quotient (IQ) by the ratio of the mental age over the chronological age. In testing growing children the question is what traits, abilities, and achievements to expect at each age. When such standards are defined, it is possible to measure what is normal for that age. This

---

[2] *The Neurotic Personality of Our Time*, pp. 13-29. This is seen to be a cultural norm, however, and the neurotic person is one who deviates from the pattern of his culture.

combines the three standards of Cattell. Cabot [3] finds growth the basic need of life. The normal is the growing, the progressing toward an ideal goal. The goal of progress is defined as perfection. If perfection is a final stopping place, it is the denial of growth. But if perfection is viewed as a fleeting goal, attained as the starting point for new progress, it becomes the dynamic lure of endless growth. Growth in quantity will reach a limit, but growth in quality of value, as in unselfish loyalty, has no limit. Spiritual growth has infinite possibilities.

Who then is normal? Can anyone attain these exacting requirements of normality? Everyone deviates a bit here and there. No one is entirely efficient. Who attains final perfection? Yet progress is possible. Not final perfection, but ideal growth. Not absolute efficiency, but practical efficiency. Not exactly average, yet within bounds. In none of these aims is the absolute attainable, but the practical standard of progress toward a worthy ideal is open to all normal persons. And in striving for such ideals everyone is capable of becoming more normal.

The normal person will not make a fetish of normality. He is willing to be different. He can accept himself as somewhat less than perfect and somewhere near efficient. Yet he cannot wisely take any true norm lightly, nor shrug his shoulders with indifference at normal imperatives. To do so is to surrender goalward tensions and to be less than one's possible best. A normal person has goals worth striving for and determination to progress toward them.

What does it mean for a person to be normally religious? That will depend upon his norm, to be sure. If the religious norm taken is the average, it will be the prevalent style of religious behavior. If the norm is religious efficiency, the normal religion will demonstrate its value in good works and effective service. If the norm is religious growth, the normal person will be known by his tend-

[3] *The Meaning of Right and Wrong* (New York: The Macmillan Co., 1933; 1936), 112-65.

ency to grow in appreciation and realization of spiritual values. One can see how sternly the orthodox condemn as heresy all deviating efforts to grow or be more efficient. Standards of efficiency and growth are better suited to promote religious growth.

The Wiemans approach religious psychology from a normative standpoint. Rather than treating the subject historically, descriptively, or experimentally, they seek the essential functions of religion in human living and the norms implicit in these functions. Valid norms, they believe, cannot be fabricated out of speculations; they arise in religious behavior to fulfill the indispensable functions of religion. Growth is the basic norm of religious living. Upon this basis they set up six specific norms by which to appraise religious growth:

1. The WORTHFULNESS of the objective. The degree to which the objective of devotion is supremely worthful for all human living.
2. The COMPLETENESS of the loyalty. The degree to which the total self, insofar as lies within the determination of the individual, is devoted to the objective.
3. The EFFICIENCY of the loyalty. The degree to which the devotee promotes and secures the values of the objective.
4. The SENSITIVITY of the loyalty. The degree to which the devotee acts with his utmost power of sensing and discriminating values in concrete situations.
5. The PROGRESSION of loyalties. The degree to which the devotion of the individual progresses through his present highest objective in an emerging sequence of ever higher value.
6. The SOCIAL EFFECTIVENESS of the loyalty. The degree to which the loyalty pervades and shapes society.[4]

These are significant norms of religious excellence, applicable to concrete situations. By these standards one may appraise the religions of the world, or the religious experience and behavior of individuals. Religious persons who have clear norms will be guided

[4] *Normative Psychology of Religion*, pp. 376-87.

thereby to more intelligent understanding and evaluation of their own behavior. By them one can measure religious progress and decline. Without norms all experience is in a fog of vague confusion. With true norms there is hope of valid growth in religious values.

Other standards of religious value in constant use are (*a*) feeling and intuition; (*b*) authority; (*c*) frequency, or popularity; (*d*) coherence; (*e*) productivity in practical consequences; (*f*) permanence of value; (*g*) comprehensive inclusiveness.[5] In this list *feeling* is similar to "sensitivity," *frequency* is similar to the "average," *coherence* is a way of defining "worthfulness," *productivity* results from "efficiency," *permanence of value* requires growth or "progression," *comprehensiveness* is equivalent to "completeness." Authority and social effectiveness are by no means identical, yet the latter may lead to the former. No single norm is adequate, for persons and values interact in mutual interdependence.

2. HEALTH AND WHOLENESS

Health and wholeness are linguistic brothers who share a common ancestry in many languages. The word "whole" appears in Old English as *hál*, in Middle Dutch and Danish as *heel*, in German as *heil*, in Swedish as *hel*, in Gothic as *hails*. The word "heal" appears in Old English as *hal*, in Old Saxon as *hêli*, in Middle Dutch as *heile*, in old High German as *heili*, and in Gothic as *hailei*. Both words are closely related to "hale" and "hail." The northern dialect of the Old English *hál* was *hale* or *heal*, while the southern and middle form was *hol*, *hole*, or *whole*. *The Oxford English Dictionary*[6] gives twelve variant English forms of "whole"—*hal*, *hale*, *hol*, *hole*, *hoal*, *hoyll*, *wholle*, *whoole*, *hoill*, *whol*, *quhole*, *whole*. The *wh* spelling first appears in the fifteenth century.

<hr/>

[5] See W. G. Everett, *Moral Values* (New York: Henry Holt & Co., 1918), pp. 219-24; and Brightman, *A Philosophy of Religion*, pp. 85-131.

[6] Oxford: Claredon Press, 1933.

The words are affiliated not only in form and derivation but also in content of meaning. "Whole" means, primarily, sound, or in good condition; in good health, free from disease or defect; well, restored to health, recovered from disease. In reference to mental powers it means sane. "Heal" means to make whole or sound, to recover from sickness or a wound; to restore a person from some evil or unwholesome condition to wholeness. "Hale" means free from injury, disease, or infirmity; in good health, robust, vigorous, whole, entire, complete, no part wanting. "Health" means soundness of body, that condition in which its functions are duly and efficiently discharged; also, spiritual, moral, or mental soundness; and well-being, welfare, salvation, wholesomeness.

From this semantic study, it is clear that health means wholeness. It is to have abundant life and overbrimming energy, the fulfillment of human capacities and the efficient functioning of all parts in unified co-ordination. Illness, by sharp and painful contrast, is the crippling disability and restraint of disease. Robinson defines illness as "a deviation from health or from a state in which all natural activities and functions are performed freely and efficiently without pain or discomfort." [7] Disease is an abnormal state of the body, recognized by objective examinations. But illness is subjective and consists of health disturbances experienced and recognized by the individual affected. Positive health, therefore, includes the normal functioning of body and mind in harmonious unity experienced as well-being or happiness. Health is the exercise and enjoyment of the powers and functions of life as a whole. Dynamic wholeness is the norm of health. It is the fulfillment of growth and efficiency.

This is not the newest discovery of medicine; Hippocrates (460?-377? B.C.), the Greek founder of medical science, saw that "in order to cure the human body it is necessary to have a knowl-

[7] *The Patient as a Person* (New York: The Commonwealth Fund, 1939), p. 3.

edge of the whole of things." [8] And yet it is one of the most significant rediscoveries of modern medicine. For specialism, valuable as it is for scientific research, has proved inadequate for medical practice. Physicians are now declaring that the whole is more than its organic parts and are re-emphasizing "treatment of the patient as a whole." [9] Psychobiology and psychosomatic medicine are demanding a holistic approach to the whole man. No man can be wholly understood without taking into consideration his social relationships and the environment in which he lives.

Health problems are not confined to organic processes. They include emotional and social factors as well; for health is a state of the whole personality, and whatever affects the person in all his relationships concerns his well-being. "Emotional disturbances form the element of illness next in importance to organic disease, and are closely related to the personal and social status of the patient." [10] H. F. Dunbar has reviewed two thousand publications, submitting evidence to show that the functions of practically all the organs of the body are disturbed by excessive or repressed emotions.[11] Whatever affects adversely any aspect of life, threatens health.

Stanley Cobb [12] finds the interaction of living processes so intricate that the popular distinction between organic and functional diseases is misleading. Organic diseases are affected by psychological factors, even as psychological disorders are affected by organic conditions. He classifies diseases by etiology into four groups:

1. *Geneogenic* disorders arising from heredity.
2. *Histogenic* disorders due to nonhereditary lesions.

[8] Quoted by C. A. Wise, *Religion in Illness and Health* (New York: Harper & Bros., 1942), p. 9.

[9] Robinson, *op. cit.*, title of the final chapter. On page 10 he says, "Man is a unity of mind and body, and medicine must consider this unity."

[10] Robinson, *op. cit.*, p. 4.

[11] *Emotions and Bodily Changes* (New York: Columbia Univeristy Press, 1935; 1938).

[12] *Foundations of Neuropsychiatry* (Baltimore: Williams & Wilkins, rev. 1941), pp. 205-25.

3. *Chemogenic* disorders from effects of chemical agents or their lack.

4. *Psychogenic* disorders arising from disturbed interpersonal relations.

Interpersonal relations are the source of emotional anxieties, fears, grief, guilt, and inferiority feelings, which are very influential in a variety of illnesses.

Robinson's study of 174 unselected patients admitted to Johns Hopkins Hospital from an urban community [13] showed that (*a*) adverse social conditions were present in 80 per cent of them, (*b*) these adverse social conditions caused harmful emotional reactions in 58 per cent of the patients, (*c*) emotional factors were the chief cause of illness in 26 per cent of these cases; and of 10 per cent more whose relation to social conditions was not established.

Thornton and Knauth studied 100 cases in the Presbyterian Hospital of New York City.[14] They found adverse social factors in 80 per cent of the patients and conditions definitely related to the illness of 65 per cent of the patients. A comparison of these two studies is shown below:

ADVERSE SOCIAL FACTORS RELATED TO ILLNESS

Social Factors	Presbyterian Hospital	Johns Hopkins Hospital
1. Inadequate physical protection (undesirable habitat, shelter, clothing, food, personal service).	44%	24%
2. Inadequate economic protection (undue effort and inadequate means to secure subsistence).	36	52
3. Faulty personal habits influencing health (unfavorable to health or following medical directions).	31	14
4. Dissatisfaction connected with family or other group relationships (broken home, incompatibility, lack of satisfying status).	30	44
5. Dissatisfaction connected with restricted outlets (lack of satisfying work, recreation, or social life).	34	12

[13] *Op. cit.*, p. 388. The table following is taken from page 34 of Robinson's book.

[14] Janet Thornton and M. S. Knauth, *The Social Component in Medical Care* (New York: Columbia University Press, 1937).

Measures taken by the Presbyterian Hospital to remedy adverse social factors in the lives of these patients indicate how far-reaching are the conditions of health.

A. Measures designed to control environment:
 1. Supplying deficiencies.
 2. Helping patient utilize available resources.
 3. Removing obstacles to care.
 4. Removing to more favorable environment.
B. Measures designed to influence conduct:
 1. Imparting information on problems.
 2. Explaining.
 3. Elucidating by reiteration.
 4. Demonstrating by example.
 5. Influencing choice by incentives.
 6. Fostering habits.
 7. Standing by and following up.

The boundaries of personality are never final as a confining wall. They are open frontiers with freedom to explore and expand into enlarging relationships. In the first chapter we defined personality as an organizing unity of conscious experience. This sets a tentative boundary at the border of conscious experience. Beyond this conscious area of dynamic relations are the unconscious relations, and beyond them the biological relations of the body, and beyond that the social relations of the human world, and beyond that the physical and metaphysical relations of the universe, including the reality that religion calls God. The relations of personality are infinite. Where can one draw a line of demarcation to declare that here a person reaches his final limit? For the limits of today are exceeded by the adventures the person may undertake tomorrow. Boundaries are useful for definition and logical distinction, but they are artificial abstractions that living persons persist in leaping over.

One of the best recent definitions of personality is offered by

Allport after a systematic review of etymology, history, and contemporary use: "Personality is the dynamic organization within the individual of those psychophysical systems that determine his unique adjustments to his environment." [15] This seems to draw the boundary at the circumference of the body and to treat all that is outside the skin as not-mine. But what of one's clothes, glasses, false teeth, artificial limb, fountain pen, radio, and other instruments of his unique adjustment to his environment? What of one's family, school, clubs, church, country, vocation, in all of which his personal values are invested? These may be classified as environment, but, if so, why not the body and the unconscious processes also? All are beyond experience and inferred as object, not known as subject. If one is to be strictly empirical, then only the conscious unity is personal. But if one is to expand the range of personality to include the biological relations of the body, is it not quite as consistent to include the physical and social relations? [16] Are they not essential to the actual sphere of personal living and integral in the organizing unity of insights and purposes?

Personality is more or less than a psychophysical system. If empirically subjective, it is less. If behavioristically interactive, it is more. From the holistic point of view personality is bio-psycho-socio-physical. A person is a complex unity of dynamic relationships among these interacting spheres of the body-mind-society-physical world. Stern rejects elementaristic psychology as removed from the concrete realities of personal experience. To mechanistic and fragmentary psychologies he opposes the concept of *wholeness*. Every experience either is itself a whole or belongs to a whole. Wholeness does not exclude internal multiplicity, nor external relationships. As an open totality the person has incessant inter-

---

[15] *Personality: A Psychological Interpretation*, p. 48.

[16] William Healy, *Personality in Formation and Action* (New York: W. W. Norton & Co., 1938), pp. 11-12, defines personality as "an integrated system of habitual adjustments to the environment, particularly to the social environment."

course with the world. His definition suggests this boundlessness of personality: "The 'person' is a living whole, individual, unique, striving toward goals, self-contained and yet open to the world around him; he is capable of having experience." [17]

To possess health, a person needs to have all functions of his multiple relationships in harmonious accord. L. J. Henderson has shown that 214 environmental conditions have to be present in accurate proportion for life to exist at all on this planet.[18] No less intricate and delicate are the internal adjustments of the psychophysical organism. Far more subtle and variable are the social adjustments of interpersonal relations, and their effects upon the individual are beyond measure. In all these interactions nothing less than a total adjustment of the inner and outer relations constitutes normal personality. When Spencer [19] defined life as "the continuous adjustment of internal relations to external relations," did he comprehend the full implications of that happy phrase? Or, in fact, do we?

3. FAITH HEALING AND MIRACLES

Faith healing has the mystery and appeal of an unexplored continent, where fact and fancy mingle. Extravagant claims and denials clash in controversy. Cures often appear miraculous, yet remain incredible to many doubters. After centuries of superstition and legend, it is no wonder that scientific medicine in the nineteenth century turned from faith to fact. Medical scientists have accumulated a vast array of accurate information on health and disease by specialized research in bacteriology, biochemistry, histology, physiology, and neurology. Now, in our time, the psychic factors, once ruled out as unscientific, are demanding attention as decisive causes in illness and health. The functional disorders as well as numerous organic diseases are clearly related to anxieties

[17] *General Psychology*, p. 70.
[18] *The Fitness of Environment* (New York: The Macmillan Co., 1931).
[19] *Principles of Biology*, I, 80.

and psychoneuroses. Faith is evidently a fact to be investigated along with other emotional attitudes in understanding the conditions of health. The question of faith in healing has new significance as emotional factors in illness are recognized. What are the facts about faith and other emotions in reference to health?

W. B. Cannon [20] has conducted pioneer studies in the effect of emotions on bodily processes. He finds that a cat frightened by a barking dog has the following bodily changes: (a) increased pulse rate and blood pressure; (b) increased adrenalin in the blood; (c) increased sugar in the blood; (d) decreased coagulation time; (e) increased muscular tension; (f) increased motor activity, restlessness; (g) deep and rapid respiration; (h) dry mouth, pilomotor and vasomotor activity; (i) dilation of the pupils; (j) defecation and urination; (k) immobility of the stomach.

In a recent study of voodoo death Cannon examines reports of death among primitive peoples following a magical spell or curse. Careful observers have seen men die within a few hours after a curse has been put upon them. The physiological reactions are similar to shock conditions arising in war, accident, or surgery. Shocking emotional stress (obvious or repressed terror) affects the sympathetic nervous system, which controls the internal organs and blood vessels. Severe emotions of fear and rage stimulate increase of adrenalin and sympathin, causing a persistent constriction of the small arterioles, inadequate supply of oxygen, and escape of plasma through the capillary walls into the perivascular spaces. This leaves the red corpuscles more concentrated, dehydrates the circulation, and reduces the blood pressure. Deterioration then occurs in the heart and the nerve centers, which become less able to keep the blood circulating effectively. In the cursed man, who believes death is inevitable, this vicious circle is fatal unless the curse is withdrawn and he is persuaded to believe he is able to live.[21] Belief controls life and death.

[20] *Bodily Changes in Pain, Hunger, Fear and Rage* (New York: D. Appleton-Century Co., 1915; 1936).
[21] "Voodoo Death," *American Anthropologist*, XLIV (1942), 169-81.

H. F. Dunbar has also conducted notable studies on emotions and bodily changes, showing that emotional factors are present in virtually all diseases. There are four ways in which emotional tensions predispose to organic illness: (*a*) by inducing accidents; (*b*) by upsetting physiological functioning by inhibiting, over-stimulating, or contracting; (*c*) by indirect emotional causation with organic complications; and (*d*) by perpetuation of physiological changes by chronic emotional stress.[22] Wise surveys emotional factors in physical and mental illness, showing that illness can no longer be considered "a specific disease of a particular organ," but a "manifestation of the whole person." [23] Diseases of the heart and circulation; asthma and hay fever; laryngitis and the common cold; diseases of the stomach, pancreas, and liver; intestinal ailments (peptic ulcer and colitis); infectious diseases such as tuberculosis and typhoid; convalescence and chronic illness, together with all personality disorders, have emotional components.

If emotional responses are so important in disease and death, they are equally so in life and health. If malignant anxiety [24] is fatally distressing, then adequate faith is specifically curative. These medical investigations give scientific answers to the question of faith healing. Faith healing is not impossible. It is a possibility wherever emotional factors play a decisive part in illness and health. Not all healing miracles are authentic. In fact, many are fraudulent, deceptive, or temporary in results. The agent employed for the healing may be as ineffectual as patent medicines or bread pills, and yet results may be surprisingly good if only the patient believes firmly enough to provide the needed emotional support.

[22] "Problems of Convalescence and Chronic Illness," *American Journal of Psychiatry,* XCII (1936).

[23] *Op. cit.,* p. 29.

[24] See E. Mira, *Psychiatry and War* (New York: W. W. Norton & Co., 1943). War is a collective psychosis, with regression to primitive emotions, especially fear and rage. The antidote for fear is not courage but love, Dr. Mira maintains. To prevent fear, men must know the truth and love their cause.

For without faith no one can be well, and with this basic confidence there is ground for better health.

Does this mean that science is giving support to miracles? Has there not been a long-standing warfare between science and theology over the issue of miracles? There have been misunderstandings to clarify. The term "miracle" has been used in at least three different senses: (*a*) a wonderful or marvelous event; (*b*) an antinatural event; one contrary to the laws of nature; and (*c*) a sign of special meaning, revealing a divine purpose. The first sense of miracle, as a wonderful event, is the ancient and original meaning. Surrounded by mysteries, primitive men were deeply stirred by the sense of awe and wonder. Not laws but powers, not natural but marvelous events, caught their attention.

The second sense of miracle—that of a deviation from the laws of nature—did not occur to biblical writers or to other men of ancient times. They thought of nature as obeying, not laws, but powers that acted freely at all times and in any ways that suited particular occasions. The idea of miracle as unnatural dates from the medieval Schoolmen, who separated nature from the supernatural. From this contrast with natural law came the view of miracle that set theologians and scientists in controversy.

Modern theologians agree with scientists in rejecting this second view of miracle. Belief in magical and irresponsible powers who violate natural laws offends both reason and morality. It contradicts the trustworthy character of God quite as much as the trustworthy order of nature. Whatever scientists know of nature upholds a system of regular events in lawful order, and whatever theologians know of God reveals a constant purpose expressed through regular events in lawful order.

The third meaning of miracle—that of a sign revealing divine purpose—is the distinctly religious conception. Those who once held that God reveals himself in unnatural and "illegal" ways were confusing religion with magic; but those who now understand that God is immanent within, and working through, the natural order bring religion and science into harmony. To the modern mind, God is more truly revealed in the marvelous order and growth of nature than in capricious disorder and violation of law. Law is a far greater miracle than magic, as universal order is a greater achievement than chaos. God is more adequately revealed in law and order than in lesser ways. Here are signs of intelligence, consistent purpose, creative organization, and faithful sustaining of values. A God so revealed glorifies the normal rather than the abnormal.

In what sense may we take faith healing as miraculous? Not in the medieval sense of something antinatural or illegal. For the emotional forces in illness and health are natural and law-abiding. They are scientifically known to operate within the natural order of personality in regular ways that reveal systematic relationships. Yet, in the original sense, the healing power of faith is a wonderful event. On this scientists and theologians can readily agree, for the true scientist is not unmindful of the wonders he finds in nature. Every new advance in science, every deeper understanding of the intricate and delicate functioning of the natural order adds to our sense of wonder and humility. All healing is miraculous, even as reproduction, birth, growth, and the amazing resourcefulness of life are wonderful. So are we led to the ultimate view of miracle as a sign of divine purpose. The marvels of science point to divine purpose, and scientific inquiry there touches religious experience.

Richard C. Cabot was a medical pioneer in whose mind science and religion met to co-operate. No one in recent times has done more to bring medical, religious, and social workers together in clinical relationship. In his book, *The Art of Ministering to the Sick*,[25] he equates *vis medicatrix naturae* with *vis medicatrix Dei* and sees the marvelous healing power of nature as the healing power of God. These healing resources are constantly at work

[25] Cabot and Dicks. New York: The Macmillan Co., 1936, pp. 118-31.

whether we are aware of them or not. Healing through faith and prayer is no more divine than healing through diet, medication, surgery, or rest. The distinctly spiritual aspect of healing is the extent to which one is aware of these beneficent influences and co-operates with them.[26]

Joseph H. Pratt is another medical pioneer in spiritual resources for healing. At the Boston Dispensary for more than fourteen years he has conducted every week a "Thought Control Class," assisted by a religious psychologist, Winfred Rhoades. Patients who have complaints without organic symptoms are referred by the physicians to this class, where they are welcomed by others who have previously joined the class and made progress. After the roll call each patient writes a brief report of his improvement, or lack of it, in the past week. The reports are considered by the teacher, with commendation or inquiry, and those who have failed to improve are scheduled for private consultation. Then follow relaxing exercises in which patients learn how to relax by methods to be used at home. The teacher gives a practical talk on the problems and methods of gaining health by thought control. This emotional re-education is followed by testimonials in which patients tell of the progress made by these methods. The results in better health for 90 per cent of the class members well justify the procedure.[27] This group therapy is not unlike the old-fashioned prayer meeting, and I have found it adaptable to church groups in these times of mounting nervous tensions.

The urgent need for emotional health has given rise to various healing cults. The most influential of these is the Christian Science Church, whose expansion since the first incorporation of twenty-

[26] See Seward Hiltner, *Religion and Health* (New York: The Macmillan Co., 1943), pp. 99-101.
[27] See Pratt, "The Influence of Emotions in the Causation and Cure of Psychoneuroses," *International Clinics*, IV (1934); Rhoades "Group Training in Thought Control for Relieving Nervous Disorders," *Mental Hygiene*, XIX (1935); S. B. Hadden, "Treatment of the Neuroses by Class Technic," *Annals of Internal Medicine*, XVI (1942); A. Hauptmann, "Group Therapy for Psychoneuroses," *Diseases of the Nervous System*, IV (1943).

six members in Boston in 1879 has been phenomenal. Coming at a time when mental factors in healing were overlooked by physicians and ministers alike, this church demonstrated the value of Christian faith in promoting health. Enthusiasm for this truth has led to rejection of other truths, denial of the reality of organic diseases, and refusal of the services of physicians. To reject medical services is to endanger the health of individuals and block public health improvement. Progress in health, public and private has come by co-operation more than by rivalry. There are signs today of heartier co-operation between medical and religious health workers. Human welfare demands larger co-operation between religious and medical services.

4. THERAPEUTIC SERVICES OF RELIGION

Health is a vital issue, basic to all human values. Organic vitality is the tide of life supporting personality in experience and expressive behavior. Wholesome interests, attitudes, and emotional responses to purposive goals are essential to every constructive achievement. Disease is for this reason a crisis, striking terror and impotency into life. Illness is a threat to the values for which men live, a danger to combat with all resources at hand. Religion is devoted to these values and committed to human life at its best. It is therefore the task of religion to promote health and wholeness.

Through the long centuries of religious history the need and art of healing have not been forgotten. In primitive communities the medicine men were priests, guardians of the mysteries where magic, medicine, and religion mingled. Scientists who reject religion because of its association with magic should examine the history of science. For science is the child of magic, which was the primitive system of controlling the forces of nature by experimenting with assumed causes and effects. Lingering superstitions have retarded both science and religion, yet in the progress both have won they stand together as allies against the errors of magic.

The art of healing has always been empirical and pragmatic.

With so many unknown factors in illness and health, it is impossible to exclude all but one causal agent and control this isolated variable. Methods of healing have developed from experience of what worked in previous cases. True and false remedies have grown up together like wheat and tares until the winnowing of time and more accurate understanding. Neither science nor religion is specifically to blame for these errors, so long as every effort is made in theory and practice to sift the true from the false.

The Ebers papyrus, dated before 1552 B.C., describes the Egyptian treatment of healing by the laying on of hands with ceremonial formulas. The Hebrews, deriving their medical knowledge from Egypt, practiced similar treatment with prayer. The Greeks practiced healing by reference to the god Asclepius before 500 B.C. Excavations at Epidaurus produced inscriptions giving the rites used. Patients brought sacrifices, cleansed themselves with holy water, submitted to ceremonial acts performed by priests, and fell into a deep sleep (hypnotism?). Visits to shrines have been popular in various religions: Moslems go to Mecca to touch the black Kaaba stone, Hindus go to bathe in the sacred Ganges, Buddhists go to touch sacred relics supposed to have healing power. Christians have also turned to shrines where healing traditions have given hope to sufferers. The shrine at Lourdes, France, has attracted wide attention, and though many go in vain enough people are healed each year to draw others.[28] Faith in persons, whether religious leaders or physicians and psychiatrists, is undoubtedly one of the most effective resources for healing at the point where emotional attitudes affect health.

The development of hospitals and medical missions is a demonstration of Christian devotion to the health of the poor. Hospital orders were formed as early as 1113, when the pope recognized

[28] See Smiley Blanton, "Analytical Study of a Cure at Lourdes," *The Psychoanalytic Quarterly*, V (1940), 348-62. For a literary account see Franz Werfel, *The Song of Bernadette*, tr. L. Lewisohn (New York: The Viking Press, 1942).

the Friars of the Hospital of St. John of Jerusalem, who maintained hospitals for infirm pilgrims, first in Jerusalem, then on Malta, then elsewhere in Europe. Other religious brotherhoods—such as the Franciscan Order founded in 1208 by Francis of Assisi—sought to serve the poor, the lepers, and sick outcasts. By the fourteenth century, in Italy and Spain, "Sisters of Charity" were organized and trained to nurse the sick and aid the poor. By the seventeenth century the "Servants of the Poor" was founded in France by Vincent de Paul for the relief of suffering. Following these early examples, hospitals and dispensaries have been developed around the world by Christian missions. In 1936 Protestant missions maintained 1,354 physicians, 4,184 qualified nurses, and 8,900 student nurses in 1,092 hospitals and 2,351 dispensaries in foreign countries.[29] Public hospitals, clinics, and health services are now expanding work which Christian churches have pioneered.

What therapeutic values, beyond promoting medical programs, does Christianity offer our generation? There is growing recognition that Christian experience ministers to health in the realm of psychotherapy. Other religions have their values too, but in order to be specific we shall consider the ways in which Christianity contributes to health. The following items are not exhaustive. Nor do they influence all Christians equally, but they are representative.

a) *The worth of every person* is a cardinal belief of Christianity. To realize one's personal worth is essential to mental health, a needed corrective to the inferiority feelings so common in our competitive society. To realize the equal worth of other persons is quite as useful in correcting the superiority feelings of ego-inflation. To view every personality as sacred corrects indifference and makes health a religious obligation.

b) *Membership in a church fellowship* is a healthy relationship.

[29] *Interpretative Statistical Survey of the World Mission of the Christian Church*, ed. J. I. Parker (New York: International Missionary Council, 1938), pp. 27-28.

Karl Stolz [30] calls the Christian church a therapeutic organism and shows how it cultivates wholeness of personality through loyalty, inclusive rather than exclusive membership, purposive activity, initiative and choice, progressive development, and free allegiance to the leader. Every person needs to belong to an intimate fellowship where values are shared and each is expected to do his best for all.

c) Invisible companionship is health-giving. Loneliness and isolation is a recurrent problem which group membership does not entirely solve. For no one can be with others at all times; moreover, there come inner separations that create loneliness in the midst of a crowd. Belief in God as a cosmic companion, who is present at all times in all places, meets this need. The sense of this intimate companionship brings an inner stability, the moral support of feeling "I am not alone."

d) Christian faith means *trust in the ultimate victory of good over evil.* Life values are constantly threatened, and at times overwhelmed, by evils. Who is not plagued by anxiety and fears, insecurity and despair? Persistent anxieties make life miserable and unhealthy. The fear of evil may, in fact, become the greatest evil of all. To these toxic emotions Christian faith offers the antidote of trust in God and the hope that evil can be overcome by good. Without faith there is insecurity and nervous despair; with faith there is hope and confidence to sustain peace of mind and health of body.

e) Worship is a therapeutic experience. For worship seeks the highest attainable reality. The individual worshiper who is earnestly sincere lays aside the hypocrisies and deceptions of daily living and tries to be honest with his Creator and himself. He aspires to become more worthy. He shares with fellow worshipers a unity of purpose and rededicates himself to a new life. He meditates upon dynamic symbols and resolves to translate ideals into

[30] *The Church and Psychotherapy*, pp. 24-27.

realities. Life may be reoriented and re-created in meeting the reality he calls God.

f) The Christian purpose is an *urge and guide to growth*. The aspiration of worship and the challenge of prophetic preaching is a rousing experience, shaking one out of complacency, rejecting the *status quo* as inadequate, and demanding further growth. Religious education guides this growth through scripture, ethical analysis, problem-solving, study of life situations, and projects for putting principles into action. We have seen that health is normal growth toward wholeness. Christian activities urge and guide such growth.

g) Christian action is *unselfish devotion to human needs*. The unselfish purpose of Christianity is fulfilled not in words but in deeds. It is not healthy to have a purpose unless one is doing something about it. The gap between theory and practice is well known. This failure to practice ideals is not so much a Christian fault as a human failure which Christianity seeks to overcome by a program of specific action and a commitment to that program. Occupational therapy finds work a means of healing human ills. The serving of human needs is the curative process of Christian occupational therapy.

h) *Confession* is a needed and difficult requisite of mental health. It is needed because the repression of anxiety and guilt increase the tensions that disturb personality. It is difficult because isolation, timidity, shame, dignity, and fear of being misunderstood block the way to expression. "There appears to be a conscience in mankind which severely punishes the man who does not somehow and sometime at whatever cost to himself, cease to defend and assert himself, and instead confess himself fallible and human." [31] The Roman Catholic Church has made confession a required institution, thereby establishing the habit and procedure for regular

[31] Jung, *Modern Man in Search of a Soul*, p. 39.

confession.[32] Protestant churches, without the formal institution, may accomplish the needed therapy by the intimate association of members and by the sympathetic interest of pastors in personal problems. The modern emphasis upon counseling and the training of pastors in such skills will facilitate confession, thus releasing tensions and promoting insight. Serious psychopathic problems should be promptly referred to psychiatrists, but a majority of the people who have psychoneurotic problems will go unaided except as pastors, teachers, parents, and friends hear confessions in permissive counseling relationships. Confession to God is recommended by Künkel as confessional meditation and reorientation.

i) Forgiveness is the essence of the Christian gospel. It is the natural human and divine answer to confession. Confession is the honest admission of one's mistakes, a first step in the repudiation of an unworthy past in order to start a more worthy future. Forgiveness is the willingness of one who has been injured to show mercy, and to be reconciled in a new beginning. Forgiveness is a therapy needed to cure the personal and social evils of guilt, resentment, and revenge. As long as men do wrong, forgiveness will be an inevitable solution. Peace cannot heal public war or private quarrels until enemies are forgiven. The family will fall apart unless husband, wife, and children are able to forgive. No one can endure to live with himself unless he can forgive his own mistakes.

j) Christianity is a *discipline, or way of life.* A promise of new life is empty without a specific program of action. No one can be healthy without rules to follow in daily living. Physicians prescribe exercise and posture, sleep and relaxation, diet and regular habits as more important in the long run than medication. Mental hygienists teach wholesome attitudes, emotions, and philosophies of life. Christians have been known as "disciples"—that is, followers who accept a discipline. This taking upon one's self a discipline is

---

[32] F. Künkel, *In Search of Maturity* (New York: Charles Scribner's Sons, 1943), p. 252, considers routine confession useless in plucking only conscious deeds while the poisonous roots remain in the unconscious.

the cure for inactivity, impulsive wandering, or self-indulgence. A major purpose or cause to live for is like an airway beacon, along whose beam the course of progress is charted. A Christian is goal-conscious, and the goal orients the regimen of daily life. Living on purpose and by rule according to well-tried methods is a therapy to heal chaotic and aimless uncertainty.

Any one of these therapies is useful, although incomplete. Taken together, they may become decisive for health over illness, success rather than failure as a human being. Jung considers religious orientation crucial for mature wholeness of personality. "Among all my patients in the second half of life (over 36) there has not been one whose problem in the last resort was not that of finding a religious outlook on life . . . and none of them has been really healed who did not regain his religious outlook." [33] One may have partial integrations, but they are apt to be unstable unless devoted to a cause larger than self-interest. A religious cause offers the cosmic co-operation and devotion that moves toward the largest integration.

5. THE GENIUS OF JESUS

Jesus is the most influential person in history. His life seems incredible. Some consider him the perfect man, others hold him divine. Some think that he is overrated, that he has been reconstructed by his admirers into a theological fiction. Was Jesus a normal personality? There are those who question his normality, pointing to certain of his sayings about himself as paranoiac. It is difficult to know whether these claims are verbatim self-assertions or whether they were acclaims of his followers, upon whose oral tradition we depend for the gospel records. It is clear that Jesus was not normal in the sense of "average"—and this is the standard by which the above critics judge him. But who can doubt he was efficient, whole, and ideal in growth? He has become a norm for more people than anyone else in history.

[33] *Op. cit.*, p. 264.

Theological questions are beyond the scope of this study. There are three psychological problems, however, that can scarcely be ignored when we consider Jesus. What makes him so great a personality? How could he change other persons? Why does he survive the sifting of time, not to decline in the perspective of history, but to increase in it? Each of these questions will be examined briefly from the human standpoint.

What makes Jesus so great a personality? (*a*) The person of Jesus was characterized by inner unity and harmony. He was unified by purity of heart and singleness of purpose, a complete togetherness that most of us long for and fail to achieve. (*b*) In all circumstances he showed trust and good will, without fear and suspicion. He trusted God as Father, men as brothers, and himself as true. He met conflict without compromise or weakness, always with love and forgiveness. (*c*) His sense of mission was unfaltering. He never wavered or turned back, but moved unflinchingly in the face of mounting opposition and danger. He was essentially unselfish, seeking not to save himself but to redeem others. (*d*) He co-operated with spiritual forces to solve spiritual problems and share spiritual values. Others have worked in the physical realm with physical forces. But Jesus chose to specialize in the highest values of intrinsic worth: truth, beauty, goodness, holiness, faith, love, and vicarious sacrifice. Identifying himself with eternal principles and meeting others at the highest level of values, he represents human life at its best.

How could Jesus change other persons? By what means did he transform life in teaching, healing, and converting? (*a*) He discovered hidden value resources in others. What others overlooked, he saw with truer insight as potential greatness. What others neglected, he developed by encouragement and inspiration. (*b*) He appealed to the best in those he met by faith in their best. He was not blind to the worst, yet he insisted evil was never final but only a prelude to ultimate good. His aim was not to destroy but to fulfill; his method was not to judge men but to redeem them. (*c*) He showed others the secret of self-development by unselfish devotion. He demonstrated the art of finding life by losing it in loyalty to a greater cause. He showed inner resources for personal growth in service to others. (*d*) He brought men in touch with eternal life, available for victorious living and dying. He set life in cosmic proportions, relating every person to his Heavenly Father in one universal family of God. Without attempting philosophical proof, it is only honest to observe that people who orient their lives as Jesus did, have a new dimension for living.

Why does Jesus survive the passing of these centuries to outlive other men before and since his time? (*a*) The social cause of his survival, without which no influence can move down the stream of history, was a faithful body of disciples. In every age it was these determined, convinced, enthusiastic followers who kept the name and power of Jesus alive. If and when the believers cease to believe, and the followers neglect to follow him through life and death, the influence of Jesus will fade to a curious legend. (*b*) The logical cause of his survival, without which his followers would long since have vanished, is the truth Jesus represents. He gave true answers to perennial human problems. The issues he faced are as vital today as they were then; the principles he set forth ring as true, and meet human needs as directly, in one age as in another. The truth of Jesus is experiential and experimental. What he experienced we can experience. And the experimental results of this truth are open to demonstration by all who care to test them in the crucibles of logic and life. (*c*) The ethical cause of his survival, without which he would long since have given place to other teachers, is his moral supremacy. Other teachers were great in their time, but they were relative to their age, dated and static in a dynamic world. The morality of Jesus is so universal that good men cannot go around it, so dynamic that progress cannot outgrow it. His ideal is still ahead of the best of us after nineteen centuries, still imperative upon the most conscientious after the rise and fall of many civilizations. Such an ideal will be ignored at our peril. What is this principle? The ethic of Jesus is a way of forgiving love—a way that is desperately needed, hopelessly denied, and gloriously attainable.

The genius of Jesus is not encompassed by these efforts at descriptive analysis. They may suggest but not exhaust his significance. It is the genius of personality to defy classification and exceed description. And the greater the person, the farther we come short of adequate understanding. Yet, although we follow afar, we gain in understanding only by following. We grow in normality only by action in the direction of the norm.

What then, after all, is a normal personality? A normal personality is an interactive unity of growing experience, guided by insight and motivated by purpose to achieve socially desirable goals. He will seek health and wholeness for all persons in a community of work and play, love and worship, that is devoted to the producing and sharing of true values.

X

The Religious Community

Society creates persons. The family is a creative society in which parents bear new life. "Two by two we marry, one by one we die." Which being interpreted means that death is solitary while life is social. Persons are born twice—first biologically and then culturally. The making of a person is a social creation in both senses. The infant is born not a person but an organism with potentialities of becoming a person. The family introduces the infant to society and awakens participating interests and actions.

How does society create persons? (*a*) Social stimuli elicit interpersonal responses. (*b*) Social actions encourage interactions. (*c*) Social examples of posture, gesture, and attitude invite imitation. (*d*) Social language provides a medium for exchange of meanings. (*e*) Social customs guide behavior into acceptable personal habits. (*f*) Social sympathy projects contagious emotions for sharing. (*g*) Social participation facilitates membership in a coacting group. In these and in many other ways society creates the person in its own image.

The religious society creates religious persons. Could one be religious in an irreligious society? It is possible, but difficult and unlikely. How could a person without social aid learn religious concepts of God, immortality, and brotherhood, or the religious behavior of prayer and co-operation for religious goals? Founded religions have had individual founders. Yet the founder was himself the heir of socioreligious traditions. Jesus was a Jew, Buddha a Hindu, Mohammed an Arabian conversant with Judaeo-Christian teachings. The religions they founded were not created out of nothing, nor could they have survived without social organization and loyalty.

The religious society creates religious persons in its image. The child of the Moslem home is a Moslem; the child of a Roman Catholic home is not likely to be a Protestant. A person may revolt against his religious tradition, as Martin Luther and Thomas Paine did. But no revolt is without its social influences—acquired in going to school, reading, talking, or observing others. A reaction is also a social response, usually for social gains. And the revolter will seek others to agree with him—and to unite with him in a new society, such as the Association for the Advancement of Atheism. Attitudes are unconsciously contagious, and the person reflects his culture more than he realizes. Moving from one cultural group to another produces inevitable changes of attitude. Studies have been made of young people in the transition from the home community to a college community.

The changing interest in religion is shown in one of these studies.[1] A group of 337 students was studied in high school and then in the freshmen year of college. Of these, 61 per cent were Protestant, 18 per cent Catholic, and 16 per cent Jewish. Nearly three fourths were church members before going to college. Before college, 74 per cent were frequent in church attendance and 26 per cent infrequent. In college, 43 per cent were frequent and 57 per cent infrequent. Before college, 46.6 per cent were active in church organizations; in college, only 18 per cent joined any religious organization.

Religion for these young people was less vital in college, as is shown by their declining participation in religious organizations, lower evaluation of religious life, decreasing interest in religious values, and slight change in religious thinking in spite of much change in other realms of thought. Probable causes for this decline are: (*a*) The most frequent comment was that "other things were more urgent," leaving little time or energy for facing the problems of religious transition. (*b*) The students felt that the college

<hr>

[1] L. B. Hale, *From School to College: A Study of Transition Experience,* ed. H. Hartshorne (New Haven: Yale University Press, 1939).

does not consider religious development among the more important things to be accomplished. Students go after what the institution emphasizes as important, both in the curriculum and in college life. (c) The religious views of their professors were not plain to the students: "I have no idea what my professors' religious views are." (d) Their break from home ties and parental supervision was followed by typical adolescent reaction to new freedom. (e) Their precollege contacts with religion were not adaptable to an enlarging knowledge of the universe.

Society creates persons, but that is not the whole truth. Persons also create society. Symbiosis (living together) is the social pattern of life everywhere. Plants cross-fertilize, insects live in colonies, animals form herds and packs, and human beings associate in families and communities for mutual aid and satisfaction. Every society is created by the co-operation of its members. By social co-operation, culture develops and civilization is achieved in the exchange of services and in the sharing of values. Inventions become industries, paths become transportation systems, signs become networks of communications, and folkways become moral codes, laws, and governments.

Persons also create religious societies—persons who, sharing values and beliefs, unite in common causes to achieve and renew their purposes. They organize cults and churches to meet their needs and to foster religious growth. Religion is a creative social force, not a passive victim of secular society. Joachim Wach[2] shows that the influence of religion on social attitudes and structures is fully as great as the influence of society on religion. Religion is a mighty force establishing and changing human associations. "One Christian is no Christian," declares the Catholic scholar Scheler. Religion is the conscious realization of mutual interdependence, says MacMurray; its function is the extension of the family unity to wider groups. "Vital religion, by its very nature, must create and

[2] *Sociology of Religion*, pp. 13, 377. The following quotations are taken from pp. 27-29.

sustain a social relationship," says Dimond.

The evidence from history is clear. Religious leaders have either formed religious societies or devoted their influence to guiding and strengthening them. Moses in religious enthusiasm led the Hebrews out of Egypt toward a new homeland, where the prophets and priests continued to direct their social development. The civilization of India was created and has been sustained for thousands of years by religious teachers. Mohammed, fired with passionate zeal for the one God Allah, welded together the diverse tribes of Arabia into a nation that has made astonishing history on three continents. The influence of Jesus led to the Christian church and a missionary movement that has left no part of the world untouched. The influence of this religion upon the Greco-Roman world, upon the rise of European culture, and upon the colonization of the Americas is, to say the least, impressive. There are those who contend that the influence of religion is based upon illusion, and predict its decline. J. F. Brown [3] declares religious behavior unnecessary, yet he cannot deny the social effects of church membership. He therefore defines religion as behavior toward a goal without physical reality but with social reality—that is, God. The cosmic reality of God is a philosophical question beyond the scope of psychology. But the social reality of God is undeniable. God is a psychological fact, and religion is a social force of the first magnitude. Religious behavior has real social effects of far-reaching influence.

Religious behavior is social interaction. Not that all social interaction is religious, but all religious behavior is social interaction. Let us observe and see. Is any religious behavior not so? What is the least social item of religious behavior? You may think of the religious hermit whose prayer is "a flight of the alone to the alone." Yet one and one equals two. The mystical communion of the hermit with God is a social experience; for God is a social reality, and

[3] *Psychology and the Social Order* (New York: McGraw-Hill Book Co., 1936).

prayer is interactive communion with another Person. Religion is essentially interpersonal.

How is religious behavior social? Religion is a social reference to social realities (persons and communities, human and divine), made by social responses (very different from mechanical push and pull) for the sake of social values (personal, yet socially approved) and reinforced by social co-operation (motivated by group membership, expectation, and loyalty). This is a more detailed analysis of our earlier definition of religion as co-operation with a trusted Creator of Values.

To be specific, how does religious experience aid social adjustment? Religion that becomes vital in personal experience

1. Awakens interest in other persons by accenting unselfish attitudes.
2. Provides common interests and mutual purposes to draw persons together, overcoming lonely isolation in significant companionship.
3. Requires sharing of values for the welfare of others.
4. Encourages service to others' needs.
5. Urges forgiveness and reconciliation to heal breaches and conflicts.
6. Furnishes standards and patterns of socially acceptable behavior.
7. Stimulates communication of ideas, creative thinking and discussion.
8. Through diversity and continuous change impels constant adjustment and growth.
9. Facilitates co-operation, mutual aid and effective social organization.
10. Brings the social heritage to the individual and puts him in touch with significant achievements and values of the group.
11. Gives social and moral support to the member, undergirding him with a sense of security and personal worth.
12. Develops institutions for intimate association, as friendships, marriage, family, church societies, thus promoting fellowship, love and mutual response.[4]

[4] Wieman, *Normative Psychology of Religion*, pp. 320-59.

This list does not exhaust the social values of religion. But it does indicate some of the psychological reasons why the actively religious person usually makes successful social adjustments. It is possible to be well adjusted in one social group and unadjusted to other social groups at the same time. A conscientious religious person may be at variance with social groups that contradict his standards of belief and conduct. Yet if his attitudes are religious in the redemptive sense of compassion and love, he will devote his energies to reconciling his enemies, blessing his persecutors, and giving his life in unselfish sacrifice to help others who have no claim upon him except his religious devotion to the welfare of all.

2. A Universal Community

Every religion tends to form a community. We have seen how religious leaders create and strengthen religious societies. There is abundant evidence that even primitive tribal groups have religious cohesion, and that living religions everywhere establish communions. Members are approved, initiated and expelled. Codes, creeds, and traditions develop in the course of time to guide the members. Records, scriptures, and rituals provide the authority and symbols of tradition. Hope and expectation, faith and labors arise as ongoing purposes of social unity.

Not all communities become universal. Few of them, in fact, ever extend so far in plan or action. Some religious communities have open membership; many do not. Some claim a mission to all peoples and hope for the salvation of all. Hinduism, Buddhism, Judaism, Christianity, and Islam have this universal outlook. Yet even with these religions universality is an ideal rather than a fact. No religious community has actually included everyone. Few have invited all into their folds or desired to be universal.

Why have a universal community? This question is less debatable every year as the tragedies of conflict and the need of world unity become more crucial. Though some deny the necessity for a world community, it is increasingly clear that the welfare of each depends upon the community of all. Modern transportation and communication, interdependent economic structures, the far-reaching effects of global warfare, the need for international organizations to resolve conflicts—all these demand a world community. In the world calamity of suicidal warfare, the human race desperately needs social salvation to uphold the interpersonal values of living together.

G. M. Stratton [5] makes a psychological analysis of causes of violence and suggests a way of liberation. He applies the scientific method of agreement and difference to regions of violence, to discover what dynamic fact comes and goes or increases and decreases, with the presence and absence of war itself. He lists areas of violence, and finds that one dynamic condition is present when violence is infrequent and absent when violence is frequent. Violence appears where the bonds of community are weak, and disappears where communal ties are strong. The decisive causal factor in doing away with conflict and violent destruction is a healthy community. These social ties are causally related to the kind of behavior desired. A community may be a family, a village, or a commonwealth of nations. But a community has power to dissolve violent impulses into good will and co-operation.

Communities have already accomplished these results in small ways, according to their dimensions. But this tragic hour of history is the time for a universal community. If we want to unite a broken world whose hostilities are rapidly destroying civilized values, a world community is indicated. If we desire to practice democracy and justice with equal opportunities for all, there is need to recognize unlimited human brotherhood—one blood and one race of mankind. If we desire to affirm monotheism, we will declare the universal ethical relationship of God and all men. Belief in one God logically requires belief in one world and one

[5] "Violence Between Nations; Deeper Sources; The Way of Liberation," The Psychological Review, LI (1944), 85-101.

family. Divisions on earth deny unity in heaven. If we desire to extend the range of human ideals and purposes we shall move toward a universal community. Local ideals are fragmentary. Science seeks universal laws; true justice, morality, and religion cannot do less.

There are many resistances that obstruct the coming of universal community. There is the intellectual anarchy of intolerant, diverging beliefs, unwilling to agree or to seek a common ground. There is the moral anarchy of exclusive practices that condemn the outsider and refuse to find a mutual code of conduct. There is the administrative anarchy of conflicting institutions that proceed on lines of absolute sovereignty, admitting no responsibility to rival groups. There is the social anarchy of selfish hostility that obstructs larger loyalties and will not choose a way of reconciliation. Religion might save us from this impasse of sterile death, for it has the creative seeds of new life. But, unfortunately, religious communities are infected with the same germs; and they, too, fall short of universality.

What prevents universality in religious communities? (*a*) Particular interests are focal in every we-group, and this ethnocentric tendency appears in religious communities also. (*b*) Local traditions may separate the in-group from the world at large. (*c*) Rival sects and religions tend to exclude others and to claim superiority for themselves. (*d*) A sense of possessing unique values to cherish as sacred prevents the likelihood of making them common in open sharing. (*e*) Pride and prejudice against outsiders are likely to arise in any group—even in religious groups whose teachings counteract such feelings. (*f*) A high threshold for admission to membership, a creed to believe, and a code to obey, naturally keep some out. (*g*) Social-cultural barriers of language, customs, beliefs, nationality, and geographic boundaries also work against the inclusion of all mankind in a universal religious community.

What are religious persons doing to enlarge their community

relations? Walter Lippmann in a widely read statement [6] reports a shrinking of religious communities in our time. Underneath the acids of modernity he finds a loss of certainty and a breakdown of religious authority. Religion, he contends, has lost one province after another where control was once exercised. Business is not regulated by religious codes, the family has forgotten religious observances, art has turned from painting religious scenes, social service and healing are carried on by secular agencies, education is now conducted by the state, and morality obeys reason rather than religious authority. He makes a convincing case for these receding religious boundaries.

But these processes work both ways. When walls of separation come down, the tides ebb and flow between religious and secular shores. If secular interests come into religious domains, so does religion go into secular fields. Religion enters all aspects of life with its ideals, permeating the whole texture of social living. It becomes less exclusive in its regulations and more inclusive in its outreach. The editors of *Fortune Magazine* [7] show how religious ideals stressing the worth of every person have become the basis of American democracy. Sorokin surveys cultural trends for 3,500 years, showing the present decay of sensate culture and the revival of ideational (religious) values. [8] In the dislocations of the second World War it appears that the only effective world-wide organizations are the religious bodies. Unifications within Christion denominations are proceeding to a World Council of Churches, with ecumenical aims and with facilities to maintain community relations across enemy lines.

There is also a waking sense of community among the supranational religions of the world. Outreachings toward mutual recognition and co-operation are evident in Buddhism, Christianity, Hinduism, Islam, and Judaism. The Parliament of Religions, held

[6] *A Preface to Morals* (New York: The Macmillan Co., 1929).
[7] *Fortune Magazine*, XXI (1940), 26-27.
[8] *The Crisis of Our Age.*

at Chicago in 1895, was an augury of this development. The International Missionary Council, meeting at Edinburgh in 1910, declared that "the missionary should seek for the nobler elements in non-Christian religions." [9] A later meeting of this council, held at Jerusalem in 1928 accepted these religions as "witnesses of man's need of God and allies in our quest of perfection." [10] The Madras Conference, held in 1938, said:

> We see and readily recognize that in them [non-Christian religions] are to be found values of deep religious experience and great moral achievement.[11]

The Layman's Missionary Inquiry, sponsored jointly by several Christian denominations in 1932, brings the viewpoint of sharing mutual values:

> As Christianity shares this faith with men of all faiths, they become changed into the same substance. The names which now separate them lose their divisive meaning; and there need be no loss of the historic thread of devotion which unites each to its origin and inspirations.[12]

Hocking [13] believes that the way to a world faith is neither through radical displacement (the traditional missionary approach) nor through synthesis (the recent liberal approach). It lies rather in the way of reconception, which is a deepening of insight through greater understanding of all religious possibilities. To follow this way of deepening insight is to discover, through increased understanding of all religions, the saving truth in each religion. To follow this way is to reach a decision to be a better vehicle of truth, in co-operation with all who care for the truth.

[9] *World Missionary Conference* (New York: Fleming H. Revell Co., 1919), IV, 267.
[10] *The Jerusalem Meeting* (New York: International Missionary Council, 1928), I, 273.
[11] *The Madras Series* (New York: International Missionary Council, 1939), I, 184.
[12] *Re-Thinking Missions* (New York: The Macmillan Co., 1932).
[13] *Living Religions and a World Faith* (New York: The Macmillan Co., 1940).

3. Religion as Co-operation

Universal religion is voluntary co-operation with all good for the good of all. At least five living religions, noted above, have universal aspirations. Yet most religions are somewhat less than universal. There are selfish religions for private advantage, tribal religions for tribal advantage (totemism), national religions for national advantage (Shinto), and ethnic religions for ethnical advantage (Judaism, Mohammedanism, Hinduism with its caste system, and Christianity that excludes Negroes). Is there any universal religion today? How universal are we? We are universal in ideal more than in practice. Every religion and culture could practice more universal freedom, responsibility, and love.

Keeping in mind the opening thesis of this section, let us consider several questions. First, is our co-operation voluntary? Co-operation of occupied countries with a conqueror is not voluntary. Military control, even in a democracy, is totalitarian: for war is essentially coercion. And whatever it may be in definition, no democracy is wholly voluntary in fact. In cities and states the citizens must obey certain laws. In homes and schools the children must obey parents and teachers. What of voluntary co-operation in religious organizations? The Roman Catholic Church requires attendance and confession, imposes penances, exacts obedience, and excommunicates offenders. Protestant churches exercise authority in the ordination and appointment of ministers, in creed, and in conduct. They are voluntary in membership—one may join or resign at will. They permit and defend freedom of conscience, and they usually recognize freedom of individual judgment as to interpretation of the faith. The church, unlike any other major institution, exists by the voluntary support of its members.

Second, do we co-operate with all good? The good means, first, God—to those who are theists. And atheists may co-operate with God by another name in seeking truth, beauty, or goodness in a cosmic order. In so far as one knows the good and desires to co-operate with good purposes in the universe he is religious. This also means co-operation with good persons, for the larger good can be achieved only by working together. Yet no one of us is wholly good, so how can we isolate the good entirely from the bad? We cannot; the only way to co-operate with all good is to work with the good in a bad context. To do this a religious person must discover good in strangers, enemies, and criminals. He will with hearty co-operation appreciate and develop the good in bad people. He will seek not to co-operate with the evil; yet some evil will be involved in human situations, and this he will try to transmute into good.

To pursue the religious thesis another step, let us ask, Do we work for the good of all? It is customary to love friends and hate enemies. Yet this is not characteristic of a universal religion. Mo Ti taught that the will of heaven is universal love. Jesus taught that we should love our enemies, but the practice is difficult. Lao Tze and Paul advocated returning good for evil, but *lex talionis* is more popular. We give of our goods to strangers and aliens in times of famine and flood, and through war relief and lend-lease—modern enterprises on a larger scale than ancient alms and charity.

Another question is needed at this point. Do we see that it is better to work with others than for others? Working for others is unselfish service, but it is not co-operation. Co-operation means working with others in free and democratic association. Much effort and many good intentions fail when decisions are made for others—pushing and pulling, correcting and controlling them for their own good. The resentment of colonials against imperialism and of children, workers, and citizens against the dominating authority is sufficient to explode the claims of benevolent dictatorship and well-meaning paternalism. True democracy respects every person too much to deprive him of the right to choose. The basic moral and religious issue in this regard is, Who decides? Shall conscience, the right of individual judgment, be freely responsible, or bound by some superior authority, without personal choice?

To test any religion, personal or institutional, by these questions is clarifying. If there is not voluntary co-operation with all good for the good of all, is the religion good enough for the democratic aspirations of our time? Have the coal miners as much right as the coal operators and the federal labor board to decide what wages are fair? Have the people of India or Cuba as much right as the governments of England and the United States to decide what political forms they will have? Has the parish priest as much right as the Pope, or the layman as much right as the ordained minister, to decide what his religious duty is? Does a church have the right to exclude anyone who desires to be a member? These questions are controversial, but they are vital to the searching of our generation for a universal religion with co-operation justly open to all.

Are religious action and religious education in our sphere democratic, voluntary co-operation? To some extent they are but a large part of both is careless repetition of second-hand traditions and habits, thoughtless following of familiar routine, with little awareness and less than complete devotion. Members of religious communities are prone to take their privilege for granted, to accept traditional issues as having been settled long ago, and to consider their part too insignificant to call forth maximum loyalty or heroic achievement. Unconvinced that urgent values are at stake or that anything great is to happen through religious means, many consider their participation a matter of no importance.

Coe has diagnosed the ill-health of Christian education as resulting from its transmissive character. If education is to succeed it must be creative rather than transmissive. Transmissive education perpetuates our errors and adds to their prestige.[14]

The creative Christian principle is the worth of persons. Personality can grow or its growth can be arrested through play and appreciation, the awakening of motives, friendship and loyalty,

[14] *What Is Christian Education?* (New York: Charles Scribner's Sons, 1929).

difficulty and opposition, defeat and suffering, mistakes and sinning, worship and aspiration. Christianity needs to assimilate the scientific attitude, to experiment and work with real causes and effects in persons and society. The growing point of creativity is the inherent radicalism of Christianity. The possibility of being born again and of remaking society is the revolutionary principle that has transformed persons and cultures where the Christian leaven has come to work. Our religious education, to be creative, must face toward social action in which persons freely co-operate to build a new world. To labor together in the unfinished tasks of the family of God will link the young with the old, the past with the present and the future. If religion is to become universal voluntary co-operation it must be more than a formal transmission of a sterile past, it must be a creative rebirth of civilization through the unselfish devotion of aroused personalities.

4. THE SOCIAL FUNCTION OF THE CHURCH

The church is a voluntary association of persons for the purpose of religious growth. It is natural, as we have seen, for every religion to form its societies. The purpose of a church is definitely social, yet not the same as other societies, for it is never merely social. It reaches into the realm of religious growth. The social aim is generally accepted wherever two or three people gather, yet not always in the same way. Is the social function of the church to save individuals or to change the world?

If the aim is to save individuals from an evil world the method will be withdrawal. The procedure will be to condemn the world as hopeless, and to put as much distance as possible between the religious person and the world. Holy men of various religions have renounced the world to go apart as hermits, or to live in monasteries, where religious orders establish retreats from the folly of worldliness. Otherworldly movements are based upon the conviction that the world is so bad or so unreal that individuals cannot be saved in the world, but only apart from the world.

According to this viewpoint the social function of the church is to rescue souls as brands from the burning, just as a fireman seeks to rescue persons from a conflagration that is beyond control.

We are now living in one of the epochs of history when this view might seem plausible. The evils of total war—oppression, persecution, separation, homelessness, famine, illness, suffering, and death—weigh as intolerable burdens upon us all. The dream of a better world has to many people become a nightmare of despair. The plans of the wisest men in every nation have gone sadly awry. With the vastly enlarged resources of modern science and invention, a good life had seemed abundantly possible for all —except for our lusts of power and acquisition and revenge, by reason of which all resources are now perverted to mutual destruction. The evils of the world overwhelm us and threaten disaster unless there is some way of escape. To remain in the midst of such evil is to be mired down in its futility. Is there no way out but the way of the refugee, dispossessed and freed of attachment, who becomes a pilgrim to another world?

Churches are known as sanctuaries. A sanctuary is a place of refuge in time of distress. A religious sanctuary is a home for the troubled and wounded spirit of man. It may be as far away as heaven, or as near as the next room. In other dark ages a pilgrim's progress was to move out of this world into a distant heaven which was the eternal home of the soul. In this era the church may serve as a sanctuary to strengthen the inner life so that whatever happens will not shatter one's central poise, but spiritual resources will enable a man to live in the world and endure the slings of outrage without dismay.

A study of Maryland young people between the ages of sixteen and twenty-four, made by the American Youth Commission,[15] reveals interesting attitudes toward the church. Of 13,528 young people studied, 65.8 per cent were from Protestant homes, 18.6

[15] H. M. Bell, *Youth Tell Their Story* (Washington: American Council on Education, 1938), pp. 193-205.

per cent from Catholic homes, 8.5 per cent from homes of mixed religious affiliation, 3.6 per cent had Jewish parents, and 2.5 per cent were from homes having no church affiliation. Of the entire group, 81.1 per cent had adopted the faith of both parents. Ninety-three per cent of the Catholic youth regarded themselves as church members, 69 per cent of the Protestant group; 66.9 per cent of those of mixed affiliation; 62 per cent of the Jewish; and 22.6 per cent of those whose parents had no affiliation.

They were asked, What is the function of the church? How often should sermons deal with current political and economic problems? Their belief in the detachment of the church is shown in the fact that 60 per cent answered "Never under any circumstances." Of those taking this view, 70.5 per cent were Catholic, 56.8 per cent Protestant, and 51.3 per cent Jewish. Some of their replies were:

Government problems should never be mixed with religion.
Preachers don't know enough about such things to talk about them.
The sermon's long enough as it is.
Church service should be solemn and sacred, not talking about law.
You can hear enough of that on the radio.
They're supposed to be preaching about the Lord.
There are plenty of other places to talk about those things.
Church should be spiritual.
I want to forget such problems in church.
A man who is a good church member doesn't have much to do with politics.

There were others, however, who felt that sermons should occasionally deal with such topics. They commented:

This old idea of Hell and Damnation gets tiresome.
I think it would be nice to break the monotony.
It depends entirely upon the minister. If he is unbiased, his talks on such problems should be useful.

Should not preach on politics, but it would help if they preached on things of *this* life instead of the next.

If they talked about more things like this, more people would go to church.

They do more good for you than all this talk about souls.

I'd much rather have sermons on current events than the same old Five Books of Moses.

There is another way besides escape from the evils of the world. Religious persons may enter the world and devote themselves to overcoming those evils with good. From this point of view the social function of the church is more than the saving of individuals; it is the entire reconstruction of society. The creation of a new world order is inherent in the program of Jesus—the establishment of the Kingdom of God on earth and the commission to baptize all nations as well as all individuals. The church has found that persons cannot be saved without redeeming the social order in which they live. Increasingly, therefore, the Christian mission has undertaken to transform the world as well as the individual. This is by far the more difficult task, but to neglect it is to fail in the whole enterprise of religious growth which is the business of the church. Totalitarian states demonstrate that freedom to worship, freedom of conscience, freedom of speech and assembly, all essential to the continuance of churches, may be crushed. The control of churches by wealth and vested interests, or by the social prestige of powerful aristocracies, also threatens the freedom of religion to do its work. To maintain its very existence, then, the church must redeem the larger society in which it lives.

The two most significant movements of Christianity in the early twentieth century have been missions and the social gospel. Neither of them has been primarily concerned in saving the church. Both have been motivated by the desire to help people less fortunate. Christian missions have gone forth, not only to save souls, but to heal bodies, to correct social ills, and to raise standards of living. The social gospel in liberal Protestantism has almost forgotten the church in its zeal to apply Christian principles to the relations of men and to transform the entire social order.

The social gospel and liberalism have been overoptimistic in assuming that men are reasonable enough to adopt the Golden Rule in business and politics when it is presented to them as the true solution. Christian principles if and when practiced, might correct most of the social ills that afflict us. Sound ethical principles have been enacted into legislation, and hopefully adopted as social reforms that ought to succeed. And yet human nature has failed time and again to live up to approved ideals, succumbing to temptation or inertia and letting reforms collapse for want of adequate support. The bitter experience of repeated failures brings the sobering conviction that man is not a creature of pure reason who will readily and naturally do what is right. A tragic contradiction in man's nature betrays him to self-defeat.

Democracy suffers from a similar illusion—that man is a creature of reason whose individual interests may balance in a laissez-faire utopia to the justice and welfare of all. A deeper understanding of human nature is needed. The psychology of the nineteenth century was too superficial to reveal the irrational forces that control much of human conduct. A more profound psychological insight is now dawning, in the light of which the task of redeeming man and reconstructing society is seen to be immeasurably difficult. Utopian schemes of social planning may be architecturally perfect on paper, but when live men and women try to work out their conflicting desires together the scene is different. The Kellogg Pact theoretically should have ended war —did not the fifty-four nations solemnly promise to have no recourse thereto? The New Deal should have outmoded economic cycles of inflation and depression by its controlled credit, public works, and social security for all. But somehow, in spite of these reasonable charts of progress, we came headlong into war, inflation, economic scarcity, and insecurity.

Social failures may lead some people to despair, but they counsel others to learn from the mistakes and to work out better solutions. The Christian church is evidently taking the social perplexities as a challenge, and seeking to meet these desperate human needs with more effective service. Denominational and interdenominational crusades for a new world order, increased giving for overseas relief and missions, lively interest in the character of the postwar world, and determination to participate actively in the forming of that world—these activities indicate that churches are not withdrawing from the social problems of our time. The ecumenical movement, issuing in a World Council of Churches, further indicates the desire to unite for Christian action on a planetary scale.

The social function of the church is consequently growing larger. The saving of individuals is not forgotten, but the reconstruction of society is more consciously accepted as the task of the church. This is not a new departure from the traditional purpose of the church in promoting religious growth in persons and society. The historical contribution of Christianity to social welfare provides significant resources for the modern task.

a) The church has a *social philosophy* which affirms the value of every person, the importance of community values, and the pattern of brotherhood.

b) The church has a *social ethic* arising from the Hebrew law and prophets, re-created by Jesus and the apostles into a code of conduct that is interpersonal and unselfish. Every virtue has a social reference.

c) The church has a *social service* that has issued in charity and relief of poverty, hospital service to care for the sick and helpless, prison service to redeem the criminal and improve his environment, education for all, social settlements and recreation, social case work and counseling, intercultural adjustment of peoples strange to each other, the elevation of women and children, enrichment of home life, and the stimulation of neighborhood activities for the mutual growth of persons in social relations.

d) The church has a *social psychology*. The Hebrew-Christian view of man is in fact a depth psychology, touching the hidden motives of behavior. The doctrine of sin recognizes irrational tendencies and uncontrolled impulses that make man, with his resourcefulness at once the highest and the most dangerous of all animals. Sin is neither accidental nor local. All men sin because it is their nature to be tempted to evil. The social fact of sin is seen as the racial inheritance and the interaction of these tendencies. The idea of original sin has been misunderstood by many, but its true meaning is that human nature has certain sinful possibilities that we make actual by personal choices and social provocations. We may be unconscious of these destructive forces until social situations call them forth in passionate outbursts or in cool deliberations to do evil. No depth psychology is more realistic about human nature, nor better comprehends the difficulty of dealing with it in order to transform its evil tendencies into good ones.

Yet Christianity does not despair of human nature. For it sees more than the evil in man—it sees also the good that can triumph over the evil. And therewith it offers a way of deliverance, in relating every man to a God who helps to redeem him from evil into larger good, and to a community that reinforces his better impulses with loving-kindness, moral support, and mutual aid for the welfare of all. There is much to discourage men and to confirm them in the bitter poison of cynicism. Such a view is fragmentary, seeing only partially some of the facts and ignoring resources otherwise available. Christian psychology sees other facts and discovers other resources that open new hope for better persons in a better society. These resources include higher loyalty, greater courage and endurance, faith in spite of defeat, heroic powers of self-discipline and self-sacrifice, a reassuring sense of invisible companionships, independence of sensate values through satisfaction in spiritual values, hope in the ultimate triumph of goodness, and a love stronger than death that is able to give all and forgive all. As we learn better to use these religious resources the psychosocial powers of creative goodness will develop in persons and in society.

5. PROGRESS AND DECLINE

All is not well with human society. Progress has been won at some times and in some places—enough to tantalize us with hopes of the better world that may be ours. But the insatiable desires of men lead to hell as well as to heaven. Having sown the dragon's teeth of conflict, they can see no way to stop the hostilities. Rivalries provoke other rivalries, vengeance invites greater vengeance, wars cease only to prepare for more total wars. The extent of destruction and human misery has reached an incomparable nadir of tragedy. What is the cause of this world crisis, and what is the direction from here on?

There are many causes, no doubt. We hear much of economic, political, geographical, and social causes. That such factors are involved is obvious; but that any one of them represents the basic cause is dubious. The basic causes of human behavior are the psychological motives that urge men to action. No matter what geographical situation, economic resources, political forms, or social status men may have, they are likely to want them otherwise. If the grass looks greener across the boundary, if the materials and markets are attractive, if the political scene obstructs desires or the social position makes one feel inferior, men will revolt. The causes of the social crisis in our world are psychological.

If the causes of social crisis are psychological, the cure will also be psychological. Whatever remedies may be attempted externally will fail until there are inner changes in the motives of men. The kingdom of man, no less than the Kingdom of God is within. Here must begin whatever change will be deeply radical enough to change the world. The new society we desire to create must be born in the hearts of men. The religious requirement of regeneration applies to societies as well as to persons. Nothing less than rebirth will reconstruct the world order to the design of justice and good will. This is not a new idea, but it is a fundamental one. It has been uttered before, but it will have to be comprehended anew in each crisis, including the present one.

In a recent book Lewis Mumford [16] diagnoses our capitalistic, imperialistic, militaristic society. The condition peculiar to man is the fact that he alone of all animals has foreknowledge of his own death, the ability to look before and after and to live in the past, the present, and the possible. Out of this disturbing awareness of the brevity of his life arises a discontent that he can assuage only by so living "that Man redeems the littleness of individual men." In the consequent historical process, man has mastered nature and transformed himself by ever new goals that emerge from and lead toward self-transcendence. In the present crisis of civilization the new barbarian threatening to reduce us to slavery is not beating on the gates from without but has arisen from within the walls. Man's animal nature, too long suppressed, turns in revolt against our hypocrisies. The basis of renewal, Mumford shows, is in man's turning his major energies from conquest of the external world to the remaking of the inner world.

Another diagnosis of the current predicament of man is made by Gerald Heard.[17] He finds two psychological principles of all living action: (a) the principle of simple growth—expansion— and (b) the principle which follows from growth—divergence. Life increases not only in size but in complexity. In man's development the speed of expansion puts his progress far ahead of that of other animals, and yet the complex divergences result in shocking disasters and collapses that do not befall the lower animals. The force of change in man's growth is almost beyond his control to moderate, and speed without control results in wrecks. Successful growth is possible only when expansion is balanced by cohesion. The more complex human culture becomes, the more strain is put upon the power to cohere.

[16] *The Condition of Man* (New York: Harcourt, Brace & Co., 1944).
[17] *Man the Master* (New York: Harper & Bros., 1941).

In the long march of history the tempo of human progress has accelerated until the modern age has become an age of revolution. Man has long since come to distinguish an inner world of values and spirit from an outer world of physical means and powers. The perception of the inner world is religious insight, in contrast to the physical grasp of material objects in the outer world. When religious insight is conservative and restrictive it does not advance with the aggressive grasp of the physical world. Then, men come to feel that religion is untrue and that the spiritual values are mere superstition. Efforts to compromise with a double truth that assigns religion to values and science to facts is an impossible division that only widens the breach. Men strive to advance their physical knowledge and possessions in disregard of their consciences. This attitude results in the collapse of an unbalanced social order in which religion is involved and in which it is discredited in the general bankruptcy of values.

Social failure results from this inability to find reality, to keep a balanced hold upon the inner and outer worlds. Democracy is weakened by opportunities for self-advancement that play upon the lust for power and acquisition until individuals forget to share the inner values that hold them together, and consequently fall apart in anarchy. Totalitarianism takes over a nation when this essential cohesion has been exhausted and no religious knowledge of the inner world has come to renew it. Communities are filled with self-conscious individuals severed from their deeper psychic resources who cannot experience social cohesion. Only the outer world seems real, and it is indifferent to moral and social values. To save society from collapse a dictator uses force to hold together what no longer coheres by consent. But dictatorships also fail, because coercion exhausts further the natural cohesion of creative consent.

Our crisis is also an opportunity; for distress can make men aware of what they have lost and of what they need. A revival of religious insight can show the deeper psychic sources of unity and motivate a balanced progress toward worthier goals. A third way lies between the horns of the present political dilemma—between democratic inefficiency, on the one hand, and totalitarian tyranny on the other. This way seeks the social goal of organic democracy, where freedom and unity meet and the outer world comes to harmony with the inner world of spiritual values. In this way, man can be the master of his future.

Predictions of the future are hazardous at any time, and especially so when world upheaval is changing everything, clouds of war make visibility low, and issues hang in the balance, undecided. The course of the future is ever hypothetical, for the future depends upon so many unknown factors. Yet the future will grow out of the present—of this we may be sure. We can know the present and so learn of the future; we can do things now to shape the future we desire. The future is a capital X in the human equation; but there are many small x's, the unknowns that will be decided by our choices, together with the choices of others. And these small x's will add up to the greater X of the future.

Two trends only will be noted here. Human efforts to achieve values move in conservative and radical directions. Conservative tendencies are those of self-defense, self-despair, and self-deception. Anxiety over values leads to futile efforts to defend them by aggression or withdrawal—either to destroy or to escape rivals. When defensive tactics fail, persons and societies are cast into despair, feeling inferior and inadequate. To escape this intolerable disgust and repudiation, they naturally seek the haven of self-deception. By repressing frustrated desires and painful memories they hope to dispose of them and be happy again. But deception will not rest; and the old anxieties, thrusting up against the ego, deny peace and perpetuate conflict. This is the vicious circle of false conservative tendencies in the human drama.

Radical tendencies are self-correcting, self-giving, and mutually creative. The radical approach to human values has nothing to defend. Freely admitting the possibilities of error, the radical method begins in the critical effort to discover and correct one's own errors. The exposing of errors is preliminary to the correcting of them by a reform, a radical one, from the root. In this process the radical is self-giving, for he gives up his pride and gives away his false pretensions. In the act of self-giving he learns the art of sharing with others. Seeing the folly of giving only what he does not want, he comes to share his values with others—the truth as well as errors, the hopes and aspirations, the insights and hypotheses that may encourage others to join the pursuit of true values. This sharing bridges the gap between individuals, establishes a basis for continuous sharing, and leads to co-operation in the social creation of values.

If a religious community is to succeed in promoting the growth of values in persons and in social relations, it may well take the radical approach. For conservative efforts, even with the best of intentions and used with the utmost caution, will tend to destroy those values they seek to save. Radical efforts, on the other hand, take greater risks apparently; but in reality they are more likely to succeed, because they are not defensive. Defense is inevitably fearful in outlook and self-centered in aim. It results in social failure through rivalry, aggression, evasion, and isolation. Religion will decay and decline along the conservative axis. Radical correction is fearless, adventurous; it dares to give up its pride, and is ready to co-operate in reforming the false and unworthy. Religion will progress and be socially creative along the way of radical reconstruction. Of such growth there is no end.

Bibliography

ALLPORT, G. W. *Personality: A Psychological Interpretation*. New York: Henry Holt & Co., 1937.

AMES, E. S. *The Psychology of Religious Experience*. Boston: Houghton Mifflin Co., 1910.

ANGYAL, ANDRAS. *Foundations for a Science of Personality*. New York: The Commonwealth Fund, 1941.

ATHEARN. W. S., *et al. Indiana Survey of Religious Education* (3 vols.). New York: George H. Doran Co., 1924.

BARBOUR, C. E. *Sin and the New Psychology*. New York: The Abingdon Press, 1930.

BARRY, F. R. *Christianity and Psychology*. New York: George H. Doran Co., 1923.

BLANTON, SMILEY, and N. V. PEALE. *Faith Is the Answer*. New York: Abingdon-Cokesbury Press, 1940.

BOISEN, A. T. *The Exploration of the Inner World*. Chicago: Willett, Clark & Co., 1936.

BONNELL, J. T. *Pastoral Psychiatry*. New York: Harper & Bros., 1938.

BORING, E. G. *A History of Experimental Psychology*. New York: D. Appleton-Century Co., 1929.

BRIGHTMAN, E. S. *Religious Values*. New York and Nashville: Abingdon-Cokesbury Press, 1925.

———. *Moral Laws*. New York and Nashville: Abingdon-Cokesbury Press, 1933.

———. *Personality and Religion*. New York: The Abingdon Press, 1934.

———. *A Philosophy of Religion*. New York: Prentice-Hall, Inc., 1940.

BRILL, A. A. (ed.) *The Basic Writings of Sigmund Freud*. New York: Random House, Inc., 1938.

BRUCE, W. S. *The Psychology of Christian Life and Behaviour*. New York: Charles Scribner's Sons, 1923.

BUTTRICK, G. A. *Prayer*. New York and Nashville: Abingdon-Cokesbury Press, 1942.

CABOT, R. C. *The Meaning of Right and Wrong.* New York: The Macmillan Co., 1933; 1936.

———— and R. L. DICKS. *The Art of Ministering to the Sick.* New York: The Macmillan Co., 1936.

CLARK, E. T. *The Psychology of Religious Awakening.* New York: The Macmillan Co., 1929.

COE, G. A. *The Spiritual Life.* New York: Methodist Book Concern, 1900.

————. *The Psychology of Religion.* Chicago: University of Chicago Press, 1916.

————. *What Is Christian Education?* New York: Charles Scribner's Sons, 1929.

CONKLIN, E. S. *The Psychology of Religious Adjustment.* New York: The Macmillan Co., 1929.

CRONBACH, ABRAHAM. "The Psychology of Religion: A Bibliographical Survey." *Psychological Bulletin*, XXV (1928), 701-18.

CUTTEN, G. B. *The Psychological Phenomena of Christianity.* New York: Charles Scribner's Sons, 1908.

DE SANCTIS, SANTE. *Religious Conversion* (tr. H. Augur). New York: Harcourt, Brace & Co., 1927.

DRESSER, H. W. *Outlines of the Psychology of Religion.* New York: Thomas Y. Crowell Co., 1929.

DURKHEIM, EMILE. *The Elementary Forms of Religious Life* (tr. J. W. Swain). London: George Allen & Unwin, Ltd., 1915.

EDWARD, KENNETH. *Religious Experience: Its Nature and Truth.* Edinburgh: T. & T. Clark, 1926.

Encyclopaedia of Religion and Ethics (ed. James Hastings, 12 vols.). New York: Charles Scribner's Sons, 1908-27.

EVERETT, W. G. *Moral Values.* New York: Henry Holt & Co., 1918.

FLOWER, J. C. *An Approach to the Psychology of Religion.* New York: Harcourt, Brace & Co., 1927.

FRIESS, H. L., and H. W. SCHNEIDER. *Religion in Various Cultures.* New York: Henry Holt & Co., 1932.

FREUD, SIGMUND. *Civilization and Its Discontents* (tr. J. Riviere). New York: Cape & Smith, 1930.

274

GARRISON, K. C. *The Psychology of Adolescence*. New York: Prentice-Hall, 1934; 1940.

GESELL, ARNOLD. *Infancy and Human Growth*. New York: The Macmillan Co., 1929.

HADFIELD, J. A. *Psychology and Morals*. New York: Robert M. McBride & Co., 1925.

HALL, G. S. *Adolescence* (2 vols.). New York: D. Appleton & Co., 1904.

HARTSHORNE, HUGH. *Childhood and Character*. Boston: The Pilgrim Press, 1919.

―――― and M. A. MAY. *Studies in Deceit*. New York: The Macmillan Co., 1928.

―――― and J. B. MALLER. *Studies in Service and Self-Control*. New York: The Macmillan Co., 1929.

―――― and F. J. SHUTTLEWORTH. *Studies in the Organization of Character*. New York: The Macmillan Co., 1930.

HEIDBREDER, EDNA. *Seven Psychologies*. New York: D. Appleton-Century Co., 1933.

HEILER, FRIEDRICH. *Prayer*. (tr. S. McComb and J. E. Park). London: Oxford University Press [1919], 1932.

――――. *The Spirit of Worship*. (tr. W. Montgomery). New York: George H. Doran Co., 1926.

HERMAN, EMILY. *Creative Prayer*. New York: George H. Doran Co., 1921.

HICKMAN, F. S. *Introduction to the Psychology of Religion*, New York: The Abingdon Press, 1926.

HILTNER, SEWARD. *Religion and Health*. New York: The Macmillan Co., 1943.

HOCKING, W. E. *The Meaning of God in Human Experience*. New Haven: Yale University Press, 1912.

――――. *Human Nature and Its Remaking*. New Haven: Yale University Press, 1923.

HÖFFDING, HARALD. *The Philosophy of Religion* (tr. B. E. Meyer). London: The Macmillan Co., 1906; 1914.

HOLMAN, C. T. *The Religion of a Healthy Mind*. New York: Round Table Press, Inc., 1939.

HOOKE, S. H. (ed.). *Myth and Ritual.* London: Oxford University Press, 1933.

HORNEY, KAREN. *The Neurotic Personality of Our Time.* New York: W. W. Norton & Co., 1937.

―――. *New Ways of Psychoanalysis.* New York: W. W. Norton & Co., 1939.

―――. *Self-Analysis.* New York: W. W. Norton & Co., 1942.

HORTON, W. M. *A Psychological Approach to Theology.* New York: Harper & Bros., 1931.

HUGHES, T. H. *The New Psychology and Religious Experience.* London: George Allen & Unwin, Ltd., 1933.

HUSBAND, R. W. *General Psychology.* New York: Farrar & Rinehart, 1940.

JAMES, WILLIAM. *The Varieties of Religious Experience.* New York: Longmans, Green & Co., 1902.

―――. *Selected Papers on Philosophy.* New York: E. P. Dutton & Co., 1917.

JOHNSON, P. E. *Who Are You?* New York and Nashville: Abingdon-Cokesbury Press, 1937.

JOSEY, C. C. *The Psychology of Religion.* New York: The Macmillan Co., 1927.

JUNG, C. G. *Psychological Types.* New York: Harcourt, Brace & Co., 1926.

―――. *Modern Man in Search of a Soul.* New York: Harcourt, Brace & Co., 1934.

KING, IRVING. *The Development of Religion.* New York: The Macmillan Co., 1910.

KNUDSON, A. C. *The Validity of Religious Experience.* New York and Nashville: Abingdon-Cokesbury Press, 1937.

KOFFKA, KURT. *The Growth of Mind* (tr. R. M. Ogden). New York: Harcourt, Brace & Co., 1924; 1928.

KÖHLER, WOLFGANG. *The Mentality of Apes* (tr. E. Winter). New York: Harcourt, Brace & Co., 1926.

KÜNKEL, FRITZ. *In Search of Maturity.* New York: Charles Scribner's Sons, 1943.

KUPKY, OSKAR. *The Religious Development of Adolescents* (tr. W. C. Trow). New York: The Macmillan Co., 1928.

LEUBA, J. H. *A Psychological Study of Religion*. New York: The Macmillan Co., 1912.
———. *The Belief in God and Immortality*. Chicago: Open Court Publishing Co., 1921.
———. *The Psychology of Religious Mysticism*. New York: Harcourt, Brace, & Co., 1925.

LIGON, E. M. *The Psychology of Christian Personality*. New York: The Macmillan Co., 1936.
———. *Their Future Is Now*. New York: The Macmillan Co., 1939.

LINK, H. C. *The Return to Religion*. New York: The Macmillan Co., 1936.

LUNDHOLM, O. H. *The Psychology of Belief*. Durham, N. C.: Duke University Press, 1936.

McDOUGALL, WILLIAM. *An Introduction to Social Psychology*. Boston: J. W. Luce & Co. [1908], 1918.
———. *The Energies of Men*. New York: Charles Scribner's Sons, 1932.

MAHONEY, C. K. *The Religious Mind*. New York: The Macmillan Co., 1927.

MARETT, R. R. *The Threshold of Religion*. London: Methuen & Co., 1909; 1914.

MARTIN, E. D. *The Mystery of Religion*. New York: Harper & Bros., 1924.

MAY, ROLLO. *The Art of Counseling*. New York and Nashville: Abingdon-Cokesbury Press, 1939.

MELAND, B. E. *Modern Man's Worship*. New York: Harper & Bros., 1934.

MILLER, J. G. *Unconsciousness*. New York: John Wiley & Sons, 1942.

MOORE, J. S. *The Foundations of Psychology*. Princeton: University Press, 1921.

MÜLLER-FREIENFELS, RICHARD. *The Evolution of Modern Psychology* (tr. W. B. Wolfe). New Haven: Yale University Press, 1935.

MUMFORD, E. E. *The Dawn of Character*. New York: Longmans, Green & Co., 1910; 1925.

MURPHY, GARDNER. *An Historical Introduction to Modern Psychology.* New York: Harcourt, Brace & Co., 1928; 1932.

MURRAY, H. A. *Explorations in Personality.* New York: Oxford University Press, 1938.

NIETZSCHE, FRIEDRICH. *Thus Spake Zarathustra.*

OLIVER, J. R. *Psychiatry and Mental Health.* New York: Charles Scribner's Sons, 1932.

OTTO, RUDOLF. *The Idea of the Holy* (tr. J. W. Harvey). London: Oxford University Press, 1923.

———. *Mysticism East and West* (tr. B. L. Bracey and R. C. Payne). New York: The Macmillan Co., 1932.

PERRY, R. B. *A General Theory of Value.* New York: Longmans, Green & Co., 1926.

PRATT, C. C. *The Logic of Modern Psychology.* New York: The Macmillan Co., 1939.

PRATT, J. B. *The Psychology of Religious Belief.* New York: The Macmillan Co., 1907.

———. "The Psychology of Religion." *Harvard Theological Review,* I (1908), 435-54.

———. *The Religious Consciousness.* New York: The Macmillan Co., 1920.

RANK, OTTO. *Will Therapy* (tr. J. Taft). New York: Alfred A. Knopf, 1936.

ROBINSON, G. C. *The Patient as a Person.* New York: The Commonwealth Fund, 1939.

ROGERS, C. R. *Counseling and Psychotherapy.* Boston: Houghton Mifflin Co., 1942.

ROYCE, JOSIAH. *The Philosophy of Loyalty.* New York: The Macmillan Co., 1908.

———. *The Problem of Christianity* (2 vols.). New York: The Macmillan Co., 1913.

SCHAUB, E. L. "The Psychology of Religion in America During the Past Quarter Century." *Journal of Religion,* VI (1926).

——. "The Psychology of Religion: A Review of Literature from a Part of the Field." *Psychological Bulletin*, XXIII (1926), 680-700.

SELBIE, W. B. *The Psychology of Religion*. Oxford: Clarendon Press, 1924.

——. *Christianity and the New Psychology*. London: Centenary Press, 1939.

SHAFFER, L. F. *The Psychology of Adjustment*. Boston: Houghton Mifflin Co., 1936.

SOROKIN, P. A. *The Crisis of Our Age*. New York: E. P. Dutton & Co., 1941.

SPERRY, W. L. *Reality in Worship*. New York: The Macmillan Co., 1925.

STARBUCK, E. D. *The Psychology of Religion*. New York: Charles Scribner's Sons, 1903.

STERN, WILLIAM. *General Psychology* (tr. H. D. Spoerl). New York: The Macmillan Co., 1938.

STOLZ, K. R. *The Psychology of Prayer*. New York: The Abingdon Press, 1923.

——. *The Psychology of Religious Living*. New York and Nashville: Abingdon-Cokesbury Press, 1937.

——. *The Church and Psychotherapy*. New York and Nashville: Abingdon-Cokesbury Press, 1943.

STRATTON, G. M. *The Psychology of the Religious Life*. London: The Macmillan Co., 1911.

STRICKLAND, F. L. *Psychology of Religious Experience*. New York and Nashville: Abingdon-Cokesbury Press, 1924.

TAFT, JESSIE. *The Dynamics of Therapy in a Controlled Relationship*. New York: The Macmillan Co., 1933.

TAGORE, RABINDRANATH. *The Religion of Man*. New York: The Macmillan Co., 1931.

THOMAS, W. B. *The Psychology of Conversion*. London: Allenson & Co., Ltd., 1935.

THOULESS, R. H. *An Introduction to the Psychology of Religion*. New York: The Macmillan Co., 1923.

TRACY, FREDERICK. *The Psychology of Adolescence*. New York: The Macmillan Co., 1925.

TROUT, D. M. *Religious Behavior*. New York: The Macmillan Co., 1931.

UNDERHILL, EVELYN. *Mysticism*. New York: E. P. Dutton & Co., 1911.
―――. *Worship*. New York: Harper & Bros., 1937.
UNDERWOOD, A. C. *Conversion: Christian and Non-Christian*. New York: The Macmillan Co., 1925.

VAUGHAN, W. F. *General Psychology*. New York: Odyssey Press, 1936; 1939.

WACH, JOACHIM. *Sociology of Religion*. Chicago: University of Chicago Press, 1944.
WATERHOUSE, E. E. *Psychology and Religion*. New York: Richard R. Smith, Inc., 1931.
WEATHERHEAD, L. D. *Psychology in Service of the Soul*. New York: The Macmillan Co., 1932.
WHITEHEAD, A. N. *Religion in the Making*. New York: The Macmillan Co., 1926.
WIEMAN, H. N. *Religious Experience and Scientific Method*. New York: The Macmillan Co., 1926.
―――. *Methods of Private Religious Living*. New York: The Macmillan Co., 1929.
WIEMAN, H. N., and R. W. WIEMAN. *Normative Psychology of Religion*. New York: Thomas Y. Crowell Co., 1935.
WISE, C. A. *Religion in Illness and Health*. New York: Harper & Bros., 1942.
WOODBURNE, A. S. *The Religious Attitude*. New York: The Macmillan Co., 1927.
WOODWORTH, R. S. *Dynamic Psychology*. New York: Henry Holt & Co., 1921; 1940.
WRIGHT, W. K. "The Psychology of Religion." *The Encyclopaedia Americana*, XXIII (1941), 348-50.
WUNDT, WILHELM. *Elements of Folk Psychology* (tr. E. L. Schaub). New York: The Macmillan Co., 1916.

Index